Our Words of Faith

Taking the Land

A Spiritual Guide to
Restoration of the Soul

By John and Glenna Miller

Copyright 2006
All Rights Reserved

JOSHUA WORLD MINISTRIES
PO Box 570428, Las Vegas, NV 89157-0428

ISBN: 1-931178-40-2

Published by:
Vision Publishing
1115 D Street
Ramona CA 92065
www.visionpublishingservices.com

The Amplified Bible (AB), Expanded Edition, 1987.
Grand Rapids, Michigan ~ Zondervan Publishing House.

Zondervan New International Version Study Bible (NIV), Fully Revised, 1985, 1995, 2002,
Grand Rapids, Michigan ~ Zondervan Publishing House

The Holy Bible, The New King James Version (NKJV), 1992,
Nashville, Tennessee ~ Thomas Nelson Publishers.

Unless otherwise noted, all Scriptures are from the New King James Version of the Bible.

CONTENTS

INTRODUCTION 7

SECTION ONE: FOUNDATIONS 15

- WHO IS GOD? WHO IS MAN? God is Triune and Creator; God is Father and Judge; Distorted Images of Heavenly Father; God is Son and Savior; God is Holy Spirit and Controller; Man is Triune Like God.
- WHAT IS SALVATION? Re-creation, Healing, Deliverance, Restoration; Fear Is a Hindrance to Salvation; Death and the Fear of Death; Salvation of the Spirit; Salvation of the Soul; Salvation of the Body; Renounce Sin and Be Delivered; Repent of Sin; Be restored as Peter Was Restored; Sample Prayer.
- CAN CHRISTIANS BE DEMON POSSESSED? We are the Temple; What About Paul's Thorn? Fiery Serpents; How Do They Get In? So Who Is Responsible? In Conclusion.
- OUR AUTHORITY: God's Authority; Authority Given to Adam and Eve; Adam Rebelled; Serpent Was Cursed; Eve Received Consequences; Adam Received Consequences; Satan Received Authority; Jesus Defeated Satan; What About Adam and Eve? Jesus Reclaimed Authority; Our Authority as Jesus' Body; Power of Jesus' Body; Our Assignment as His Body; Sample Prayer.

SECTION TWO: ROOT CUTTING 55

- GENERATIONAL SIN AND INIQUITY: Iniquity Accumulated; Cultural Sin and Iniquity; Territorial Spirits; Cultural Beliefs and Distinctions; We Can Be Free; Sample Prayer; Who Can We Pray For?
- SOUL TIES AND SPIRITUAL TRANSFER: Godly Soul Ties; Satan's Counterfeit, or Ungodly Soul Ties; Sin and Iniquity in the Flesh; Spiritual Transfer; Many Generations Defiled; Sample Prayer.
- DEDICATIONS AND BAPTISMS: Questionable Dedications and Baptisms; Christian Baptism; Sample Prayer.
- CURSES OF GENDER, IDENTITY, AND DESTINY: Curses Through Family Line; Curses of Names; Curses of Nicknames; Curses from Others; Curses from Family Members; Purchasing Curses for Ourselves; Cursing Ourselves; Cursing Others; We have an Alternative; Curses of Physical and Emotional Trauma; Substance Abuse, Escape, and Counterfeit Healing; In Conclusion; Sample Prayer.

SPIRIT OF ANTICHRIST: Antichrist Denies Messiah; Antichrist Diminishes the Work of Jesus; Antichrist Attempts to Replace Christ; What About Created Ones? What is Love? What About Created Things? What About Spirits that Imitate the Holy Spirit? Sample Prayer.

SECTION THREE: THE SOUL 113

DEFINING THE SOUL: Soul in Hebrew—in Greek; Heart in Hebrew—in Greek; Definition of Mind; Planting Seeds in the Soul; Germination and Growth; Fruit Development; God Commands; Conflict in the Soul; Sin Causes Damage to the Soul; Can We Lose Control of Our Soul? Soul Damage Affects the Body; Hasn't the Work Already Been Done? Old Programming Versus God's Truth; Work Out Our Own Salvation? Confess and Be Cleansed; Sample Prayer.

METHODS OF DISSOCIATION: Dreams, Fantasies, and Imaginations; Consequences of Dissociation; Familiar Spirits; Familiar Spirits of Death; We Do Have Other Options; Restoration of Our Soul; Now What? Sample Prayer; Can You Be Like God?

SECTION FOUR: SOUL FRUIT ISSUES 161

CAN YOU JUDGE LIKE THE FATHER? Unwillingness to Forgive; Effects on the Body; Fearful Responses; We Assign Blame; Sample Prayer.

REJECTION AND ABANDONMENT: Sample Prayer.

SHAME, WORTHLESSNESS AND PRIDE: Worthlessness, or "The Tortoise"; Pride, "The Hare"; Defilement; Wrong Perceptions; Idealized or Idolized Self; Our True Identity; Sample Prayer.

WHAT ABOUT THE FIRST YEAR? The Deepest Roots; Spiritual Death Transmitted; Sample Prayer.

IMAGE OF THE FATHER: Believing Heavenly Father like Earthly Father; Sample Prayer; Idealized Images, Good and Bad; Who Am I Supposed to Be? Desire to Be the Judge; Sample Prayer. The Father's Blessing.

CAN YOU SAVE LIKE THE SON? Failure Motivating Actions; Fear of Failure; Are We Institutionalized? Potential for Failure; Hopelessness and Despair; Programmed Failure; Guaranteed Failure; Need to Be Perfect; Need to Perform; Sibling Rivalry and Competition; Competition for Parents' Attention; School Activities and Sports; In the Media; In Marriage; In Business; In the Church; Are We in Savior Mode? Emotional Vampirism; Have Any Jobs for Me? Desperate Needs; Emotional Starvation; Self-Destructive Behavior; Satan, the Blackmailer; What Is Wrong with God? How About This for That? Refuse Satan's Offer; Our Conclusions; Desire to Be a Savior; Sample Prayer.

CAN YOU CONTROL LIKE THE TRUE HOLY SPIRIT? Injustice Produces Rebellion; Rebellion Equals Witchcraft and Lawlessness; The Importance of Vows; Gender Defilement; What is Honor? Religious Environments and Programming; Alternatives to Rape; How Can We Be in Control? We Are Never in Control; Sample Prayer.

CONTROLLING THROUGH SICKNESS OR INJURY: Is Sickness an Illusion? Sample Prayer; Desire to be the Controller; Sample Prayer.

YOU CAN BE EVERYTHING HE CREATED YOU TO BE! Righteous; Free from the Law of Sin and Death; Heirs of Christ; Guaranteed God's Love; His Divine Nature; Sample Prayer; In Closing.

BIBLIOGRAPHY 287

INTRODUCTION

The preparation for this book started a half-century ago. Glenna and I now see how the Lord has prepared us for today. He has used events in our lives, our training as a teacher and an engineer, to equip us for the challenges we now face. A brief look at our backgrounds might be helpful.

Before Glenna entered my life, I had been involved with new age metaphysics. While wandering in these spiritual weeds, I was involved with many dangerous things. I was on a quest, and was being driven in ways I didn't understand. My quest had begun in junior high where I was encouraged to develop my *natural* psychic abilities.

I would have told you I was searching for truth and for God. All I was really searching for was power. I wasn't seeking the true God because I did not want to give Him control of my life. I wanted the same thing Adam and Eve wanted: to be like God and to wield the powers of the universe according to my will instead of His!

My desire for control had begun because I grew up in a household that was far from idyllic. My mother was an occasionally active Catholic who appeared to have a genuine relationship with Jesus. I believe my father would have called himself a Christian, because his mother had required him to attend church when he was a child. In spite of this, I saw more fruit of witchcraft and rebellion in him than Christianity.

As a result of my home environment, I grew up with massive insecurities, bottled-up rage, and an overpowering sense of despair and hopelessness. I was convinced I was a failure and inadequate in every aspect of my life and being. This produced a sense of powerlessness that caused me to crave being in control of my life, the lives of those around me, and the very forces of nature.

During my time of psychic discovery, I was married and divorced twice. These relationships were destroyed, to a great extent, because of my emotional and spiritual issues. These issues were magnified by my journey into the metaphysical. With a deep sense of regret, I look back on the years when I responded to my family, wives, children, and stepchildren in ways that remind me of my father. I also engaged in relationships with other people, both men and women, which proved to be painful and destructive.

After many years, I was working in Mesa, Arizona, as a project engineer. My spiritual explorations had included the use of familiar spirits to engage in spiritual warfare against those I perceived to be enemies. Occasionally my familiar spirits would suggest others who should be attacked in specific ways. If I refused, my familiar spirits would express their anger in a variety of ways. As time went on, I realized that the spirits I had considered to be my servants, actually considered me to be their servant.

I was getting very little sleep at night. I would wake up in a cold sweat and the hair would be standing up on my body. I could feel their presence and their hatred being projected at me. I would turn the lights on and sit in the middle of my bed willing them to go away. I had been taught that I was in control and they had to do what I wanted; but I wasn't in control, and they didn't do as I willed.

One night, in absolute desperation, I looked up and spoke to God. I had always known He was there but had not chosen to acknowledge Him. My quest had always been to establish *my* power and control in all things. On this night I was sufficiently terrified and beaten to finally give Him control. I said, "I don't know if You are really there, but if You are, I need Your help." I knew that I had found the end of myself and needed more.

The next morning, someone in the office gave me a book they said I needed to read, so that evening I began reading *The Beautiful Side of Evil*, by Johanna Michelson. It was about a young woman who had grown up surrounded by magic and witchcraft. She, too, was tormented by spirits, and some Christians told her how to be free of the torment.

I closed the book, resolving to sleep, but as soon as the lights were off my tormentors were back. I was filled with fear at their presence and by the intense hatred I perceived they were directing at me. At first I was immobilized, but my fear was mingled with an intense anger resulting from many months of harassment. At the top of my lungs I yelled, "In the name of the Lord Jesus Christ, you get out of here!" I was greatly relieved when they, along with the intense feelings and emotions, were instantly gone. I was amazed by the power of that Name.

My lifelong quest for power had come full circle, to the God I had dismissed as unimportant. The power I had sought was nothing compared to the power of that Name. I had finally found what I was looking for. The next night I saw a man on television whose name I do not remember. He pointed into the camera, looked directly at me and said, "This is your night to receive the Lord Jesus Christ." He was right. I sat in a puddle of tears on the floor in front of my easy chair for a long time.

Glenna grew up with parents who demonstrated the concepts of Christianity. They lived by and taught their children the Golden Rule, to treat other people as you would like to be treated. She experienced standards, work ethics, and family values that were amazingly healthy compared with the norms of society. Her parents really tried to instill love and security in the hearts of their children. Though there was never an abundance of money, her family experienced many forms of wealth.

In 1989, I met Glenna in Winslow, Arizona, at a Bible study. I had been sent there to help with a construction project for my engineering firm with the Arizona Highway Department.

During the next ten months, we became good friends and enjoyed visiting several churches as well as our own home church. Our goal was to open a study group and invite people from other churches to help break down the walls of separation. The group that gathered represented different churches and backgrounds. As a result of this eclectic group, we began to involve ourselves with spiritual warfare and related subjects. It was a great growing experience for all of us.

One day at lunch, Glenna and I were discussing how much we enjoyed being together. I was feeling regret that the construction project would be completed in just a few more weeks and I would be leaving Winslow. I was amazed by how much I had enjoying our times of fellowship. I was already feeling a sense of loss. Glenna shared these feelings. A week later we were married and, shortly after that, we moved into my condo in Gilbert, Arizona.

The moving process completed, we began to consider our options. We were both professionals with experience overseas. Glenna had taught school overseas for the Department of Defense. I was a registered civil engineer with a significant amount of experience in construction. We decided to seek foreign employment.

In 1990 there were big construction projects all over the world. I had been told that they were hiring anyone with even a meager amount of experience. As a result, Glenna and I put together our resumes and sent them out to several potential employers. We expected it would only be a matter of time before the offers came pouring in.

We decided to ask the Lord to help us with what was, certainly, going to be a complicated decision. We explained to Him our well-thought-out plan. We would certainly receive many offers and would be required to choose the one representing His highest and best for us. We knew we could not trust ourselves to make the best choice, so we asked the Lord to close all the doors that were not His best. We asked Him to leave open only the one door that represented His best, and we promised to go through that door.

After many weeks had passed, we received one letter with a short reply thanking us for our inquiry. They appreciated our interest but had nothing to offer at that time. We were both feeling pretty frustrated. Then, my boss invited me into his office to explain that, during the time I was in Winslow, the job I had previously done had been distributed to others. The company would be willing to help me find a new job or I could go to Las Vegas and help pioneer a new office there.

That evening Glenna and I agreed Las Vegas was the last place on earth we wanted to go. Glenna had been there before and did not want to go back. My father was a gambling addict, and I had vowed to never go to Las Vegas because of my negative attitude about anything associated with gambling.

We were, however, reminded of our previous prayers. We had asked the Lord to open only one door and we promised to go through it. We saw only one door and would have loved to find a loophole in the agreement. The Lord had totally ignored the wonderful plan we presented to Him, to work overseas for a short period of time, make lots of money, bank the extra money, then travel and serve Him as missionaries. Instead, in the fall of 1990, we headed for Las Vegas.

The Wilderness

We arrived in Las Vegas and spent several months looking for a home church. We finally found a church that was beginning a week of marriage renewal meetings, ending with a rededication of marriage, on our first anniversary. We both felt the Lord had confirmed this was to be our home church. We found we were unable to connect with most of the people attending this church.

After several months of this relative isolation, a faint glimmer of hope appeared. One of the pastors announced a class for training new home group leaders. We had experience in home group ministry, so we signed up and attended all the classes, hoping for the opportunity to serve by leading a home group.

When we were first married, we told the Lord that we would do anything He offered as ministry. We had no idea that He was again going to ignore our plans and recommendations of how we could best serve Him.

We discovered we had volunteered for what was being called deliverance ministry. In all the ways we had proposed to serve the Lord, we never mentioned deliverance. We knew nothing about it and preferred to keep it that way. The idea of dealing with demons, one-on-one, was totally repugnant and intimidating. Again, He ignored our plans, knowing what was really best for us.

During the next year or so, we were on a very steep learning curve. We read books and listened to tapes. We were given the opportunity to minister with some **very special people**. If what we were told was true, some of these people had come from family situations beyond our wildest imaginings. This was on-the-job training in the Lord's school of hard knocks. He was very patient to put up with all of our whining and complaining.

Every time we read a new book, we would try the ministry methods it described. Sometimes we observed good fruit and sometimes we did not. We cried out to the Lord to show us how to minister in a way that would best serve Him. We were very uncomfortable with some of the models for ministry that seemed to be abusive. We were frustrated and felt battered spiritually, emotionally, and physically.

Crossing Over

One night we were complaining to God. We thought we were serving Him in valuable and important ways so His master plan could come to fulfillment. We were suffering and He wasn't doing anything about it. We had done all the warfare we knew how to do, with no apparent effect. We had complied with many of the formulas for prayers gleaned from the books we read. Nothing seemed to help. I was angry and I wanted Him to know it.

As a result of this turmoil and confusion, we pulled back from ministry with other people and went back to reading and studying, hoping to find resolution for these issues. This was a time of decision, because the temptation to quit this frustrating ministry was very compelling.

Throughout this time, the Lord was faithful to show us issues still affecting our hearts and bodies. As He revealed things for which we needed *deliverance*, we would make lists and address them. We attended seminars and conferences to learn more about the soul and what was being called satanic ritual abuse. We found new ministry models and experimented with each other.

Some of the models produced good fruit and some did not. The ministry models developed for people with extraordinary backgrounds seemed to be a blend of many things. We found that Satan's methods for shattering people's souls applied to everyone. Our previous attitudes and tendencies to strictly label and categorize people were being quickly eroded.

As our pastor sent people to us for ministry, we tried the new techniques and models we were learning. We would throw some things out and keep other things. Our desire was to remove everything we considered abusive and ineffective, and to keep all those things that were producing good fruit.

At this time, our pastor proposed that we produce our own ministry seminar. I responded in rebellion, as a result of my fears and insecurities, and refused to consider it.

Occupying the Land

Before long, it became necessary to put aside our rebellion, fear, and insecurities. In 1995, we produced the first seminar outline for *Taking the Land*. We combined the strengths of other ministry models we had read about or experienced, and presented it to our pastor. He instructed us to schedule our first seminar.

With much trepidation and dry mouths, we presented our first *Taking the Land* seminar at our home church. We were surprised to receive a great deal of positive reinforcement. One person told us of always feeling both an attraction and an aversion to being around us, but after the seminar the aversion was gone. Since then we have received many similar comments.

Along this path of travel and ministry, we've experienced many ups and downs. It has really been hard to let the Lord be in charge. He refuses to follow our agenda and is always faithful to show us our many headstrong ways.

At one point, I did what I suppose many people have done. I waved my Bible at the ceiling and told the Lord I was confused and frustrated and wanted to know what was going on. I dropped my Bible on the table, and it fell open to Isaiah 58. My eyes focused on verse 6 and I read to the end of verse 12. In this, the Lord proclaimed the fast he had chosen. It didn't have anything to do with our religious observances.

He told us to do our part to break the yokes, to untie the cords, to remove the heavy burdens, and help the oppressed go free. He told us to share our bread and offer hospitality, to clothe the naked, and never hide from our fellow men in need. He told us that if we would do these things our light would break forth, our healing would come speedily, our righteousness would go before us, and the glory of the Lord would be our rear guard. He told us that we would be called the repairers of the breach and the restorers of streets to dwell in, because He would be working through us. He was clearly telling us what He wanted us to do.

These verses have become keynote Scriptures for our ministry. Our Lord wants His people to be free of all forms of bondage. He wants us to function as His ambassadors, to represent Him, and to assist in the process of setting His people free from the burdens of darkness and death.

We spent the next couple of years pursuing this new vision with all the energy we could muster. As we would present seminars in various locations, more and more people approached us with requests for catalogs of books and tapes. We didn't have a catalog, because we had no books and tapes for sale. All we had was the teaching outline we used for our seminars.

We had a big box full of audiotapes of seminars we had given, but they weren't organized. We would take orders for the tapes of the seminar we just gave, and fill those orders. The idea of writing books was too intimidating. I decided we were too busy to get involved in projects I didn't feel adequate to accomplish. I told the Lord if He really wanted us to write books, He would have to show me clearly, never really expecting Him to do so, because I was just an engineer. He obviously enjoys using the least likely to accomplish His will. This book is proof.

There are many deliverance ministries. Most focus on a particular part of the ministry spectrum. In that part of the spectrum, they seem to be effective. In other parts of the spectrum they focus less attention. Our goal has been to provide a ministry model with as broad a spectrum of effectiveness as possible. As a result, we have combined what we believe are the best attributes of a group of ministry models. We think of our model as a broad-spectrum treatment for spiritual infections. We also have come to believe that deliverance, alone, is not enough.

In our view, it is necessary to combine deliverance with restoration so the salvation process is complete. A form of restoration occurs when the spirit is re-created. We believe further restoration should occur during the salvation of the soul and the body. We will discuss these processes of salvation, deliverance, and restoration throughout this book.

We offer examples of issues and situations we have encountered. We have a strict code of conduct that we have imposed upon ourselves. We can never violate the trust of a person who has come to us for ministry. As a result of this, the examples will be composites representing real ministry situations. They will accurately represent situations and ministry issues we have faced. They will not be specific to a particular person unless they pertain to our personal ministry to one another.

There may be some ideas and ministry methodologies presented in this book that could conflict with the reader's beliefs or theologies. We ask you to check our Scriptural references to verify that we haven't perverted, or taken out of context, anything we have cited from the Bible. We also ask the true Holy Spirit to shine His light of truth and clearly display any error we are teaching or proposing. We have endeavored to study thoroughly the material we present and we trust that the reader will find we have accurately represented the truth of the Bible.

It is our earnest prayer that many people will read this book, pray the prayers, and be loosed from the bonds, the heavy burdens, and every yoke of darkness and death. The Scripture promises, *"Whenever two or three agree as touching anything, it shall be done for them"* (Matthew 18:19). Glenna and I are in agreement with you as you read the prayers in the book. Since there are two or three in agreement, we expect our Lord to honor these prayers anytime anyone reads them!

JOHN MILLER

In order to begin this book, it is necessary to establish some foundations. We are Christians and, as such, we present all the following information from our Christian perspective. This includes the belief that there is a God, the pre-existing One, who is responsible for all creation. Hebrews 11:6 tells us we need to believe that He is, and He rewards those who diligently seek Him. Everything we present in this book as fact is based upon our understanding of what the Bible says, as well as our experience in ministry with thousands of people around the world.

Throughout this book, our prayers are directed to our Father in heaven. In the book of John, Jesus states, "In that day you will ask Me nothing. Most assuredly, I say to you, whatever you ask the Father in My name, He will give you" (John 16:23). Jesus said, "Your Father knows the things you have need of before you ask Him. In this manner, therefore, pray: Our Father in heaven..."(Matthew 6:8-9). We conclude from these Scriptures that we are to pray to the Father, not specifically to Jesus or the Holy Spirit; therefore, the model in this book is to follow the instructions of our Lord Jesus.

SECTION ONE: FOUNDATIONS

WHO IS GOD? WHO IS MAN?

God Is Triune and Creator

(Isaiah 42:5) The Scriptures say God is One, in three primary identities. He is defined as eternally being Father, Son, and Holy Spirit. There are many names attributed to God throughout the Bible. However, for the purposes of this study, we are speaking of the three-in-one Godhead.

In Genesis, we see two manifestations of God, Who created the heavens and the earth. The Spirit of God was moving over the waters. (Genesis 1:1-2) The Hebrew word that is used for God in this passage is a plural form.

John, the apostle, began his gospel with a description of the third manifestation of God, and His part in these activities, *In the beginning was the Word... and the Word was God. All things were made and came into existence through Him; without Him... not even one thing was made. In Him was Life, and the Life was the light of men* (John 1:1-4 AB).

As we look at the process of creation, we can picture God the Father, Who had the really good idea of creating the universe. Then the Son, the Word of God, defined the universe with His words. Finally, the Holy Spirit used His infinite power to cause what was spoken to come into existence. They worked as a team to manifest creation. Each of the manifestations seems to have had a specific function in the overall plan of creation.

There are those who don't approve of His creation. Many people see inequities and injustices in issues that pertain to their own lives and the world around them. They want to know why a Creator God seems incapable of correcting all the obvious problems on earth. If He is so loving, why is He unwilling to cause everything to reflect His goodness?

These normal people want to know, "Why does He allow all the bad things of this life? Or more precisely, "Why did He allow all these bad things to happen to **me**?"

All these things really do reflect His goodness and love! God does not want us to function like puppy dogs or robots. God, in His infinite love, has given us the free will to choose. He has told us to choose death or life, to choose darkness or light, to choose Satan's kingdom or His kingdom. It isn't a game. The choices we make will affect us forever. God has given us the right and the responsibility to make the choices. (Romans 11:29)

Suppose it is time for the national elections. When you go to vote, you discover there are five candidates for president. Candidate one is John Miller. Candidate two is John Miller. Candidate three is John Miller. Candidate four is John Miller. Candidate five is John Miller. You are instructed to vote for one of the candidates.

Does this validate your freedom of choice? In order for free will to be validated, there has to be a **real choice**. God gave us the right to choose, and He won't take away that right. God allows us to make good decisions and bad decisions, do bad things, hurt other people, and experience being hurt. He must allow all the terrible things people do in the world, and bad things to happen, even to us!

He created life and death, light and darkness, and the reality of two distinct eternal kingdoms, heaven and hell. Only by doing so does He validate our right to choose. So, you see, it really is all about love.

(Isaiah 14:12-15) He created Lucifer knowing he would rebel. After he was banished from heaven, Lucifer, son of the morning, became Satan, the enemy of God and all of humanity. God created the Lake of Fire as the eternal destination for Satan and his followers. Satan can't take away our right to choose, because he is bound by God's laws.

Many people have interesting ideas concerning the nature of God, and have expressed a viewpoint that sounds similar to what is taught in some Eastern religions. For example, God is a force existing everywhere in the universe. He is omnipresent and, therefore, exists as both infinite good and infinite evil. He created the universe to function according to a set of defined rules, but He doesn't have interaction with His creation. It is our responsibility to learn and grow so we can become the god identity, even if it takes many lifetimes.

Another commonly held view of God portrays Him as an angry old man. He has a long white beard, flowing robes, and a bundle of lightning bolts in one hand. He sits malevolently on His throne waiting for some member of His creation to do something bad. He hurls lightning at them. He kills, destroys, and makes their lives generally miserable. This wrathful God offers a gift of salvation with one hand and, with the other, threatens to snatch it away again if someone doesn't perform perfectly.

We once knew a woman who apparently viewed God in this way. One day, while leaving church, she tripped on the sidewalk and fell onto her hands and knees. I went over to help her up and ask if she was hurt. Even though she wasn't hurt, she sat there crying. I asked her what was wrong if she wasn't hurt.

Through her sobs she said, "God must be mad at me." She actually believed that God was angry and caused her to trip on the sidewalk. We were distressed because she had this distorted image of God and tried to convince her He wouldn't do that to her. We don't believe she was ever convinced concerning His true, loving character.

These are just a couple of examples expressed by people who are confused about God. They have believed so many misguided teachings that have nothing to do with the Bible, and have no idea who God really is. Unfortunately, much of this garbage is believed, even by Christians, and produces many distorted images of God.

God Is Father and Judge

God, the Creator and Father, is also defined as the infinite Judge. David wrote, *Search me, O God, and know my heart* (Psalm 139:23). The apostle, John, describes, *I saw a great white **throne** and Him who sat on it....the **dead were judged*** (Revelation 20:11-15). Peter warns, *They will have to give an account to Him Who is ready to judge and pass sentence on the living and the dead* (1 Peter 4:5). The writer of Hebrews declares, *To God [Who is] **Judge of all*** (Hebrews 12:23).

Although Scripture clearly identifies God as the only Judge, many of us judge others, ourselves, and particularly God, based upon our experiences.

Most people, who believe there is a God, accept Him as Creator but heart issues arise concerning His identity as Father. Has anyone ever met a perfect father? We don't believe anyone alive has seen one.

We know there are men who really try to be good fathers. Even so, we don't know how any man could hope to fulfill this role when they've never seen an example of a perfectly functional father. Because of this, we conclude that all earthly fathers are dysfunctional to some extent. This is not meant to be an attack, merely an observation.

Distorted Images of Heavenly Father

We believe the greatest misconceptions of God, the Father, are based on life experiences. We all have had normally imperfect fathers and we probably concluded that all fathers are like our earthly father. This is understandable, but presents a problem with regard to our heavenly Father. Many people find it difficult to establish a relationship with God because of this confusion between the two images.

There is also another source of concern. We see from the Bible that the king or priest in authority over a nation will define the spiritual personality of the nation. The husband and father of the household is the priest of the house. His dysfunction in the administration of his responsibilities will affect the family, so that unhealthy behaviors and interactions are the result. He will establish the spiritual personality of his home and family.

My dad demonstrated constantly that he was incapable of functioning as a husband or father. I grew up with him as the example of what I was to *become*. I remember being terrified when I discovered I was going to be a father. The fear of failure overwhelmed me because I didn't want to be like that man I had always called Dad. I feared I would do to my wife and children what had been done to my family and me.

The result of this programming and self-imposed curse was that I did and said many abusive things to my wife and daughters. There are others, also, who were dependent upon me for a healthy male role model. When I look back, I know I failed miserably and sincerely hope they have been able to forgive me and receive healing.

I still struggle when *the voice* comes to remind me of things I said and did. These reminders fill my heart with regret. I consider myself fortunate in having found a measure of peace through the love of my heavenly Father. I believe He has told me I can turn those people over to Him for healing.

What about men who never discover the healing power of the Holy Spirit? They do terrible things to their children, because they are broken, full of fear and anger, and don't know how to do anything else. We don't believe the people involved are evil. We do believe they are, to some extent, being controlled by evil. We are not making excuses for anyone, merely stating the way we see it.

Every time a man goes out drinking or womanizing, returns home drunk, and abuses or molests his family in any way, the accuser is there to blame. Every time he is gone when the family needs him or treats someone unjustly, the accuser speaks into the hearts of his children. He might say, "See, this is how all fathers are. They will always reject, abandon, abuse, and molest you. They yell at you and treat you unjustly. This includes the heavenly Father."

All of these things could apply to any authority figure including mother, brothers, sisters, any other family member, a teacher at school, a policeman, or a minister. The reason we focus on dad is because we believe Satan is working diligently to defile our relationship with our heavenly Father. The way he can most easily accomplish this is to defile the image of earthly father.

Even when mom or others are the abusers, dad is responsible because he is the head of the household. He is the one responsible for providing protection and security. When he actively or passively allows abuses by others, he retains the responsibility for the abuse, both in God's eyes and in the eyes of the ones being abused.

Normal people tell us, "I just go through the motions. I don't understand why I don't experience God's touch." When we ask the Holy Spirit to search their hearts so we can discover the truth, we often find that deep inside is a child who is very angry or afraid. They continue to respond fearfully to intimidation, manipulation, yelling, and various threats. They might remember themselves hiding under the bed, in the closet, in a back room, or out in the yard, because they are so afraid of their father.

Children grow up with a normal, imperfect, and dysfunctional daddy, and conclude that daddies aren't safe. They can't be trusted or depended upon. A child might think all daddies are angry and mean, so it's best to stay closer to mommy. Could this explain why so many people would prefer to have a feminine God?

There are several Scriptures that define God as the Father: *Whenever you stand praying...forgive...that your Father in heaven may also **forgive you** your trespasses* (Mark 11:25). *Be merciful, just as your Father also **is merciful*** (Luke 6:36). *All that the Father gives Me will come to Me, and the one who comes to Me I will **by no means cast out*** (John 6:37).

These Scriptures speak of the nature of our heavenly Father who has been forgiving, merciful and accepting. When speaking to Philip, Jesus proclaimed that anyone who has seen Him has seen the Father (John 14:9). While on this earth, Jesus demonstrated the love, the righteousness, and the divine nature of the Father. We have only to study the way Jesus dealt with situations and people, to have a clear understanding of our Father.

God Is Son and Savior

There are many religious organizations willing to accept the Lord Jesus Christ as a great man, prophet, and teacher, but are unwilling to accept Him as the Son of the living God and Savior (John 1:1-4; Luke 2:11).

In the first chapter of the book of John, Jesus is described as the Word. He was with God, and was, Himself, God. He was responsible for creating everything (John 1:1-4). Throughout the book of John, there is a deliberate emphasis placed on the deity of Christ. We believe it takes a great deal of effort to miss the significance of these statements and, yet, many people are successful in doing so.

Jesus came to **represent us** as righteous to the Father, to function as our ambassador to bring **peace** (John 14:27) and **reconciliation** (Romans 5:11), so we can come boldly to the throne, without fear. (Hebrews 4:16; Romans 3:22-26)

Jesus also came to serve as God's ambassador and to **represent the Father** to us. (John 14:9) He came to demonstrate the love, and the true nature, of our heavenly Father so we will be willing to go before His throne. The role of Jesus, **as Savior**, is to represent both sides to the other and, in so doing, end the warfare. (Zechariah 8:17; Proverbs 8:36; Revelation 21:7-8; Ephesians 2:13-18)

In John, chapter four, Jesus is described as the Savior of the world. We are told that He accomplished the awesome work of paying for all the sins of the world. He sprinkled His own blood on the mercy seat in heaven, and thus nullified the power of sin. There are many other Scriptures naming Jesus as the Savior of the world. (John 4:42; Acts 5:30- 31; 2 Timothy 1:10; 1 John 4:14)

In spite of these proclamations from Scripture, we meet people regularly who seem determined to function as a savior. Maybe they simply gave up on Jesus at some time in their life. Maybe they never had any concept of Him as the Savior. Maybe their need is to be a savior so they can be in control, can claim credit, and can boast. *By **grace** you have been saved through faith...it is the **gift of God**, not of works, lest anyone should **boast*** (Ephesians 2:8-9). [Emphasis ours]

There are many reasons to explain why people have chosen to be a savior. It is the same now as it was in the Garden of Eden. The snake is still saying, "You can be like God." Then we agree and proceed as though it were true. The problem is that no one is qualified to be the *Anointed One*, any more than we are to be the Judge, so we're taking upon ourselves a job that is impossible to accomplish.

God Is Holy Spirit and Controller

The biblical evidence suggests the Holy Spirit is infinitely powerful. In the beginning, He was hovering over the empty universe and it was His power that produced everything when the command was given. (Genesis 1:2; 1 John 4:13; 1 John 5:6; Romans 15:19) He was, and is, the motivating force bringing all of God's spoken proclamations into reality. He is the spiritual power Who raised Jesus from the dead. (Romans 8:11)

We are told that He is capable of doing things that are infinitely beyond anything we can think or even imagine. (Ephesians 3:20) As Christians, we now have Him dwelling in our hearts making it possible for us to relate to God as our Father. (Romans 8:15)

We have other great Scriptures defining His role in the Father's master plan for redemption. He is the motivating Force, the infinite Power that causes God's Plan to manifest. He is our Tutor, our Trainer, our Comforter, and everything else we need. He is in control of absolutely everything.

In spite of this fact, normal people believe we are supposed to be in control. Because of our life experiences, our programming, and our desperate need to survive, we strive to be in control. We dare not trust God to control our lives because we don't have any frame of reference for giving that kind of control to anyone. *The voice* tells us that the only way we will survive is to be in control. Therefore, we try to be like God and take control, even though we are not qualified and face the guarantee of failure.

Man Is Triune like God

Man is created to reflect the **image** and have the **likeness** of God. (Genesis1:26) Although this doesn't seem to be critical to our biblical understanding, Scripture seems to make a distinction between the creation of animals and the creation of people. As far as we can tell, people are the **only** creation in the image of God and with His likeness.

In the book of Genesis, we find that God gave animals two distinct parts of their being. He gave them a body and something called the *living soul*; and these parts define their being. God breathed the breath of life into both man and animals. (Genesis 2:7) A word study tells us that spirit, defined as breath or wind, in one sense, only applies to rational beings. We conclude that God has inserted something into man that wasn't given to animals.

We know that God has three primary parts, so it is reasonable to believe that human beings must have three primary parts. The Bible says that we were given spirit, soul, and body. Scripture tells us that the word of God is sharper than any two-edged sword and divides between the soul and the spirit. This clearly indicates that the soul and spirit are distinct, because otherwise nothing could be put between them. (Hebrews 4:12)

We don't believe in making it complicated. If the Bible says we have three primary parts, we accept this as truth. (1 Thessalonians 5:23) When we combine that with the image in the likeness of Him, we see that people are distinct in His creation. We know of no other being or entity that was created similarly.

Who is man? God has commanded us to choose. (Deuteronomy 30:19) This ability to choose is important because it has to do with relationship. Man was created to be the Lord's **friend** and **companion**. We conclude that we, alone, are able to experience this unique fellowship with our Daddy, God. (2 Corinthians 13:14; John 15:14-15; 1 Corinthians 1:9; 1 John 1:3). Furthermore, we are told that we are God's **eternal children** and are **joint heirs** with Christ. (Romans 8:16-17) As if this weren't enough, we have the following:

*He **has not** put the world to come, of which we speak, in subjection to angels. But one testified in a certain place, saying: "**What is man** that You are mindful of him, or the son of man that You take care of him....You have **crowned him** with glory and honor, and **set him over** the works of Your hands. You have put **all things** in **subjection under his feet**." For in that He put all in subjection under him, He left **nothing** that is not put under* *him. But now we do not yet see **all things put under him** (Hebrews 2:5-8). (Also, Psalm 144:3)*

This must be why Satan and all of his followers hate us so intensely. We've been given something they never had, nor ever will have, and it must enrage them.

Previously we stated that Jesus came as the ambassador of God the Father to represent the Father to us in an effort to end the warfare. As **God's ambassadors** in the world, we have the same commission as Jesus. We are to present the offer of peace, not war, to the people and the world around us. Wherever we go, we are to offer a treaty of peace between the heavenly Father and people, His highest and greatest creation.

WHAT IS SALVATION?

Re-Creation, Healing, Deliverance, Restoration

There are many religious belief systems that describe a variety of processes defined as, or necessary for, salvation. Eastern religions seek the state of Nirvana and atonement for sins based upon many lifetimes of work. Other religions teach that salvation is based on discovering all the secret knowledge of the universe. This reminds us of the offer Satan gave to Adam and Eve. There are also religious systems that dwell extensively on doing good works and giving gifts.

There is one common factor associated with these religious belief systems. In all of them, it is necessary for the individual to earn salvation through a variety of means, including good works and abilities. Because these systems employ self-salvation, these philosophies are united by the gospel of antichrist.

When people indicate the desire for prayer to receive the gift of salvation, they may close their eyes. They may cry or mumble prayers while the minister is praying for them. They may stand stoically, or have a look on their faces that seems to plead, "Please, let this be real for me." We look on sadly because they apparently don't understand the simplicity of receiving the gift of salvation.

Some Christians seem to think salvation is one-dimensional and occurs only at some uncertain point in time. They're not really sure, and they haven't been taught how it happens; they just hope it really does.

In order to present the concepts of deliverance and restoration, we need to help clear up the **question of salvation**. The meaning of the name, Jesus, in Greek, and, Joshua, in Hebrew, describes our Lord's identity and destiny as **Savior**. It means **He will save**. (See Strong's, H 3442 and G 2424)

By definition, the word, salvation, has many facets. It is like a wonderfully cut gemstone. No matter how we view it, we see the glory of it reflecting the light of truth. Included in the meaning of the word are such things as deliverance, aid, victory, prosperity, health, help, and welfare. (See Strong's H 3444)

The Bible tells us to meditate on the things of God, or chew on something mentally. Our study of a thesaurus added greater dimensions of this word. When we looked at the amplified list of definitions for salvation our understanding expanded.

Scriptures tell us **we were chosen** and the **names were written** in the Book of Life, either "before the foundation of the world" or "from the foundation of the world." (Ephesians 1:3-4; Revelation 17:8)

This prompts a very important question. What must we do to have our name written in the Book of Life? How many lifetimes must we live; how many good deeds must we do; how much money must we give; or how much secret knowledge must we accumulate? What is the price God has placed on having our name written in His book? If our name was written in the book before, or from, the foundations of the world; there is nothing for us to do.

People try to accomplish, in their own strength, what He has already done.

Jesus, by the shedding of His own blood, has made **atonement**, has **paid**, for **all** the sins of the world, **forever**, meaning forever past, forever present, and forever future. Many people are greatly deceived and believe the sins they have committed are so great they cannot be saved; neither can their sins be forgiven. We would ask which of the sins of the world don't fall into this category of **all** and **forever**? (1 John 2:2; Hebrews 10:12)

It is not because of anything we can do, our goodness, our kindness, our money, good deeds, or anything else, that our sins are forgiven. God has forgiven our sins **for His name's sake**. Can you see how comforting this is? (1 John 2:12)

Jesus has perfected a covenant, and God honors it, in spite of our inability to fulfill our part. For His name's sake and righteousness, He has guaranteed to fulfill His end of the deal.

We don't have to feel condemned by our inadequacies or imperfections. We acknowledge them, and regret them, but know that nothing we do, or don't do, will affect His ability to maintain the covenant. (Hebrews 9:15; Titus 1:2)

Our sanctification is not totally accomplished, but we are His works in progress. (Hebrews 10:14) He has promised to complete that work He has begun in us. Can you see that this is another awesome promise?

Let's look at what we have already discussed. He has written our names in His Book of Life before the foundation of the world. He has paid for all the sins of the world, including all of our sins. If we look in the books of Romans and Galatians, as well as much of the rest of the New Testament, we find that salvation is a gift. It doesn't cost us anything, and there's nothing we can do to earn it!

The blood of the covenant provided for our sanctification. The word sanctified means to make holy, to purify, or consecrate. When Jesus completed His work on the cross and sprinkled His blood on the mercy seat, the effect of sin was nullified for those who accept the gift of salvation.

If we have been given righteousness as a gift, can the law of sin and death still hold us in bondage? Paul proclaims there is **no condemnation** to those who are in Christ Jesus. The **law of the Spirit of life** in Christ Jesus has made us free from **the law of sin and death.** (Romans Chapter 8)

God has commanded us **to choose** life or death, light or darkness, His kingdom or Satan's kingdom. The Spirit of grace offers the gift of salvation. If a person considers the blood of Christ to be a common thing, and the gift of salvation undesirable, they are insulting the Spirit of grace and refusing their only hope.

If they continue to refuse throughout their life, the time will come when the gift is no longer available; they remain a child of darkness and receive eternal judgment. Therefore, refusing the gift of salvation is the unforgivable sin. (Hebrews 10:26-29)

Fear Is a Hindrance to Salvation

A number of years ago, when I was working on a construction project, I was talking to one of the workers. He was big and strong and everything about his demeanor spoke of masculinity. The conversation somehow shifted to spiritual matters. He told me about his beliefs, and I told him about my Christianity. When I asked him if he would like to accept the gift of salvation, tears welled up in his eyes and he said, "I just can't do it now. I'm afraid. Maybe I will some other time." His response was a surprise to me. In spite of this man's demeanor and the image he projected to everyone else, he didn't receive the gift of salvation that day because of fear.

There are many others like him. They rationalize they'll be able to earn salvation, someday, by their good works. They may say, "I'm not a bad person; I've never killed anyone or robbed a bank. I believe in God, in Jesus, and in what Jesus did. I'm sure God will take all this into consideration and find a place for me." Have you ever heard, or perhaps said, something like this?

Satan, all the fallen angels, all the demons, and those who serve Satan also believe in God, in Jesus, and in what Jesus did. In spite of their belief, all these beings will spend eternity in the lake of fire. Believing philosophically is not enough.

Many people prefer a feminine god, because she isn't so intimidating. They imagine her as loving, nurturing, and accepting, like a good mommy. They imagine she would be everything their earthly dad never was.

The greatest hindrance to receiving the gift of salvation is fear, resulting from misunderstandings about Father God and His true character, or divine nature. Most of us believe God is like our earthly father, mother, or some other authority figure we have known. We may believe He would do to us what those others have done. As a result, we are wary and reluctant to expose ourselves to danger from this heavenly Father.

In our opinion, fear is a common motivator for all sin. The bondage to fear can prevent us from receiving salvation, deliverance, healing, and, even, fellowship with God. There is no fear in love and no thought of punishment, as we grow into love's complete perfection. (I John 4:17-18)

When we read there is no fear in love, we also conclude there is no love in fear. Where fear rules, love cannot exist. Since we were given dominion in this realm, we are the ones who decide to embrace either fear or love.

Do you remember, as a child, telling ghost stories, playing games that elicited fear, and enjoying the energy and excitement of fear? Do you remember hiding from one another and jumping out suddenly to elicit the maximum fear response? What about carnivals, haunted houses, and scary rides? Do you remember that goose bumps and hair standing on end were desirable responses? Do you also remember that those choosing not to participate were called names like wimp or sissy?

Everyone would think we were having a good time. However, suppose the little door opened, and a creature entered, promising to give us the sensation of fear any time **we** wanted. So we turned parts of our mind and nervous system over to this creature. In doing so, we gave it the right to fill us with fear whenever **it** wanted. As a result of this simple contract, we can experience a life filled with many fears. Forgetting our childish games, we blame God and wonder why He doesn't free us from this spirit of fear.

God is honoring us by honoring our decision to allow fear to take a place in our heart. Just as we have the right to choose life or death, we have the right to choose love or fear. This is not complicated. God tells us, *He who overcomes shall inherit all things, and I will be his God and he will be My son. But the* **cowardly***, the unbelieving...shall have their part in the lake which burns with fire and brimstone, which is the second death* (Revelation 21:7-8). Isn't it interesting that He begins the list with those controlled by fear?

Many Christians don't believe in the manifestations of the Holy Spirit, nor do they believe in His gifts. They don't believe that God would interact directly in their lives by providing healing, deliverance, victory, or prosperity. They may believe that "God helps those who help themselves." They often want someone else to pray for them, so they won't have to approach God personally.

This is understandable; it is also a problem. God says that anything which is not of faith, is sin. If we don't believe what He says about Himself, concerning His divine nature of love, grace, and mercy, we have a problem. Once again we go to Scripture, and find, *Beware, brethren, lest there be in any of you an* **evil heart of unbelief***...(and)...***they could not enter in because of unbelief** (Hebrews 3:12-19). [Emphasis ours] (Also see Luke 19:12-27, The Parable of the Ten Minas; and Matthew 25:14-30, The Parable of the Talents)

Death and the Fear of Death

We have studied what the Bible says concerning death and the role it plays in our lives. It appears to have been one of the first of Satan's weapons. God told Adam if he ate of the fruit of the tree of the knowledge of good and evil, he would surely die.

The serpent contradicted God, telling Eve she would not surely die. She ate and gave to Adam who was with her and they received death into themselves. (See Genesis 3:4-5) We are also told that Death is the last enemy that will be destroyed. (1 Corinthians 15:25-26) Once again, death is described as a primary enemy here on earth.

Scripture helps define the job God gave to Jesus, which was to defeat Satan. We are told that through death He destroyed him who had the power of death, and released those who, through the fear of death, were subject to bondage. (Hebrews 2:14-15) The power of fear has been overcome in Jesus Christ! There is no reason for fear to continue to rule in our hearts or in our lives!

In summary, all fear is sin because it is the opposite of love. (Romans 8:15; 2 Timothy 1:7) There is no reason for us to allow fear, death, or the fear of death to rule in our lives. We can, instead, choose to allow love to rule in our lives; and God is Love.

There are three major stages in the process of salvation. As we overcome our fears concerning accepting the initial gift of salvation, we begin a journey of discovery, empowered by our freedom of choice, and guided by the Holy Spirit.

Salvation of the Spirit

In order to understand the process of salvation, it might be useful to look at the model of the Temple we have been given for comparison. When Moses was commanded to build the first Temple for God, he was given a very clear and precise shopping list for all the component parts, as well as a program for construction that outlined the steps in the process.

Phase one consisted of constructing the Holy of Holies, and providing all those things associated with it. Phase two was the construction of the inner court with all its furnishings. Finally, the outer court was completed. This is our model of construction for the Temple of God.

We are told that, as a part of the **new** covenant, **we** are the temple and residence for God. Because those things associated with the old covenant are defined as shadows of the new covenant, we believe this also applies to the Temple. Therefore, God's program would be to construct the three parts of the Temple. He would logically begin with the Holy of Holies, then the inner court, finally, the outer court. If we equate **our spirit** with the **Holy of Holies**, we have a starting place.

We believe salvation of the spirit occurs in an instant, through grace, and not by anything we can earn. When we accept the gift of salvation, the spiritual being we were ceases to exist and a new spiritual being is created. We believe our spirit, in an instant, becomes united with the Holy Spirit.

(Ephesians 5:8-9; Ezekiel 11:19; 2 Corinthians 5:17) From God's perspective, our previous moral and spiritual condition has ceased to exist.

Jesus told Nicodemus, the Pharisee, he would have to be born again. When He was questioned, Jesus explained that it was not a physical birth, but a spiritual rebirth. This new spiritual creation, who once was a child of darkness, is now a child of light, clothed with righteousness and holiness. (Ephesians 4:24; 1 Corinthians 1:30; 1 Corinthians 6:11; Romans 8:35-39, 11:29; and Ezekiel 18:31)

There is no discussion in Scripture concerning the body being re-created as a part of this salvation experience. We know the Scriptures concerning this event can't be referring to either our soul or our body. We have never met anyone who doesn't continue to have thoughts and physical desires that don't come from God.

The focus of God's creativity in this moment of initial salvation is our spirit, our personal holy of holies. It has been **saved, washed, sanctified, justified**, and **created anew**. Phase one is accomplished.

Salvation of the Soul

We believe that, at this point, all things pertaining to our spirit have become new. However, our soul-man still has many of the same thought patterns, attitudes, beliefs, feelings, and desires it had before we were saved. Throughout the Scriptures we find references to the sad condition of the soul before salvation. (2 Corinthians 3:14; 4:4) We have all seen brothers and sisters in Christ whose life is far from victorious.

Generally, our old heart programming is not in keeping with God's truth. There appear to be levels of consciousness of which we are not aware. As a result, we respond to other people, events in life, and God in ways we don't understand. Often our thinking process has become automatic, because our thoughts are based in old programming.

The heart is the center of physical function as well as moral and spiritual function. It is the center of the soul. Scripture indicates that most of us don't know what is going on in our own heart, which is deceitful, and desperately wicked. (Jeremiah 17:9; Mark 7:21-23; Proverbs 23:7). The things we believe about ourselves, other people, and God, represent the reality in which we live.

These concepts, planted in the heart and expressed in our words and actions, often become self-fulfilling prophecies. We may respond explosively to seemingly unimportant events, and are surprised at the fervor of our outburst. We proclaim, "Gee, I don't know where that came from." Programming, put in place many years ago, could be stimulating automatic responses to certain events. We react in ways we believe are necessary for our survival, or to have our needs met. In our opinion, **no response is accidental**.

After receiving the gift of salvation, we are still dwelling in a clay body and functioning in this world. As a result, both our soul and our body are still being affected, to some extent, by the influences around us. With all the old programming being normal to our understanding, we continue to respond **normally**.

We are programmed with old ideas and traditions in many areas: life, family, politics, church, and others. Traditions concerning the church and religious issues seem to control, even if they can be proven wrong from Scripture. Old beliefs concerning life and *the way things ought to be* seem to rule our hearts, even when they don't make sense.

Are you familiar with the story of the young wife? Her husband was watching her prepare the ham. Before placing it in the pan, she cut about three inches off the small end, and placed that in the pan next to the large end. As her husband watched, he asked her, "Why did you cut the small end off?" She thought for a minute and replied, "I don't know, it's what my mother always did." He suggested she call her mom and ask.

Her mother answered, "I cut the bone off because my mother always did. I'll ask her why she did that." Later, mom called back, embarrassed and chuckling as she explained, "Your grandmother told me she had to cut the end off the ham because her pan wasn't big enough." This is humorous and, at the same time, not so humorous.

We respond to many situations in our lives in an automatic, possibly irrational, way. We've always done it this way, so we continue the pattern. It's time to question why we do what we do, and why we believe what we believe. Is it beneficial, or is there a better way? Did it really come from the Spirit of God, or is it just old programming?

Perhaps it's time to make a change, to make note of our beliefs, our responses, and our thoughts. This is not complicated. We judge our thoughts, based upon the Word of God, and accept them or cast them down and reject them.

Paul gives us some insight concerning our thoughts, and where they may come from, when he proclaims, *We do not war according to the flesh. For the weapons of our warfare are... mighty in God for* **pulling down** *strongholds, casting down arguments and every high thing* that exalts itself against the knowledge of God, bringing *every thought into captivity to the obedience of Christ* (2 Corinthians 10:3-5). [Emphasis ours] In this passage, strongholds could be systems of thought or programming which are spiritually inspired.

We are not able to accomplish these things in our own strength. We are rooting out spiritual strongholds in our own souls, and we are being opposed by evil spirit beings described as "every high thing." In order for us to succeed in this exercise, we need the active participation and power of the Holy Spirit.

There was an expression coined early in the computer age that applies here: *garbage in, garbage out*. How we **spend our time** and what we **see** and **hear** greatly affect our heart and soul. While some activities may have a positive effect on us, these same activities can influence us negatively, as well: TV, music, videos, books, video games, magazines, and virtual reality, to name a few.

If we allow our emotions, soul, or body to **respond sinfully** to what we see or hear in any of these areas, we become guilty of the sin and receive the spiritual consequences of the sin. (Matthew 6:22-23; Luke 11:34)

Paul states that if anyone **cleanses himself**, he will be sanctified and prepared for every good work. (2 Timothy 2:20-21) This cleansing would, naturally, include everything that represents our chosen environment.

When we are saved, and the process of reprogramming begins, our soul is being cleansed of the darkness as the true light moves in. As we feed on the Word of God, which is the Word of Life and Light, the process continues.

The Bible calls this reprogramming, **renewing the mind**, and is very clear about it being an important step in the process of salvation of the soul. (Hosea 4:6) God's word also equips us with the knowledge necessary to accomplish this. (Romans 12:2; Colossians 3:10; Ephesians 4:23) This renewing of the mind is similar to the reprogramming of a computer.

When we install new software or update old software, we want to delete the old version. When we push the delete button, the computer sends up a box with the question, "Are you sure you really want to delete this?" We have to be persistent in getting rid of the old software, so we can replace it with the new.

New software won't upgrade the computer's performance if it remains in the box on the shelf. It has to be installed and used in order to improve operations. In the same way, we must apply God's Word to our lives for us to benefit from its wisdom.

Jesus has made Himself responsible to **complete that work** He has begun in us. (Philippians 1:6) We are not told specifically when that process will be complete. Therefore, we believe the salvation of our soul requires us to take an active role if we want to **speed up the process**, **minimize the discomfort**, and **walk in a greater degree of victory** now.

As the process takes place, we see the construction of the **inner court**, or **the second phase** of the temple being completed as a part of His master plan.

Salvation of the Body

It is possible for us to experience a measure of healing and restoration in our bodies as we are healed and restored in our souls. During our years of ministry, we have received testimonies from people who experienced these healings after soul restoration. We always rejoice when we receive such a report and yet we know there is much more.

The Bible describes the fulfillment of our re-creation. When Jesus was preparing to go away, He told His disciples His Father's house contained many mansions, and He was going to prepare a place for them. (John 14:2) Mansions are large, imposing residences.

Paul refers to his earthly body as a humble dwelling place, a tent. Paul also proclaims that we will one day receive the completion of our inheritance in the new, glorified body. This new body, created with celestial material, will undoubtedly be far beyond our current capacity to understand. We believe it will have capabilities and powers we can't imagine.

There is a much greater dimension applicable to the salvation of our bodies. We believe total salvation of the body is achieved at the time we receive a glorified body as promised in Scripture. (Romans 8:23; 1 Corinthians 15: 40-49; Philippians 3:20-21) It will be our graduation present, given to us by our Daddy in heaven. When we receive our new body, God will have completed the construction of the **outer court** or the **third phase** of His temple. (2 Corinthians 5:1-4)

Renounce Sin and Be Delivered

The Word of God tells us wonderful things will occur if we confess our sins. (1 John 1:9) When we confess our sins, we acknowledge that we are desperately wicked. We admit we have no hope of salvation if it's based upon our ability to comply with the law. We confess that our only hope is to depend on His mercy, grace, and finished work of salvation. (1 Peter 1:13-15) When we stop depending on our own ability and depend on Him entirely, He is capable of doing everything necessary.

When we confess our sins, we take responsibility for having agreed with the kingdom of darkness through our words and actions. We begin to recognize which patterns of our behavior are displeasing to God and are harmful to us and to others. We disown those behaviors and attitudes. We are counseled to declare our confessions to one another. (2 Corinthians 4:2; James 5:16; Revelation 12:11)

As we will discuss later, we know that he who sins becomes a slave of sin. If we want to be free of the spiritual slavery, we must renounce our sins. This is a legal process whereby we nullify the agreement we made with the kingdom of darkness. Before Jesus fulfilled His commission, this was impossible; but now, because of what He did, we can be free by exercising our free will.

When we renounce our sins and nullify Satan's legal claim, we ask the Lord to deliver us and free us of the power of sin. He rescues us from bondage to sin and releases us from spiritual imprisonment. His completed work includes the past, present, and future, providing us with perfect security. (Luke 4:18; Colossians 1:13; 2 Timothy 4:18; 2 Corinthians 1:10)

Repent of Sin

In the Bible, the message of repentance was for all men, saved and unsaved. (Revelation 2:4-5; Revelation 2:22; Revelation 3:19; Matthew 3:8; Acts 26:20) We believe this applies even more today, since the Lord Jesus has paid for all the sins of the world.

While we are slaves of sin, our decisions to stop sinning are merely an effort of willpower, like all those New Year's resolutions that fade away after just a few days. After we renounce our sins, taking away the legal claim held by the kingdom of darkness, we are no longer slaves of the power of sin. When we are no longer slaves, it is possible to repent of those sins.

Repentance is not saying, "I'm sorry." **Repentance** is making a decision to **change** our **behavior**. When we receive freedom and renewal of our mind opens our understanding concerning our sins, we repent and put aside those sins. No longer a slave to sin, we determine to go in a new direction.

We change our pattern of behavior, conforming to the path laid out for us by our Lord.

Be Restored as Peter Was Restored

We believe complete healing cannot be accomplished without restoration, as it is a vital component of the process. (Psalm 23:3). In Hebrew, the word for restore, primarily, means to return or bring back. (Strong's, H 7725)

In our view, the whole process of restoration is returning everyone to wholeness, as Adam and Eve were before the fall. Because of our sinful reactions to things we have experienced, we believe that we have turned parts of our soul and humanity over to the control of the kingdom of darkness. We will discuss this much more completely in Section Two.

John 10:10, tells us the thief comes only to steal, kill, and destroy. Our object is to take back all that has been killed, stolen, and destroyed. To illustrate, when he was in prison, Peter was asleep, chained between two guards. An angel entered the cell and told Peter to get up and put on his sandals. When Peter did, the chains fell off.

Technically, Peter was delivered at this point. All the restraints holding him in bondage were removed. The angel didn't stop at deliverance. He told Peter to follow as he led him out of the cell, past more guards, and out the iron gate of the prison, that opened by itself. (Acts 12:6-10) The angel restored, or returned, Peter to the streets of the city and the relative freedom he had enjoyed before his imprisonment.

The goal of this ministry is to help people retrieve all their soul and humanity lost to Satan's control through deception and sin. Parts of our soul and humanity have been left in bondage, or spiritual imprisonment. Through the power of the Holy Spirit we are led through the process of taking back everything belonging to us.

We offer this sample prayer for you to fervently proclaim to both your soul and the spiritual realm. There are similar Sample Prayers in this book. Each time you come to one, we strongly encourage you to read it aloud.

Sample Prayer:

I renounce all the sins of my past. I renounce all the hidden things of shame, and the power of those things to control me. I renounce all of my decisions and choices that have turned my soul or humanity over to the control of Satan's kingdom.

Heavenly Father, I thank You for the gift of salvation through the Lord Jesus Christ. I thank You for setting me apart. I thank You for the gift of righteousness and the gift of grace by which I am washed and justified.

I know that the Lord, Jesus Christ, has delivered me from the power of darkness. I thank you that I am no longer subject to condemnation or to the Law of sin and death. I have been freed from captivity by the Law of the Spirit of Life and restored into Your loving care.

I thank You for Your living Word that renews my mind and destroys the power of deception that has controlled me. I thank You for cleansing and restoring my soul and for giving me the ability to prosper in all things, even as my soul prospers.

I praise Your Holy Name! Amen.

CAN CHRISTIANS BE DEMON POSSESSED?

Now that we have determined what it means to be a Christian, we need to deal with a troublesome question. For many years, Glenna and I have dealt with this question at seminars and in conversations with pastors and other Christians. It would be impossible to determine how many times we've been asked, "Why is deliverance necessary for Christians?"

There is a general perception that, as Christians, we should be immune to demonic infestation. We are, after all, the Temple of God. We have been told that it is impossible for God and those serving Satan to dwell in the same house. Light and darkness cannot dwell in the same place. These voices proclaim loudly that a Christian absolutely cannot be demon possessed.

For the purposes of our discussion, possession would indicate ownership. If this is true, we need to determine how legal claim of ownership can be established. Because we are triune, it seems we would need to determine the qualifications at all three levels of our being.

The fact that God is the Father and Creator of our spirit proclaims ownership. (Isaiah 42:5; Zechariah 12:1; Ecclesiastes 12:7; 1 Corinthians 6:20) God says all souls belong to Him. (Ezekiel 18:4) He also claims ownership of our body and of the earth. (Psalm 24:1; 1 Corinthians 10:26) Since our body is made of the dust of the earth, He maintains a prior claim on both the earth and our body. Furthermore, as Christians, we have become the purchased possession of God through the Lord Jesus Christ.

Most of us don't like the idea of being anyone's property. We want to feel free and independent so we can have a greater measure of control. On the other hand, this is extremely comforting. This contradicts the position that God is just a force in the universe, uninvolved in the lives of people. Rather, it suggests that He will maintain an active role in the happenings on earth, because He has a vested interest in those things that affect His property.

If He claims ownership, either passively or actively, it stands to reason that He protects that which belongs to Him. The One claiming ownership is the all-powerful and all loving King of the universe. He has a vested interest in preventing *His flock* from utterly destroying itself. He is motivated to help us find good food and water, and protect us from disease, bugs, and parasitic organisms. It pleases Him when we are healthy and content. (Ezekiel 34:12-16)

Speaking of bugs and parasitic organisms, we don't believe Christians can be demon possessed. Because of the price He paid, the Lord owns us. It is **impossible** for us to have another owner. Maybe we can give access to the spiritual bugs and parasites. Thus we can be tormented, harassed, or even infested by those things, just as any house could be infested with roaches.

We Are the Temple

The Bible says we represent a house, the present day temple of God. In Proverbs 20:27 we are told that the spirit of a man is the lamp of the Lord, searching all the **inner depths of his heart**. The literal translation speaks of *the rooms of the belly*. So our heart apparently consists of multiple compartments. This is an interesting parallel.

The first tabernacle for God had three defined spaces or rooms. Moses was instructed to construct the Holy of Holies, then the inner court, and, finally, the outer court. In the book of Ezekiel, chapters eight through ten, God showed the prophet a variety of activities taking place in the temple built in Jerusalem.

He observed abominations occurring in the outer court. Then he was instructed to dig a hole into the wall so he could witness the activities of the inner court. He peered in to see *wicked abominations* occurring in the inner court. He saw the idols of the house of Israel, images of creeping things, and abominable beasts portrayed on the walls. He witnessed seventy of the elders giving sacrifice to the images and the idols.

After this, God directed his attention to a place where women were sitting and weeping for Tammuz. In modern terms, these women would be weeping for the Antichrist. Again, God took Ezekiel into the inner court where men were worshiping the sun, or the sun god Baal, toward the east. God proclaimed this to be an even greater abomination.

For those who are convinced God and Satan can't dwell in the same house, we would like to make this point. God was resident in the Holy of Holies while the abominations and demonic activities were occurring in both the inner and outer courts. We don't know how long He shared this house with satanic activity. We are told, in Chapter 11, that He finally removed Himself to a mountain east of the city. (Ezekiel 8:4-6, 9:3; 10:4, 18, 19; 11:23)

We, the present-day temple, also have three compartments: our spiritual core, which is the Holy of Holies; our soul, which functions as the inner court; and our body, the outer court. If we draw a parallel with the other temple, we believe that the Spirit of God does dwell in our holy of holies. This is true in spite of the fact that demonic activities can still take place in both our inner and outer courts.

God tells us He never changes. What was true for the temple of old should also be true for the present-day temple. (1 Corinthians 3:16; 6:19-20, and 2 Corinthians 6:16)

What About Paul's Thorn?

We've also been told that references to the old Temple are not relevant. That structure existed before the new covenant so, in spite of God never changing, it doesn't apply to us. Once again, these voices are very insistent that a Christian cannot *have a demon*! Our response has to be the question, "What does the Bible say?"

Paul writes that he was given a thorn in the flesh, a messenger from Satan, to buffet or beat him. He indicated it occurred so he would not be exalted inappropriately as a result of the revelations God had given him. Paul said he *might desire to boast* so he may have been tempted by pride, which is sin. The thorn apparently functioned as a countermeasure against pride. (2 Corinthians 12: 6-10)

The word messenger used here is the same Greek word normally translated as angel. A messenger from God would be an angel; one from Satan would be a demon. The Scripture clearly states that Paul's thorn, this messenger, came from Satan.

This demonic messenger was not like Casper, the friendly ghost, floating alongside Paul. It was *in the flesh*, afflicting and tormenting Paul. He prayed to God to remove the thorn, but God refused, saying His grace was sufficient for Paul. We interpret this as meaning God was being glorified through Paul. He was forcing Paul to accept a humbling place of weakness.

We also believe God was saying the thorn was necessary for Paul's good. Paul appeared to understand this when he proclaimed he would take pleasure in infirmities, reproaches, needs, persecutions, and distresses. In being humbled by all these things, Paul would be less subject to the sins of pride and self-exaltation. God could use him in a greater way.

We believe that our sin limits God's ability to utilize us in His highest and best way. As a result, He responds in love by allowing us to experience the consequences of our sin. If our sin causes us to experience a thorn, or affliction, we might respond the way Paul did. When we are **motivated** to forsake the sin, God can raise us up to a higher and better place. We think this is a good thing.

Fiery Serpents

As God's chosen people traveled in the wilderness, they complained against God and against Moses. God heard their complaints and responded by sending fiery serpents. The serpents bit the people and some of them died. The people then went to Moses asking him to tell God that they were sorry for their sin. They wanted God to take away the fiery serpents. (Numbers 21)

When Moses prayed for the people, God told him to make a serpent of bronze and hang it on a pole. If the people were bitten, they could look at the serpent and live. He would not take away the fiery serpents.

He might have said, "The serpents are good for you, because they motivate you to seek the healing provided by the bronze serpent on the pole." [This was a foreshadowing of the coming Christ]. "They **motivate you** to maintain a closer relationship with Me. They also **motivate you** to keep moving forward toward the Promised Land. This is all good for you."

We can see that pain can bring about good. There is a disease that inhibits a person from experiencing pain. When someone with that disease damages their body, they don't feel the pain, so they are not motivated to seek medical help. This damage could lead to death.

God gave our bodies the ability to experience pain. It motivates us to do what is beneficial for our survival. There are a number of good ways to treat an injury, as long as we know it is there. That is why we say **pain can be used for good**.

We believe this also applies to both the spiritual and emotional levels of our beings. A thorn in the flesh can be perceived as good, because it is very motivating. Spiritual and emotional harassment can also be perceived as good because it will **motivate us** to seek God. When we seek God, we receive the healing and restoration He has provided through His master plan of salvation.

God set up a perfect system to help us survive our time on planet Earth. In His mercy, He allows unpleasant circumstances to work out issues in the hearts of His children.

God proclaimed, *"I form the light and create darkness, I make peace and create calamity; I, the LORD, do all these things."* He went on to say, *"I, the LORD, have created it. Woe to him who strives with his Maker"* (Isaiah 45:7-9)! *Behold, I have created...the spoiler to destroy"* (Isaiah 54:16).

In the next verse He also proclaimed, *"No weapon formed against you shall prosper, and every tongue which rises against you in judgment you shall condemn. This is the heritage of the servants of the LORD, and their righteousness is from Me"* (Isaiah 54:17).

God created calamity, darkness, and the spoiler or destroyer. Does this make Him the angry, vengeful tyrant many believe Him to be? No. When He declared those things, He offered the alternative in the next verse. We believe this is all a part of His plan for salvation. It is part of the purpose of giving us the freedom to choose and allowing us to experience the consequences of those choices, both good and bad. This makes us stronger, as individuals, and strengthens the body of Christ, in general. (1 Corinthians 10:13)

How Do They Get In?

If Paul can receive sin into his flesh, why can't we? Are we greater than Paul? If not, how do spiritual bugs gain entrance? Can we receive demons from a dirty potty seat or from other conditions in our environment? Can we receive them through eye gates, ear gates, or mouth gates? Can we receive a spiritual virus simply by having association with people who possess it? Can demonic entities hop from one person to another?

We've been asked all these questions. We've read books and accumulated a great deal of material on the subject. Because of the ministry with which we've been involved, we've heard some very strange things. We finally decided we needed to disregard complicated formulas and look for an answer from the Source. In doing so, we found our answer by looking at both ends of the Book.

At the **back end** of the Book, in Revelation 3:20, Jesus proclaims that He knocks **on our door**, which, we believe, is the door of our heart. When He knocks, and **we open our door**, He will come in. He will have fellowship with us, eat with us, and establish covenant with us. Maybe the door only has a handle on the inside, so we are required to open it. Regardless, we are convinced He won't open the door, because that would disregard our free will, our right to choose.

In the Song of Solomon, the King (also called her beloved shepherd) came and knocked, but the Shulammite woman didn't respond quickly enough. When she finally did respond, He was gone. (Song of Solomon 5:2-6) This demonstrates that He honors our right to choose.

This might also apply to others who represent the Lord. If we pray for a spirit of wisdom, we believe wisdom will knock on our door, and it is up to us to allow wisdom access. If we're seeking other things from Him, is it up to us to open our door so we can receive what, or whom, He sends? It is always our responsibility to open the door in order to receive from Him.

At the **front end**, in the book of Genesis, the sacrifice Cain offered God had been rejected, and he was angry. God's response was to ask, "Cain, why are you so angry? Don't you know that, if you do well, you will be accepted? If you do not do well, sin lies at your door. It wants to come in and have you, but you are supposed to have dominion over it." [Author's paraphrase, Genesis 4:6-7]

This is a very significant statement. Cain is not a Christian, so he doesn't have the blood of Christ, the name of Christ, or the power of the Holy Spirit. In spite of this, God tells Cain he is supposed to rule over this thing called sin. This verse uses wording based on an old Babylonian word that described an evil demon crouching at the door of a building, threatening the people inside. (See NIV Study Bible note for Genesis 4:7)

In this case, it is sin that threatens and, also, the demonic penalty for sin. The word **sin** used here means an **offense** and its **penalty** or **punishment.** (Strong's H 2403) It also means the **state of being wicked**. This literally means to **absorb** or **take in** like a sponge or a wick. It results from the act of lawlessness, giving one a **predisposition** to commit sin. This sin can be received as a result of our own bad decisions and willful acts of sin.

In accordance with this example, as we commit sin we take into ourselves the penalty or punishment for sin. When we take this thing, called sin, into ourselves, Scripture says we become the slave of sin. (John 8:34) Remember that sin was lying at Cain's door waiting for an **opportunity to enter**; an opportunity provided by Cain when he chose to sin.

Now we have a word picture. Cain is feeling rejected and angry, and there is an evil demon crouching at the door of his heart. We imagine this creature with big yellow eyes, pointy ears, horns, teeth, and claws, seeking access into Cain. God told him he didn't have to let it in. He could have said no and refused to open the door. Instead, he let sin in and killed his brother.

This gives us an idea of how spirits get in. They knock; **we open our door** and allow them in. God won't barge in without our invitation, and Satan can't barge in without our invitation. He, and those who represent him, can knock on our door and hope to receive access, but they can only come in as we allow.

Who Is Responsible?

So how do demons get in? **We let them in.** Then they have a legal dwelling place in the rooms of our belly. They receive legal status because we give it to them. When they knock on our door, it is as though they offer us a contract.

They offer to provide us with strength, rage, or whatever we need, in order to deal with a person who has wronged us. They offer to help us defend or protect ourselves, or defeat an enemy. In return, they want residency in **our condo project**. They may also require a part of our soul or humanity we don't value, telling us we'll never miss it.

We regularly hear people make statements such as, "He broke my heart; She offended me; He **made me** sad; someone hurt my feelings; or they **made me** angry." These expressions proclaim that someone else **made us** say, do, or feel something. To say this implies that we have lost our free will, which is impossible. It is like saying, "Someone made me a Volkswagen."

No one else can make us anything, not sad, angry, offended, or even happy. We decide how we will respond to a word, a comment, a situation, or anything else we experience. No one else can control our emotions. We are the only ones who decide when and, and for whom, we open our door. Remember, God gave us free will, and the gifts and the calling of God are irrevocable.

The system God established was illustrated when He warned Cain that sin was lying at the door. The system God established never changes and the temptation to sin is ever present. Peter said that our adversary, the devil, roams the earth seeking whom he may devour. (1 Peter 5:8) Paul also warned us to withstand the fiery darts of the wicked one. (Ephesians 6:16) [Author's paraphrase]

These are all warnings to Christians as well as to the unsaved. We are under the constant influence of the god of this world. Satan and his minions come to kill, steal, and destroy. It is up to us to guard our door very carefully and only allow access to those who seek our good.

In Conclusion

We are influenced by the demonic in our souls and bodies, but Satan can only take the ground we give him. Each time we react to circumstances and the deceptions of Satan in a sinful way, we open a door for enemy forces to move in. Our task is to **use our authority** to evict the deceivers and **take back** the **promised land** of our soul, so we can walk freely in the Spirit of God.

Before Jesus came to the earth, there was no hope. In Joshua 9, when the people of God made an unwise covenant, they were obligated to that covenant, even though they had been deceived. Since He has come, and paid for all the sins of the world, we can now escape from everything we entered into through deception.

Once we make peace with the idea that demonic entities have gained access to **our condo**, we can do something about it. When we understand that we are the ones who opened the door, we can take responsibility for our actions. As we realize that these entities only have access because of contracts to which we agreed, we can nullify the contracts. **Deliverance really is easy.** We invited the *bugs* and *parasites* in, and **we can evict them.**

The power of the blood of Christ is available to free us from the effects of our unwise decisions. The eternal consequence of sin, and the demonic infestation that results from sin, can be removed. The fact that we chose to open the door no longer condemns us to permanent consequences. We are no longer slaves to sin, because the legal claim is no longer valid. This is a glorious part of the good news of the Gospel of Christ.

OUR AUTHORITY

Our understanding of our authority in Jesus is very important. When we start teaching about the devil, demons, satanism, and witchcraft, some people become fearful. They sometimes say, "Let's not talk about those things, because if we do, they might get angry and hurt us." This fear filled Christian might propose that we hide in our prayer closet and pray for the rapture.

That reminds me of a movie I once saw. In this movie a melon farmer antagonized a hired killer. The killer came into a restaurant where the farmer was having breakfast. He started telling the farmer how he planned to slowly kill him, and how he wanted him to suffer. The killer went on and on. Finally, the farmer said, "Well, I guess it doesn't do any good to try and get on your good side." He put down his coffee cup and slugged the killer, who went rolling across the floor.

The killer didn't have a good side and neither does Satan. There is nothing we can do to appease him. He and his servants are entities without the capacity for love, mercy, pity, or grace. They are motivated exclusively by evil and the desire to steal, kill, and destroy. There is no place to hide from these rulers of darkness and hosts of wickedness in heavenly places.

One of Satan's greatest weapons against us is fear. If we fear him, he has already won the battle. He doesn't rest or sleep; he is ruthless and extremely persistent. When our defenses are down, he is sure to attack. Knowing this, we should wage an **offensive war** using all the weapons we have. Keeping him on the defensive is much more effective than cowering in the closet.

We can wage war against Satan's kingdom using the weapons and armor with which the Lord has armed us. Scripture describes a belt of truth, breastplate of righteousness, footwear of the gospel of peace, the shield of faith, the helmet of salvation, and the sword of the Spirit, which is the Word of God. We are charged with praying always. (Ephesians 6:12-18)

Our most powerful, offensive weapon is prayer. Our words and proclamations, aligned with the Word of God, are an effective sword and will overcome him. (Revelation 12:11) How do we go on the offensive? With God's authority!

God's Authority

God's authority was made manifest at the time of creation. He said, "Light be," and the process of creation began.

Amusingly, even the theory of the Big Bang describes a similar event. There was once nothing in the universe except one little spot of matter, too small for us to imagine. It contained more density and energy than anyone could understand. For reasons the proponents of this theory can't explain, this spot of energy exploded and became all the matter in the universe.

Based upon an assortment of assumptions, these proponents estimate the time since the Big Bang, and the amount of energy and matter in the universe. It takes a massive amount of blind faith to believe all their theories.

We believe it takes much less faith to believe the Word of God in Genesis 1:1. When we look at the universe, the miraculous machine we live in, and the world around us, it is obvious it could only have been accomplished by a Being worthy of the title, God. (John 1:3)

We find it reasonable to accept that the One who created everything has infinite authority and should be considered the Owner of all He has created, (Psalms 24:1) We don't think it's arrogance for Him to proclaim, *Thus says the LORD: "Heaven is My throne and the earth is My footstool"* (Isaiah 66:1).

Authority Given to Adam and Eve

God has not allowed His creation to be in subjection to angels. This includes all the fallen angels and the king of the fallen angels. (Hebrews 2:5-8) These are powerful supernatural beings with the wisdom of having been there when God created the heavens and the earth. Then, after creating all things, He put it all under the authority of people **wearing clay bodies**. This must have been terribly frustrating for Satan and his angels!

The purpose of God was to create companions for Himself, as well as caretakers of His creation. After He created them, the Lord stated that Adam and Eve were given dominion in this physical realm. Dominion proclaimed sovereignty, authority, and power.

In doing so, He made it necessary for all things to be accomplished through the authority He had given them. Once He made that declaration, God was bound by His word because, "The gifts and the calling of God are irrevocable." (Genesis 1:26; Ephesians 1:5; Isaiah 43:21; 1 Samuel 15:29; Romans 11:29)

This is extremely important, because the one with dominion is the only one who can decide what will be done. Like God, the one with dominion can delegate decisions or actions to others, but will always be the responsible party. Therefore, if we delegate our authority and dominion to Satan's kingdom, we will still be responsible for what is done with that authority.

Adam Rebelled

Scripture reads, "God commanded the man." There was no mention of the command being given to Eve. Adam received the command and was responsible for it. Later, when Eve was deceived by the serpent and ate, Adam also ate. Adam rebelled against the only command given him. (Genesis 2:17; Genesis 3:6)

Scripture does not say that Adam was deceived; therefore, his was the sin of rebellion. Verse seven says their eyes were opened, they knew that they were naked, and they made themselves aprons. Finally, when they heard the sound of God walking in the garden, they hid in fear. As a result, God confronted the serpent, Eve, and Adam. (Genesis 3:7-8)

Serpent Was Cursed

The serpent, Satan, was cursed for his actions. The Lord said He would put a mutual hatred between the serpent and the woman, and between his seed and her Seed (Jesus). The Lord also proclaimed that her Seed would bruise the head of the serpent. The word bruise suggests much more than the skin discoloration, it suggests that his head would be shattered or crushed. (Genesis 3:14-15)

Eve Received Consequences

The curse that God placed upon the serpent demonstrates that Eve has not been cast aside, but has been given a very important place in His master plan. It's interesting that God said the Seed of Eve would be the one to crush the serpent's head, not the seed of Adam. (Genesis 3:16) In spite of popular opinion, we find no evidence that Eve, or womankind, has been cursed.

God did say there would be consequences as a result of her being deceived. He told her there would be multiplied sorrow and pain associated with childbirth, that her desire would be for her husband, and her husband would be put in a place of authority over her. Although many women have **perceived** this as a *curse*, we would like to look at it from a different perspective.

We have heard much about the differences between men and women. Men generally function more in their left-brain, employing "male" logic and rational application. Most men are not normally as inclined to focus on the emotional, or touchy-feely, aspects of a situation.

Women generally tend to function more in the right brain, reflecting more emotional response and heightened creativity. Women seem to be more intuitive concerning spiritual matters. There is an expression that applies to this, *women's intuition*. We generally view women as being more tuned in to the spiritual than most men. We see this reflected in normal church attendance. Because women are more tuned in to the spiritual realm, it would be easier for the supernatural creature, "the serpent," to deceive them.

We believe God chose to place Eve under the spiritual authority of Adam to protect her from the consequences of being deceived. When a man and woman function together as a team, there is a great blend of logic, emotional response, rational application, creative viewpoint, and spiritual intuition. This seems to be a wise and loving way to combine the strengths of both genders.

Was it God's purpose to punish Eve and all women when He put them under the authority of their husbands? We don't think so. We view it as an expression of His love.

Adam Received Consequences

When confronted by God for his rebellious act, Adam did what any normal man would do; he blamed Eve, and God. (Genesis 3:12) God ignored Adam's attempt to avoid responsibility and continued to list the consequences of Adam's sin.

These consequences were much more profound, from our perspective, than the others. Through Adam's sin, a curse was put on the ground. We believe the entire physical creation was included in the curse, because we are told the entire creation is waiting for the reversal of this curse. (Genesis 3:17-24; Romans 8:19-22)

When Adam chose to rebel, death came in as God predicted, along with rebellion, fear, shame, rejection of God and His law, and fear of rejection. All these demonic forces began exerting some control. He had been given free will but with each sin the spiritual influence became stronger. His ability to resist diminished along with his ability to make right decisions.

Because of Adam's initial bad decision, both he and Eve were defiled by death, were made slaves to sin, and subjected to spiritual bondage. (John 8:34; 2 Peter 2:19) There is a spiritual law which proclaims we will receive the same as we give. As a result of rejecting God, Adam and Eve received rejection and were kicked out of the Garden.

Can you see that image in your mind? God looked at them with absolute fury. He dragged them to the gates of the Garden and hurled them into the dirt. Then to reinforce His indignation, He made it impossible for them to return. Isn't that the way most people view God?

We understand why people might view God this way and yet, we are convinced the real issue is perfect love. God saw that the man and woman had experienced spiritual death as well as having received death into themselves. They would no longer be able to enjoy His companionship but must now experience separation from God. If they had, then, eaten of the tree of life, there would be no hope. They would have existed eternally in this state of spiritual death.

Father God manifested His infinite love for those who rejected Him by protecting them from this terrible fate. He placed guards east of the Garden to guarantee that these fallen people could not have access to the Tree of Life. He already had a perfect plan to redeem them, and all of mankind, from the powers of sin and death. All it took was Jesus coming to do His awesome job of salvation, once for all. (Genesis 3:22-24; Hebrews 7:27)

Satan Received Authority

As a result of Adam's sin, he and all of his descendants would be subject to satanic control. Adam and Eve produced Cain and Abel and the sin of murder was added to the growing list.

The process continued, until the Lord saw so much wickedness among men, His heart was grieved. (Genesis 6:5-7) Once again, many people view this statement as proof that God is filled with hatred for His highest creation. We don't accept this conclusion, because it doesn't represent the nature of our heavenly Father. We see His love being displayed again.

Because people are slaves of sin, they continue to give greater control to those who have become their masters. As each generation comes into the world and continues to sin, Satan uses methods such as fear and deception to gain even greater control. The more they sin, the more they turn their natural dominion and authority over to Satan and his kingdom. (Ephesians 2:2)

The longer the process continued, the more enslaved the people became. The people, whose minds had been blinded, continued to slide deeper into the jaws of death. It was necessary for God to stop the accumulation of iniquity if His master plan was to manifest. (Genesis 6:12) The most loving thing God could do, at that point, was to bring the flood. He chose eight people who could be saved, and greatly reduced the accumulation of iniquity in mankind. (2 Corinthians 4:4)

When Jesus came into the world, there had been many generations since the flood for Satan to deceive and bring into bondage. He was working his will from a place of authority within people. When Jesus was tempted in the desert, He didn't dispute Satan's claim of authority over the kingdoms of the earth. He knew that Satan did possess all the authority **delivered over to him** by normal people. (Luke 4:6) He simply refused the offer.

Jesus Defeated Satan

Despite all of the efforts of Satan and his servants, Jesus was able to accomplish everything His Father sent Him to do. In His life, Jesus defeated Satan absolutely, thus fulfilling prophecies made generations earlier. (1 John 3:8; Matthew 11:5; 26:56; John 19:28; Isaiah 61:1; 35:4-6) Jesus never received anything from Satan into himself. (John 14:30)

This statement reveals that He was free from the control of those who had become the masters of all other men. Because of this fact, Jesus was chosen before the foundation of the world to be the sacrifice for all sin. In paying the price for sin, it was essential for Him to experience the consequences a normal sinful person would experience.

When we consider what Paul said in Ephesians, we conclude that Jesus would have to descend into the lower depths of the earth. In order for the payment to be fair, He would have to experience the fires and torments of Hell. He would have to experience the torments of Satan's kingdom, not as God, but as the Son of Man. (Ephesians 4:8-10)

As terrible as this would be, there would be something much worse! Just as a normal sinful man is separated from God, Jesus would have to be separated from His Father. This is the separation Jesus experienced on the cross, when He cried out, "Why have You forsaken me?" Prior to this moment in time, Jesus had never been separated from the presence of His Father. This must have been far more terrible than the physical and emotional punishment He experienced!

Jesus spoke of the *least* in the kingdom of God; therefore, there must also be the most. We believe that, just as this is true, there must also be the least and the most in Satan's kingdom. If, because of our greater works of righteousness, we receive higher rank, and glory, it stands to reason that for the greatest works of depravity, or evil, a person would also receive the greatest measure of torment. We don't know how this works, but it seems logical.

Paul said Jesus descended into the **lower parts** of the earth. We believe this indicates a lower part of Hell, with associated torment. When Jesus entered into that place carrying all the weight of the sins of the world, just like the most depraved human being, it must have been terrible beyond comprehension.

We might wonder what happened there. We imagine Jesus bent over with that terrible weight on His back. The minions of hell danced around Him celebrating, while the king of Hell sat on his throne gloating. They believed they had defeated Christ and the master plan of God in Heaven. Then, something incomprehensible happened.

We imagine that when Jesus straightened up and dumped the load of sin off His back, the partygoers stopped their dancing, wondering what was going on. When a glimmer of light appeared in the eyes of the Lord, then grew and intensified in, on, and around Him, we imagine all the others cowering and hiding their eyes. (Colossians 2:15)

Paul's wording, He led captivity captive, in Ephesians 4:8, suggests a victory parade. We imagine this procession to be similar to those the victorious Roman army held when they returned to Rome with all the booty and the slaves chained together. They paraded through the triumphal arch riding proudly in their chariots. Similarly, Jesus made a public spectacle of His enemies, triumphing over them. Then He ascended far above all the heavens, that He might fulfill all things.

God's critic might ask, "What kind of God would put His only begotten Son through a terrible ordeal like that?" An absolutely loving God paid for all the sins of the world through His only begotten Son. He also glorified and exalted His Son to a place **far above** all the heavens.

That which Jesus experienced, He counted as joy for the result that would be for eternity. Now and forever the Lord Jesus has the position and authority and no one can take it from Him. (Ephesians 1:20-23) Jesus was the first one with a **glorified** physical body. The angels and all the created beings in heaven don't have them; God, the Father, doesn't have one. Jesus, the **glorified** Christ, is the only One to whom John could possibly be referring. (Revelation 14:14)

What About Adam and Eve?

We are convinced that Jesus also visited the place called Paradise, before ascending on high. At His crucifixion, Jesus spoke to one of the criminals with whom He was crucified. He told the criminal that he would be with Jesus in Paradise. (Luke 23:42-43) Paradise means a place of future happiness. (Strong's 3857)

We are reminded of the story Jesus told about the rich man and the poor man who both died. The rich man went to a place of torment, while the poor man went to a place Jesus described as "Abraham's bosom." We believe this is the same place described here as Paradise.

This place seems to be a temporary holding place for those who died before Jesus ascended. Prior to His death and resurrection, no one was qualified to go to heaven after they died. The Lord apparently created this place called Paradise, Sheol, or Abraham's bosom, for those who would be qualified after Jesus completed the job only He could do.

Jesus allowed Himself to be tortured, killed, and taken into the bowels of the earth. He was raised from the dead. He ascended and sprinkled His blood on the mercy seat. When He sprinkled His blood on the mercy seat, He did what had to be done to pay for **all** the sins of the world. (Hebrews 9:19-21-23) As a part of this process, we believe He preached the Gospel of Life to all those who were resident in Paradise.

With their sins paid for, there was nothing to keep them out of heaven. Those who accepted Jesus as their Savior, left that place with Him to find their place in His eternal kingdom. We believe Adam and Eve were also freed of the consequences of one bad decision. (1 Peter 3:19-20)

Jesus Reclaimed Authority

He lived with the weaknesses of a normal man, tempted in every way, but never giving in to temptation. He was brought to life again by the power of God. After which, He proclaimed, He had the keys of Hades and death. (2 Corinthians 13:4; Revelation 1:18) Satan no longer possessed the power of death; Jesus had defeated him. (Hebrews 2:14-15)

Jesus, a Man without sin, legally claimed back authority over the earth when He defeated Satan. After His resurrection, Jesus appeared to His disciples and declared, **all authority** has been given to Me **in heaven** and **on earth** (Matthew 28:18). [Emphasis ours] This might be the most dramatic statement Jesus had uttered up to that point.

Now we have the absolute guarantee that Jesus **reclaimed the authority** that was given to Satan by sinful people. We don't believe Jesus ever lost His authority in Heaven, but God had given the authority of this physical realm to people in bodies of clay. Because He had worn a clay body and defeated Satan, He received all authority on earth, also. He took it back legally, thus maintaining His righteousness. Satan couldn't go before God and complain, "That's not fair!"

Our Authority as Jesus' Body

Because of what He did, we may die physically, but we are no longer doomed to experience spiritual death. (Hebrews 2:9) Our authority as Jesus' body is defined in the New Testament. How can a person not be confident when we read this proclamation? *"We are children of God, and if children, then heirs–heirs of God and joint-heirs with Christ"* (Romans 8:16-17). (Also see, Ephesians 1:3, 11-13; 2:4-10).

He chose as many as would receive Him as Savior to be a part of His body. We have been told that we are His body, the fullness of Him who fills all in all. Since He has been raised up above all things, we, who are His body, have also been raised up to take the place we were created to have in our Father's kingdom. (Ephesians 1: 19-23; Hebrews 2:5-8)

When He took back the authority that had been given to Satan by sinful people, He chose to do a most amazing thing. He, again, delegated that authority to people. He proclaimed that He was giving us authority over all the power of the enemy and those things that serve him. (Luke 10:19)

We have so many promises from the Lord that there isn't any reason to fear. Being born into a clay body has **given us dominion** in this realm, and being His has **given us awesome authority**. (Matthew 16:19)

The Power of Jesus' Body

Scriptures reveal the power within believers in Jesus Christ. As the book of Luke is closing, we find Jesus explaining to His disciples what has happened. Jesus said, *"It was necessary for the Christ to suffer and to rise from the dead...Behold, I send **the promise** of My Father **upon you**; but stay in the city of Jerusalem until you are **endowed with power from on high**"* (Luke 24: 45-51). *"I will pray the Father and He will give you **another Helper**, that **He may abide with you forever**--the Spirit of truth...you know Him, for **He dwells** with you and will be **in you**"* (John 14:16). [Emphasis ours] (Also see John 14:26 and 15:26)

His followers are given the promise that they will receive power from on high. We know from the Scriptures that Jesus was referring to the Holy Spirit. He is able to do **exceedingly** and **abundantly** beyond anything we can ask **or even think**. (Ephesians 3:20) We believe the reason exceedingly and abundantly were combined suggests this is a magnitude for which the writer didn't have a word. Maybe we could use the word infinitely.

How big is that? I can close my eyes and see galaxies spinning together and exploding. I can imagine huge black holes in space, and whole galaxies being sucked within them to disappear forever. In my imagination, I can see wild things happening, and just about anything is possible. Yet, Paul says this Spirit can do **infinitely** beyond anything I am even capable of thinking!

This isn't a power *out there* in some distant corner of the universe. The Holy Spirit can do it according to the power that works *in us*. Because our spiritual being is now one with the Holy Spirit, the Spirit that **dwells in us** can do infinitely beyond anything we can imagine.

We get hung up over little things while we have the power that created the universe working in us. The same power that freed Jesus from Satan's grasp and raised Him from the dead is in every one who is truly a Christian. Because Jesus has gone to His Father, and we have received the presence and power of the Holy Spirit, we should be on the offensive.

We should be invading the areas Satan considers his, and driving him out of our lives, our families, homes, churches, businesses, and cities. Jesus has proclaimed that we are capable of doing even greater works than He did while on earth. (John 14:12) We don't have to be afraid of, or intimidated by, demonic spirits. We don't have to be concerned that acknowledging their presence is going to give them glory. Our job is to acknowledge they are here, and run them off, giving God the glory.

However, fear can limit us. Death tells us lies and creates illusions. Even though we are told that infinite power dwells in us, we can accept the lies if we choose to.

As we travel, we meet challenges from various sources. We encounter people involved in witchcraft: those who are functional satanists belonging to a formal coven, and others who are practical satanists without a coven. We deal with representatives of governments, with those involved with the travel industry, and with people who belong to churches. All are functioning as a result of their brokenness. In these interactions we experience a great deal of spiritual harassment.

This seems normal because we live on battlefield Earth. We don't respond in fear or paranoia. We consider spiritual warfare a part of our normal prayer activity. On the other hand, if it weren't for what Jesus has already done, some of these things could be very daunting.

Our Assignment as His Body

God proclaimed that life is in the blood. (Genesis 9:4; John 6:53) When Jesus was hanging on the cross, and His side was pierced, a mixture of blood and water touched the ground. The blood of the Son of God, containing **infinite Life** that comes from God, Himself, was poured out into the earth. The curse of death, put on the earth by Adam's fall, was overcome. Therefore, all of creation has technically, and legally, been set free from the curse of death.

Even so, creation is still waiting to be delivered from the bondage of corruption by the revealing of the **sons of God**. (Romans 8:19) As the Lord's ambassadors, representatives, and priests on this earth, we know the debt has been paid. When we look around our cities and see Satan in control, claiming death as his legal ground, it is obvious what we are to do. We have been raised up together with Him, and we are His body. **We are the ones** in the world who can do the warfare and all the other things He empowered us to do.

There are so many Scriptures pertaining to the promises of God for us, we can't possibly include them all. Our goal is to demonstrate clearly the magnitude of what has been given to us. Having received the gift, and the awesome blessings and privileges of it, we also need to make note of **our responsibilities**. Remember, to whom much is given, much is also expected! (Luke 12:48)

Whatever your level of faith is now, you can get stronger. You can exercise more dominion tomorrow and next week than you did today. This is a learning process. You will discover more of what it means to be a child of the King of the universe. You might discover that living on battlefield Earth is really just the process of training to become all we should be.

We glorify our Lord by walking in the victory He gave His life to provide for us. When we go into battle, it is good to remember that the weapons of our warfare are mighty in God (2 Corinthians 10:4). When we make the decision and are willing to fight the battles, the Lord defeats our enemies. He lays them down before us, so we can put our feet upon their necks.

Then, He destroys our enemies. (Joshua 10: 24-26) This is what makes us **more than conquerors.** (Romans 8:37)

Jesus tells us, *"**Go therefore** and **make disciples** of all the nations, **baptizing them** in the name of the Father and of the Son and of the Holy Spirit, **teaching them** to observe all things that **I have commanded you**; and lo, I am with you always, even to the end of the age"* (Matthew 28:18-20). [Emphasis ours] This was never meant to be a suggestion; this is a command.

This isn't some theological mystery. It is very simple. Jesus also said, *"**If you love Me**, keep My commandments"* (John 14:15). [Emphasis ours] We either love Him, or we don't.

We are either going to keep His commandments, or we are not. We either stomp the enemy, or we don't. We either chase him out of our family, our church, and our territory, or we don't. These are very clear options. This is a good time to pray.

<u>Sample Prayer:</u>

Heavenly Father, I praise You for blessing me with every spiritual blessing in the heavenlies.

I praise You for the privilege of being raised up a child and joint heir with the Lord Jesus Christ. I praise You for the awesome power of the Holy Spirit working in me. I praise You for the spiritual weapons and authority You have delegated to me. I praise You for making me to be more than a conqueror!

I ask You to do what ever it takes for my mind and soul to receive the revelation of these truths so I can serve You in a greater way.

I thank You for giving me the faith, courage, and confidence to use this authority to bring You an abundance of glory and honor. Amen.

SECTION TWO: ROOT CUTTING

What Is Root Cutting?

In Genesis, chapter one, God, in the process of creation, proclaims in verse 11, *"Let the earth bring forth...the **fruit tree** that yields fruit according to **its kind**."* Then, verse 12 reads, *"The earth brought forth...**the tree** that yields fruit, **whose seed is in itself,** according to its kind."*

Trees, plants, seeds, branches, vines, roots, and fruit are mentioned many times in the Bible. There are also references to gardening and gardeners, beginning with the Garden of Eden and continuing throughout the Gospels and Epistles.

The Garden of Eden contained both the tree of life and the tree that produced death. (Genesis 2:8-9) From the beginning, God established a contrast for the purpose of giving mankind the freedom to choose God, or not. (See John 15:1-5)

In Matthew 13, people are referred to as seeds planted in the world. There is a contrast between the seeds that are the sons of God and those that are the children of Satan. (Matthew 13:37-38) As the seeds develop into plants, some produce the good fruit of God, and some produce the bad fruit of wickedness.

Paul identifies good fruit as love, joy, peace, long-suffering, kindness, goodness, faithfulness, gentleness, and self-control. (Galatians 5:22-23) These are called the fruit of the Spirit. Jesus said, *"A tree is known by its fruit."* (Matthew 12:33) Jesus also described people as trees bearing fruit with a contrast between the types of fruit they produce. (Matthew 7:16-20)

When John the Baptist was confronting the Pharisees and Sadducees, he referred to them as a brood of vipers and commanded them to bear fruits worthy of repentance. He told them the trees that don't bear good fruit would be cut down and thrown into the fire. (Matthew 3:7-10)

The writer of the book of Jude expressed concern regarding *certain men* who had crept into the church unnoticed. He referred to them as ungodly men, dreamers, defiling the flesh, rejecting authority, and speaking evil of dignitaries. He called these men waterless clouds, late autumn **trees without fruit**, for whom was reserved the blackness of darkness forever. (Jude 4-13) Because of the fruit of sin, they were condemned as dead trees. (Also see Matthew 15:13-14) They were like the fig tree that produced **no good fruit**, so it was cursed and dried up.

We see sin as a seed. The circumstances of life are the process by which the seed of sin is planted in the fertile ground of our soul. The original circumstance and all similar, subsequent ones continue to feed the plant, which grows accordingly. The plant, then, begins to produce fruit. Since the seed is sin, the fruit will be sin, possessing the seed of sin.

Attack Roots to Kill Tree

We know from the Bible and our experience that some trees produce bad fruit, some trees produce good fruit, and some trees function like normal Christians. These trees produce good fruit some of the time and bad fruit the rest of the time. This is because the spiritual core of our being has been re-created, but our soul and body continue to be works in process.

We see many different examples of how Christians tend to deal with one another. One of the more common methods is to function as an *official fruit inspector*. This person scans all the trees around them. When they see a member of the body who is, at that moment, producing bad fruit, they strike. They pull out their sword of self-righteousness, hack at the fruit, and damage the tree.

We have ministered to many wounded Christians who have experienced this kind of treatment. How many times have you heard it said, "Why is the church the only army that regularly shoots its own wounded?" We have met many disenfranchised Christians who left the church, because *the world* treats them better. Some have told us, "I will never again set foot in a church with all those self-righteous hypocrites!" Does that sound familiar?

Does the *sword of self-righteousness* method sound like something Jesus would do? Didn't He say, "Let him who has no sin cast the first stone?" If anyone had the right to look down on other people as sinners, it was Jesus, but He didn't. The ones He rebuked were the ones who looked down on others and refused to acknowledge their own sin.

If the goal is to stop the production of bad fruit, using the sword of self-righteousness as a pruning tool isn't efficient. Gardeners know that removing the fruit from plants stimulates the growth of more fruit. If the fruit isn't picked, often the plant will just go to seed and stop producing fruit for a time.

If we spend all our time plucking or hacking at the fruit, and don't deal with the roots, the plant may produce more fruit than ever. The same principle applies to deliverance, restoration, and healing. Unless we have thoroughly dealt with the root of a sin issue, how it got there, and Satan's legal claim, the fruit of sin could multiply. Then the person could be in even worse condition than they were before. Remember the example of someone who started with one demon and ended up with seven more? (See Luke 11:24-26)

Jesus dealt with a fig tree that hadn't produced any fruit by saying it would never produce fruit again. (Matt. 21:19) The next morning, the disciples saw the fig tree had **dried up from the roots.** (Mark 11:21)

The perfect Teacher gave us an example of how to deal with a tree bearing bad fruit. We should kill the root system instead of focusing on the fruit or branches. We want to starve them by cutting off their source of nutrients.

In our spiritual trees, nutrients could be the things with which we surround ourselves: friends, reading or viewing choices, activities, and attitudes. These nutrients are the sources of sustenance for the roots, primary trunk, branches, and fruit. If we cut off the flow of nutrients from the roots, the fruit will wither naturally.

After we have ministered to deep soul issues, a person may report that one or more physical problems have diminished or completely disappeared. This is evidence that we serve an awesome God who heals all our wounds and hurts. This is also evidence that there is a correlation between soul healing and physical healing. Both aspects of healing are part of the salvation process.

Root cutting requires digging beneath the surface and removing the roots of evil.

GENERATIONAL SIN AND INIQUITY

There is an interesting distinction between two commonly used words, *sin* and *iniquity*. **Sin** is an **act** or acts in violation of the laws of God. It is wrongdoing, frequently bringing about **unpleasant consequences**. The word **sin**, in Genesis 4:7 and many other times in Scripture, means an **offense** and its **penalty** or **punishment**. (Strong's H 2403)

Iniquity is the inclination to sin. It also means **wickedness**, or the quality or **state of being wicked**. This literally means to **absorb** or **take in** like a sponge or a wick. It results from the act of lawlessness, giving one a **predisposition** to commit sin. Iniquity can be received from our fathers, grandfathers, and great-grandfathers, or as a result of our own bad decisions and willful acts of sin.

As we commit sin, we take into ourselves the penalty or punishment for sin. Remember that sin was lying at Cain's door waiting for an

opportunity to enter, an opportunity provided by Cain when he chose to sin.

God discusses the transmission of generational iniquity in Exodus 20:5, *"I...am a jealous God,* **visiting the iniquity** *of the* **fathers** *upon the children to the* **third and fourth generations** *of those who hate Me."* [Emphasis ours] (Also see Exodus 34:7 and Numbers 14:18) This statement indicates that the fathers had taken the spiritual iniquity into themselves and that inclination to sin is transmitted to their children through their loins.

Is it fair that men are held responsible for all the sin that is passed down through the generations? We all know that women carry their fair share of sin and iniquity. In spite of this, God chose to give the responsibility to fathers. When we observe that the iniquity is being passed down to the third and fourth generation, we note that there is a dovetailing of generations. This means we can follow this chain all the way back to Adam and the iniquity for which he is responsible.

God said, *"You shall not eat flesh with its life, that is, its blood"* (Genesis 9:4). We pondered this proclamation many times to try to understand it. Does it mean that the blood contains the substance we would call life force, or does it mean that the blood contains spiritual stuff, like the consequences of sin? Does that iniquity actually flow in our bloodstream with our blood?

We have been told that the drinking of blood during a satanic sacrifice is very important, because satanists believe it is where they receive their spiritual power. If so, this is a good reason for God to tell His people not to eat the blood. We believe satanists receive into themselves the spiritual stuff of death when they consume the blood of sacrifice.

On the other hand, Jesus instructed us to drink that which **represents** His blood, in order to receive His **infinite life**.

Medical science tells us a baby receives the life, or blood, from the father. We understand the sperm, alone, enables the fetus to produce its own blood. The mother's body provides nourishment, but her blood does not enter the baby.

This is a good time to offer a hypothetical scenario for consideration. During World War II, my dad was stationed in San Diego, California. There came a point in time when he was put on board a ship for transport to the islands of New Guinea where he would become involved in the war.

Based on his stories, they spent months traveling a meandering route to their destination.

Being normal people, let's say my dad and those other soldiers became lonely during the trip. We can imagine that, at some point in time, my dad might have discovered that the fellow on the next bunk was also lonely. So we ask, what if they decided to comfort each other sexually and, in doing so, received into themselves the spiritual consequence of iniquity.

Many years later, my dad met my mother; they were married and produced children. I was born into the world as little *Johnny boy* and as the years went by, I discovered other little boys were sexually arousing. When I became an adolescent, this arousal became obsessive and I found I needed to defend how I felt. If challenged, I would proclaim, "I have always been this way so it **must be from God**!" Does this sound familiar? Haven't we heard this proclamation used to justify a lifestyle of homosexuality?

Fortunately for me, this scenario is just hypothetical. If we reject God and His word, it is necessary to find some other explanation for things that are clearly dealt with in His word. Our humanist culture and the gospel of Hollywood are quick to find explanations based upon assumptions and *blind faith*. Then, once these assumptions have been established, it is necessary to find a way to validate them.

Scientists have been trying to find the homosexual gene, the murderer gene, the rapist gene, the robber gene, and others. In our opinion, they will not find them, because iniquity isn't physical. It is the **spiritual condition** resulting from action against God's laws. It is being passed down through the loins of the fathers.

Some studies indicate criminal inclinations are passed from generation to generation. For example, a small child can be taken away from a home with criminal activity and raised in one without it. These studies indicate this child is more likely to engage in criminal activity. This is not strange. The child was conceived with spiritual iniquity resident within his or her being.

Again, normal people would perceive this to be unfair and we agree. The answer to this is found in Exodus 20:6, *"[God is] showing* **mercy to thousands [of generations]***, to those who love Me and keep My commandments."*

That means the blessings of Abraham are passed down to his physical, and spiritual, children. It also means that we can receive the blessings purchased by Jesus when we accept Him. In doing so, we become an heir as part of His family. These blessings are available to thousands of generations. That isn't fair either, but **we like it!**

Because Abraham pleased God with his faith, and because Jesus fulfilled His part of the plan that was made before the foundation of the world, we are blessed. We don't want fair; we want grace and mercy. We want the blessings that come to us in spite of ourselves.

Iniquity Accumulated

The first root of sin and iniquity originated with Adam and has been passed down to each succeeding generation. Many generations after Adam and Eve were in the Garden, God recognized there was a problem. The load of iniquity being passed down from fathers to children had been increasing since Adam. (Genesis 6:5-7)

Adam committed the first sin of rebellion against God. He felt fear and shame. That is why he and Eve hid from God. After being expelled from the garden, he would have felt guilt, condemnation, rejection, and other things. His children inherited his iniquity. One of them, Cain, murdered his brother, because he was jealous, and added jealousy and murder to the core of iniquity that has been passed from generation to generation.

The apostle Paul said that we were once children of darkness, born in a state of spiritual death. (Ephesians 5:8) When a man and woman join together sexually, they share the iniquity they received from their fathers. Each of their fathers received the iniquity of two fathers, his and his wife's. This began with the children of Adam and Eve and continued to the people described in Genesis six, who had been affected by the iniquities of many fathers.

It wasn't a simple accumulation, as in one, two, three, etc. It included fathers to the third and fourth generation, each having two fathers from whom to receive iniquity; so there was a geometric progression: two, four, eight, sixteen, etc. The progression grew until God saw that all their thoughts and motives were evil.

The flood was an act of love. It greatly diminished the multiplication factor. However, fathers in ensuing generations passed their iniquities to the ones that followed. This accumulated iniquity affects us all. It is because of God's mercy that we can be freed from the spiritual consequences of the sin and the iniquity we inherited.

The spiritual components of sin and iniquity continue to accumulate. Spiritual death is transmitted through the blood from the father to the child. This is why the virgin birth was so important. If Jesus had been fathered by a mortal man, He would have carried the man's core of iniquity. He was conceived by the Holy Spirit, therefore, He was born without sin.

Cultural Sin and Iniquity

Throughout Scripture, people groups and their nations suffer because of sin and iniquity. In Jeremiah 44:1-6, God describes calamities He brought upon Jerusalem and all the cities of Judah because of their wickedness in serving other gods. He tells the children of Israel living in Egypt, that because they also worshipped other gods, they would **cut themselves off** and become a curse and a reproach among all the nations of the earth. Note that God has not cursed them, but has proclaimed that they have cut themselves off and become cursed as a consequence of their actions.

We find judgments on Ammon, Moab, Edom, and Philistia, in Ezekiel 25. In Matthew 11:20-24, Jesus rebukes the cities of Chorazin, Bethsaida, and Capernaum in which great works were done; and still they did not repent. Towns not receiving the seventy were to experience grave consequences. (Luke 10:10-12) When He approached Jerusalem, Jesus wept. (Luke 13:34)

Can you hear the heart of God in all these things? He has continually demonstrated His love, grace, and mercy. He sent His teachers and prophets, only to have them stoned to death by the religious leaders who wanted to maintain control. He made His appearance in a clay body, but was rejected by people who would not repent. He cried in mourning for all the judgments that must come upon the earth because of the hardheartedness of people.

We used to watch the movie about Moses and the Exodus from Egypt and feel anger toward all those people who saw God's miracles and continued to rebel against Him and His appointed leader. Now, after these years of ministry, we conclude that nothing has changed. Some believe that humanity is improving, but we observe people are the same today as they were then.

Territorial Spirits

At this point, a natural question would be, "Why do the people of the nations continue to act the way they do?" The answer is that there are territorial spirits influencing, or reigning over, geographical areas, such as kingdoms, countries, states, cities, towns, etc. We believe these spiritual entities affect everyone within their area of influence, to some extent.

Twice in the book of Daniel, **Jesus** is referred to as the Prince. In 8:11, He is called the Prince of the host, in 8:25, the Prince of Princes. We interpret this as meaning the host of heaven, including all those angels who have not fallen with Satan and are still serving God. (Jesus later received a promotion to King of kings)

There are three other spiritual princes specifically mentioned in Daniel. He refers to **Michael**, the prince of Israel, who serves Jesus. He also tells of the **prince of Persia** who wars against the angel of God and the **prince of Greece,** who will be coming. The angel proclaims that Michael will uphold him against both the prince of Persia and the prince of Greece. This is ample evidence of spiritual rulers influencing this world. (Daniel 10:13, 12:1, 20-21)

In the book of Ephesians, Paul exhorts believers to be strong in the Lord and in the power of His might. He identifies our spiritual adversaries using titles that indicate there are ranks involved with the spiritual hosts. This describes a spiritual army of darkness with varying degrees of power and authority. (Ephesians 6:10-12) These forces influence nations and people.

Cultural Beliefs and Distinctions

We have discovered another aspect of generational and cultural iniquity that combines the two in a unique way. It has to do with specific aspects of bloodlines and cultural heritage, as well as astrological signs, personality types, emotional inclinations, cultural distinctions, and psychological categories. In the minds of some, these labels define their identity and destiny, either positively or negatively.

Some have shown great pride in their bloodlines and cultural heritage. They have told us they have royal blood and that the spirits dwelling within them are royal spirits. They represented significance and importance, and, in some instances, they felt the spirits were necessary for their survival. These people believed the royal spirits provided for their needs as well as protection.

Many believe their significance is dependent upon being a member of a particular group, club, or secret organization. We have even met people whose identity was wrapped up in being a member of a certain historical society.

Still others belonged to a particular branch of the military and fought in a war or conflict. Although they have been discharged, they are convinced they will always be a part of that organization. It has become an essential part of their identity.

Whether it is a royal bloodline, a secret organization, or a career path, it can represent identity and destiny. If a person is convinced this identity establishes his or her significance, he or she will hold onto it, no matter what. This is a problem if the identity and destiny is assigned by man, and not by God.

Astrological signs can also establish identity and destiny. We've met a number of Christians who continue to define themselves by an astrological sign, and tell us how this identity affects their lives. At times they have surprised us by the intensity with which they hold to these beliefs.

When I was told I was a Virgo, I read books to discover who I was supposed to be, and the way I was supposed to respond to people, events, and life around me. For many years, my view of reality was colored by these beliefs.

When I accepted Jesus as my Savior, I decided to learn everything I could about being a Christian. Many Scriptures identified my previous activities as witchcraft. All forms of divination, necromancy, giving credence to the stars in astrology, and functioning as a medium, were described as abominations to the Lord. After many years and prayers of renunciation, the control and influence of these things have become dim memories.

Occasionally, someone will still ask, "What's your sign?" At first, I had no idea how to respond, and would say something sanctimonious like, "Oh, I'm a Christian. That doesn't apply to me anymore." Inevitably, I would receive a look of puzzlement, or maybe disapproval, ending the conversation. Then, one night, someone asked me that question, I received a flash of revelation and responded, "I'm a Christos!"

That person's facial expression clearly asked, "What is that? I've never heard it before." In response, I told them I had previously been a Virgo, but had become a Christos. I explained I had received the gift of salvation and was a new creation.

The issue is identity. When I became a new creation, by God's miraculous power, my identity changed. No longer am I under the control of a spirit representing an astrological sign. No constellation is needed to control anyone's life, because the Creator of the constellations has offered us a new identity.

Environment frequently determines how people feel about themselves. Someone who grew up in a dysfunctional family assumes their dysfunctional behavior is normal, because it has always been that way.

Personality traits and emotional inclinations are considered permanent, as though they were given to us by God and can't be charged.

This is a deception. The apostle Paul says that God is taking us from glory to glory. (2 Corinthians 3:18) He also assures us that God is faithful to complete the work that He has begun in us. (Philippians 1:6) That includes the salvation of our souls. Finally, we are told that we can be partakers of His divine nature. (2 Peter 1:3) Since this is true, our personality traits and emotional inclinations should be changing as He accomplishes this work.

There are people who believe they are controlled by cultural distinctions. They attribute their irrational behavior to one ethnic group or another, believing there is nothing they can do to change it. They might say, "I respond this way because I belong to this or that cultural group. Everyone knows redheads are hot tempered! There's nothing I can do about it."

Do we believe there's a curse on the entire culture or classification, or are we just using it as a *copout*, so we don't have to be responsible? Regardless of the reason, none of these distinctions should control our identity or destiny after we become a Christian.

Someone may be twenty minutes late to everything, because they are a Latino, an African-American, a Filipino, a Frenchman, or a member of a particular church. Everyone knows churches run on *church* time. Then we have the issue of *girl* time, with flexible minutes and the length of the minute changes, depending upon the situation and inclination of the individual. In this case, five minutes can mean almost anything. Of course, the same can also be true of *guy* time or *family* time.

People also take psychological tests in the workplace and in churches, and describe themselves as type A, B, C, D, phlegmatic, choleric, sanguine, etc. This seems to be another convenient excuse to dodge responsibility for our responses or behavior.

In these cases, we have allowed our identity to be defined by a system that has nothing to do with God. It has to do with secular psychology and the world's belief system. We are convinced that any identity or destiny that doesn't originate with our Creator becomes a curse on our lives. When we accept these counterfeit identities and destinies, we accept the curse.

It is time to evaluate. Are we blindly accepting the world's labels as descriptions or definitions of who we are? How do they compare to what our Creator says about us?

We Can Be Free

The solution is simple. If any of these counterfeit identities or destinies still have **control** of our lives, we need to get saved. Once we are saved, none of these things really matter. Bloodlines, cultural heritage, astrological signs, personality types, emotional inclinations, cultural distinctions, and psychological categories have become incidental. As we receive the **mind of Christ** and except the **identity** and **destiny** established by the Manufacturer, all else fades into insignificance.

*"But **you are** a **chosen** race, a **royal** priesthood, a **dedicated** nation, [God's] own purchased, **special people**, that you may set forth the wonderful deeds and display the virtues and perfections of Him Who called you out of darkness into His marvelous light"* (1 Peter 2:9, Amp.) (See also, Ephesians 1:3-8, 2:4-10 and Romans 8).

Through the blood of Jesus, we can be freed from bondage to generational and cultural iniquity. Jesus was the perfect, sinless sacrifice that, **once and for all**, nullified the power of iniquity. (1 Peter 1:18-19; Galatians 1:3-4)

We must appropriate the power of the shed blood of Jesus to cleanse us from all the power of sin and iniquity in every aspect of our lives and beings. This was done for our spirit when we became a new creation. It is important to use our authority to obtain freedom in our inner and outer courts, in our soul and body.

Whether or not you believe yourself to be a Christian, we believe this prayer will be extremely beneficial for you. We encourage you to read it aloud. There will be similar opportunities for you to pray throughout the rest of this book.

Sample Prayer:

In the name of the Lord Jesus Christ, I proclaim the destruction of all generational and cultural curses upon any part of my life or being.

I renounce all generational and cultural sin and iniquity I inherited from all my ancestors. I claim the power of the blood of Jesus Christ for the destruction of all spiritual connections between any of the sins of my ancestors and me.

I renounce everything serving Satan's kingdom associated with cultural heritage, birthrights, nobility, royalty, significance, blessings, and gifts I have received as a result of my physical bloodline, ancestry, or culture. I bind and

renounce everything serving Satan's kingdom that I received from my earthly parents by any means.

I renounce all sinful personality traits associated with any people group. I renounce viewing anyone as being less or more important or valuable than me. I renounce all pride, arrogance, attitudes, expectations, perceptions, beliefs, and lies that have deceived any part of my soul or humanity.

I renounce any royal spirits, spirit guides, and familiar spirits I have received from my earthly ancestry or by any other means. I renounce all real or perceived benefits I have received from these sources in any way, and I renounce giving any part of my soul, humanity, or energies over in return.

I now command everything serving Satan's kingdom to leave every part of my life and being, release everything claimed as a result of sin, and go, now, wherever the Lord Jesus Christ sends them. I also command Satan's kingdom to give the Lord Jesus Christ everything received from me as a sacrifice because He has paid for all my sins.

I claim back all my soul and humanity killed, stolen, or destroyed. I ask the Lord to restore to me all my soul, humanity, gifts, abilities, dignity, self-respect, health, wellbeing, and my true identity and destiny as His child and friend.

I proclaim that I am a child of God Almighty, the King of the universe, and that is my only source of royalty or heritage. I am also a member of the body of Christ and this fact defines my identity and destiny.

I ask You, Heavenly Father, to do whatever it takes to manifest these things and make me whole, as you created me to be. Thank You. Amen.

Who Can We Pray For?

We are not responsible for those things that are not a function of our free will, such as generational or cultural iniquity. We are not entirely responsible for soul ties. In most cases, we are not responsible for the roots that are the base of our problems.

These Root Cutting Prayers can be modified, just slightly, or similar prayers can be created, that will affect the lives of others. The people for whom you pray do not have to be present for your prayers to have effect.

We believe there are *degrees* of authority in prayer. Our greatest authority is in our own life. The next greatest authority would include our spouse, because we are one flesh, and then our children. For our under-age children, particularly, our prayers would be nearly as powerful as if they were saying them. In the case of adopted children, or blended families, parents have spiritual authority, because they have the responsibility over the lives of all their children.

Beyond our immediate family would be extended family members. The next group might include church members and friends. These prayers would have some effect, although not as much as if they prayed for themselves.

We also pray these prayers for unsaved loved ones and others we want to see saved. This might give them enough freedom to accept Jesus Christ as their Savior. We have heard a number of testimonies suggesting this is true.

An example is Glenna's father who was totally closed to the Gospel and would not listen at all. Any time the subject was introduced, he would argue. She had been praying for him for years. We prayed these prayers for him and continued to love him and speak things into his life. As a result, a few years before he died, he accepted Jesus Christ as his Savior with no argument.

SOUL TIES AND SPIRITUAL TRANSFER

The terms, *soul ties and spiritual transfer* are not found in the Bible. However, we believe it is appropriate to use them. In order to make this discussion more understandable, and for the purposes of praying effectively, we believe it is beneficial to attach a label to these complex concepts. We can also demonstrate that Scripture makes mention of them in a variety of ways.

Godly Soul Ties

In many places the Bible describes connections between Christians, saying we are all members of one body and spiritual structure. We are also told that what affects one of us, affects us all. (1 Corinthians 12:12-13, 26; Ephesians 2:18-22) We don't understand how this works. We estimate there are hundreds of millions of Christians around the world. Since we are not connected physically, we must be connected in some other way, through the power of the Holy Spirit.

As we consider these mysterious connections, we find Scriptures that indicate there are events when people demonstrated an extraordinary unity of heart and soul. (Acts 4:32) Some would say this sounds like ESP, with all these people sharing consciousness, thoughts, will, and emotion. We don't accept that term, but we do see connections between people that are beyond normal.

These links are also mentioned in the Old Testament. The souls of David and Jonathan were knit together. (1 Samuel 18:1; 1 Chronicles 12:17; Deuteronomy 13:6) The verses indicate that two **intangible souls** can be bound together in love, mutual esteem, friendship, and loyalty to one another. The verses also indicate that married couples, parents with their children, and siblings can also experience a knitting of souls. (See Genesis 2:24) We can almost see a tapestry being created, weaving many souls together as one.

We see evidence that husbands and wives frequently seem to know what their spouse is thinking. At times, a brother or sister knows when something is happening to a sibling miles away. We've heard stories about mothers who suddenly knew there was danger for their children and hurried to rescue them. Once again, we reject the idea this is just another demonstration of ESP.

We have ample scriptural evidence that God created a system to join us together in ways we do not understand. They must be designed to strengthen and protect us, to provide oneness with the body of Christ, as well as with family members, relatives, and close friends. Because we know He loves us infinitely, we know these connections are for our good.

Satan's Counterfeit, or Ungodly Soul Ties

We have heard much about ESP, mind control, and mental telepathy. There are celebrities on television claiming they can read people's minds. Those involved in the different aspects of metaphysical sciences employ methods that seem to imitate the works of God.

Satan is not the Creator; he is a counterfeiter. He can imitate something that God has created. It is reasonable to believe he would counterfeit, pervert, and defile what God has done, by devising his own system for connecting souls. Logically, he would choose a harmful method that would serve his purpose of bringing death and destruction.

For example, someone may still be connected in some way with a dead person. This connection might involve memories that trigger negative emotions. Hearing familiar phrases and sayings could prompt fear or anger. Some individuals have actually taken on the personality of another person after that person's death. After they pray to destroy ungodly soul ties, they are set free.

One couple had a daughter, in her early teens, who had befriended another young woman whose parents had recently divorced. The friend was angry and rebellious. Although the couple's daughter wanted to help the other teenager, she also began to exhibit rebellious mannerisms and attitudes. The parents were distressed and wondered what they could do to help their daughter.

We led them in prayers to destroy all the soul and spiritual connections that would affect their daughter. The next day she announced she had decided to end her relationship with the other young woman. She realized she was being negatively affected, and seemed to be having no positive effect on the other young woman.

We conclude there are spiritual connections and soul ties between people. Some are good and some are harmful. Our goal is to maintain those that are beneficial, and sever the harmful ones.

Sin and Iniquity in the Flesh

As Christians, our spirits are free from iniquity because Jesus paid for it. We are now children of light and are going to spend eternity in heaven. However, we still have a soul and body that want to do things that are not of God; things our spirit does not want to do. Do you remember Paul's expression of anguish concerning his own inclination to sin? (Romans 7:15-25, 8:1)

Paul proclaimed that with his mind, he was serving the law of God. For the good that I, **the spiritual man**, *will* to do, I, **the flesh man**, do not do; but the evil that I, **the spirit man**, will *not* to do, that I, **the flesh man**, practice. Paul was struggling with his dual nature, part of which desired to serve God, and part of which didn't. (Romans 7:19) [Author's paraphrase]

This seems to be true for any normal Christian. Our spirit wants to function perfectly, in accordance with God's will. We don't want to engage in sin, yet we find ourselves doing so. We don't like it and we want it to be gone, but it is being inspired by iniquity, which was resident in our soul and body before we were born. We have sin that **dwells in us**, just as Paul did.

Spiritual Transfer

The Lord has commanded us to refrain from sexual impurity. Why? Is it because He is a cosmic killjoy? One of the Ten Commandments tells us not to commit adultery. (See Exodus 20:14) God has also stated some very hard things concerning fornication. He seems to lump together fornication, adultery, and harlotry with **all sexual impurity**. (1 Corinthians 5:1, 6:18-19; Galatians 5:19; Ephesians 5:3)

In the Old Testament, God commanded that people caught in these sins be taken outside the camp and stoned to death. Based on modern situation morality and the religion of Hollywood, this would seem extreme. Our world population would be radically affected if all those guilty of fornication and adultery were stoned to death. Why would God tell His people to do such a radical thing? Is it another case of God demonstrating His dark side, or should we look at this from another perspective?

There may be many methods of establishing spiritual union with other people. In ministry we've heard some interesting things, but we believe the most effective way is through sexual relations. In some translations of the Bible, the word *joined* is translated as cleave, which means to become one. Based on this, *in marriage* doesn't mean you go through a legal ceremony; it means to join sexually. When one is joined to another they shall **become one flesh**. (Matthew19:5-6)

Sin dwells in our flesh. Remember Paul and **the thorn** or messenger from Satan? Paul lamented about **the sin** that dwelled **in his flesh**. (Romans 7:17, 18, 20, 23) The word sin means the act of sin and the **spiritual consequence** (the creature that comes in).

When two people have sexual relations, they become one flesh, and spiritual *stuff* is given opportunity to migrate. This is because the two **become one flesh.** (1 Corinthians 6:16) When two join together, they receive, **into themselves,** the iniquity of their actions and are **being filled** with all unrighteousness. For the purposes of this discussion, there is no difference between joining man-man, woman-woman, or man-woman. (Romans 1:26-31)

It would be like taking two glasses of water, putting one color of dye (iniquity) in one and another color of dye in the other. If these two bodies of liquid are joined, or made one, the attributes of both colors combine, making a blended color. Typically, once these colors are combined the process cannot be reversed. As this relates to the spiritual issue, once the iniquities are **combined**, the result would be terrible.

This was disastrous for mankind until Jesus was resurrected and sprinkled His blood on the Mercy Seat. This is because it was impossible to undo the spiritual damage done in the joining. In answering the previous question, we don't believe God's command was a demonstration of His dark side. We are convinced this is another demonstration of His love.

Many Generations Defiled

In order to demonstrate why we believe this is a manifestation of love, maybe this is another good place for a scenario. Suppose I decide to agree with the concepts of situation morality and seek out a prostitute for sexual gratification. After all, Hollywood says it will be OK as long as it's between two consenting adults. And yet, before I go on, maybe we need some clarification.

I once heard a story that defines a prostitute. A man went into a bar, sat down on a stool next to a good-looking woman, and offered to buy her a drink. She accepted, so he continued the conversation. After a while he asked her, "If I paid you one million dollars, would you go to bed with me?" She thought for a while and finally said she would.

Then he asked her, "Well, would you go to bed with me for fifty dollars?"

She was offended and yelled, "What do you think I am, a whore?"

"We have already established that," he responded, "Now we're just haggling over the price."

We can view this from the world's view or from God's perspective. It doesn't matter what the price is, or what kind of currency is used. It may be a million dollars or just fifty, two drinks and a dinner, a movie and dancing, or soft words spoken into a shell pink ear that bring comfort to the soul. What matters is that men and women choose to defile themselves and **function as whores**, both physically and spiritually. Now, let's get back to the scenario.

Let's say I negotiate a contract with the prostitute, I pay what has been agreed upon and we consummate the contract. Afterwards, we go on with our lives. This seems to have been a very simple process except we need to look at it from the perspective previously discussed. What are the consequences of my joining with this prostitute?

Prior to joining with me, this prostitute may have joined with hundreds of others. In becoming one flesh with each of them, the prostitute would have received the combining of iniquity. Some of them may have had homosexual experiences, had sex with dogs and cats, committed murder, or done other weird and perverted things I have never considered doing.

The prostitute would have functioned as a receptacle by receiving and sharing iniquity with them. If they had joined with many others, they received the iniquity of each of those others. Those others had also received from everyone with whom they had joined. The numbers are exponential and the iniquity is received from just one joining.

In pursuit of a few minutes of *enjoyment*, I can receive the iniquities of hundreds, or possibly thousands of people and bloodlines. From an engineer's perspective, this is certainly a very efficient way to defile one's self.

At a later time, I join in intimacy with my wife and share everything I received. Should we produce a new little Johnny boy, he might think it is *normal* to find other little boys attractive, to fantasize about torturing and killing people, and find dogs and cats sexually exciting. When questioned about these things, he might say, "I've always been this way, so **it must be from God!**"

Have you ever heard that statement used as an explanation for a perverted lifestyle? In our culture, God can be blamed for sinful activities and perverted lifestyles, but it is the earthly daddy's fault. He chose to defile himself, his wife, his children, their children, and their children, with the accumulated iniquity.

Although the physical consequences of promiscuity can be grave, the spiritual consequences are much worse. Once we receive the iniquity, we receive the inclination to commit the sins represented by demonic spirits. By receiving these spirits, many have become the slaves of the sins. The defilement continues through the generations until the blood of Christ is appropriated to end the curse.

Apologists call prostitution a *victimless crime*, in order to justify it. We strenuously disagree. Multitudes of people have been defiled and kept in bondage through prostitution. There are physical diseases, sometimes resulting in death, as a consequence of this practice. There may also be divorce, with the emotional tearing and trauma. More than the other consequences, an **entire bloodline** will be **defiled** when one person joins with one prostitute.

It is easy for God's critics to condemn Him for taking such a hard stand on this issue. When He told us not to engage in this type of activity, it wasn't because He is nasty and mean. It was because He knew the terrible consequences mankind would experience. That is why He established His umbrella of protection, the covenant of marriage.

When an earthly daddy tells his children to stay away from the stove, it is because he loves them and doesn't want them to get burned. A mother tells her children not to go out in the busy street, because she wants to protect them, not spoil their fun. Establishing logical rules is the job of a good parent. He is our Father who loves us, and wants good things for us!

Our heavenly Daddy does His job perfectly, and establishes perfect rules for our protection. He tells us to choose life or death, what is good or what is bad. We are responsible for **spiritual transfer** that occurs as a function of our will. Fortunately, because of what Jesus did we can be free from the consequences of our bad decisions. We can pluck out the roots of all those things that have kept us in bondage. Once again, it is time for you to exercise your authority and pray.

Sample Prayer:

In the name of the Lord Jesus Christ, I proclaim the destruction of all ungodly soul ties, demonic connections, and spiritual transfer between me and any other person, place, object, substance, or being by the power of the blood of Jesus Christ.

I renounce and bind everything serving Satan's kingdom that I have received from any other person or source at any time, by any means, including sexual relations. I command all these to leave every part of my life and being and go, now, where the Lord Jesus Christ sends them.

I renounce giving anything to Satan's kingdom as a result of my sin. I command everything serving Satan's kingdom to give the Lord Jesus Christ all energies and everything else received from me, because He alone has paid for all my sins and He alone is worthy to receive these things.

I reclaim all my soul and humanity, including everything killed, stolen, or destroyed, and everything turned over to Satan's control through any ungodly soul tie or ungodly spiritual connections.

Heavenly Father, I praise You for the sacrifice of the Lord Jesus Christ, and I give You all honor and glory for freeing me from spiritual bondage associated with these things. Amen.

DEDICATIONS AND BAPTISMS

To dedicate something is to set it apart, or designate it for a new or different use. In the world systems, there are different kinds of dedications serving to **establish claims and authority**. In our Scriptures, dedications can mean to cleanse, consecrate, or sanctify.

Anything can be dedicated. People, things, and actions can be dedicated. Hannah dedicated her male child to God, even before he was conceived. (1 Samuel 1:11) Articles of silver, gold, and bronze can be dedicated. Buildings and geographical locations can also be dedicated. (2 Samuel 8:10-11; Ezra 6:16) The statue of Nebuchadnezzar was dedicated to something. (Daniel 3:1-3)

Because of the dominion and authority given to people, anyone can dedicate themselves, or anything over which they have spiritual authority, to anything. To the extent we have spiritual authority we can, and should, be exercising that authority. We should consciously dedicate our families, our properties, and ourselves to the God of creation. By not doing so, it is possible we are passively dedicating them to the god of death, by default.

We believe Satan can be given legal claim to parts of a person's life or being, and to property, as a result of such **default dedications**, even though a person may not be aware of it.

Questionable Dedications and Baptisms

In Jeremiah, the Lord determined to burn the city because the children of Israel offered, or dedicated, incense to Baal and drink offerings to other gods. (Jeremiah 32:29) Based on His response, it is apparent the Lord views dedications as being significant.

Since the children of Israel did not have the cleansing power of the blood of Jesus, the power of His name, or the Holy Spirit, the Lord cautioned them strongly against having commerce with pagan peoples. The things they would receive through such trade could be defiled, or infested, with spiritual influences.

Although the blood sacrifices in the Temple covered the sins of the Hebrews, it did not set them free from the spiritual influences. They had no way of being freed of demonic bondage, once they were infected. The only solution was death or destruction. When God instructed His people to destroy all these **infected things**, including people, His motivation was love. Once again, He was protecting people from the spiritual consequences of sin.

Throughout history, dedications and baptisms to false gods and entities other than the living God have been common. Because of the unique nature of our ministry, we have read books that were not written for Christians. One evening, we were studying a book pertaining to the Druid religion because we were dealing with someone who claimed to have that background.

The author described a particular ceremony for dedicating a child using oaths and pledges. We were startled by what we read. The father of the child would present the baby to the priest, giving him spiritual authority. The priest would dedicate the baby and all his issue, or offspring, to the great oak tree, or whatever represented his god.

We became concerned because we both have Northern European roots. We may have had Druid ancestors who dedicated us to **something**, many generations before we were born and we would never know it.

Something might proclaim, "You belong to me because you were given to me twelve generations ago. I'm going to influence your life in every way possible, for as long as I can. If you get saved, I will continue to harass you until I'm forced to leave." Once again, the past can affect us.

From a present perspective, our families may dedicate us to **something** represented by a statue in a church, and ask *it* to protect us. The statue may look very pretty, but it's just a piece of wood or plaster. Our concern is the **spiritual entity** that might be hiding behind the statue.

The parents feel they have done their child a good service; yet, something malevolent may become a companion for the child through life. The belief of many Christians is that we are to dedicate our babies to the God of creation, so He can provide for and protect them. There is no reason to believe we should dedicate babies to a dead person.

Some people are taken to a practitioner of witchcraft, to receive blessings, healings, or dedications. This is a problem because God says all forms of witchcraft are an abomination. They are all works of Satan's kingdom. This is not a good thing to do for a child.

Through religious systems such as Oriental martial arts, Yoga, Eastern religions, and other similar spiritual activities, people regularly dedicate their bodies or energies. From our perspective, these dedications represent the potential for spiritual bondage.

There are even *religious organizations* that practice baptizing dead people, and possibly others, without receiving permission. We don't know the effects of these baptisms but, from a Christian perspective, they represent a source of concern.

Often, people bind themselves through membership in *religious organizations* without realizing the spiritual implications of such dedications. There are groups around the world with affiliated branch organizations that serve gods other than our heavenly Father and reject the Lord Jesus Christ. Some of these organizations compel their members to dedicate themselves, their families, and their businesses to the gods with which they are affiliated.

If people have been deceived into dedicating their families and businesses without full understanding, they may be serving Satan's agenda without knowing it. Jesus warns us to be sure the light in us is not *darkness or false light*. (Luke 11:35; Matthew 6:23)

People swear oaths and make pledges to nations, governments, financial institutions, corporations, or military organizations. These proclamations may give that entity, or the spiritual power over that entity, lifelong influence over their lives.

How much more powerful are the dedications of Christians, who are working within the will of God in dedicating their lives, families, businesses and possessions to Him? These dedications give God an opportunity to bring blessings into a person's life, with or without their knowledge.

Christian Baptism

John the Baptist describes two kinds of baptism, with water and with the Holy Spirit. (Matthew 3:11) In the modern Christian church, to be baptized is usually to be immersed in or washed with water. We believe this particular baptism symbolizes our sharing in the death, burial, and resurrection of Jesus, our Savior. (Romans 6:3-4) This symbolizes our being **born again**.

Just as with dedications, baptisms can be performed for many purposes, not all of which identify one as a member of the body of Christ. It is our purpose to nullify those dedications, baptisms, oaths, pledges, and spiritual debts that may have placed us into spiritual bondage. It is our purpose to firmly establish ourselves in covenant with the Lord Jesus Christ, because we have been purchased by His shed blood.

The objective of the next sample prayer is to free us from *the power and control of Satan's kingdom*. If the spiritual authority over any entity or organization does not come from the Lord of all creation, we want to be free of its influence.

Jesus said we are to *render unto Caesar what is Caesar's*. (Matthew 22:21) Therefore, we must honor the legal contracts we established and the debts we have incurred according to the laws of the land, without placing ourselves into spiritual debt and bondage.

We must also dedicate every part of our being, all of our energies, and every part of our lives to our Creator. In doing so, we can *render unto God what is God's*. We now have the blood, the name, and the authority of Jesus, everything we need to be set free. This is a good time to pray.

Sample Proclamation:

I proclaim, by the power of the blood of Jesus Christ, the destruction of all baptisms and dedications placed upon my life or being at any time, by any means, subjecting me to the power and control of Satan's kingdom.

I renounce and nullify all oaths, pledges, and contracts between any part of my being and any entity that binds me spiritually to Satan's kingdom. I renounce any claim of ownership of any part of my life or being by any spiritual or political entity, corporation, government, organization, or financial institution.

I renounce and bind everything serving Satan's kingdom that is affecting my life or being as a result of any of these things. I command everything serving Satan's kingdom to leave every part of my life, my humanity, and my being, now, and go where the Lord Jesus Christ sends them.

I command that all my spiritual, emotional, and physical energies, received by Satan's kingdom, be given to the Lord Jesus Christ, because He paid for all my sins, and is the only One worthy to receive them.

Because of the finished work of the Lord, I reclaim all of my heart, soul, mind, nervous system, organs, and body parts, as well as everything killed, stolen, or destroyed as a result of sin.

I proclaim that every part of my spirit, every part of my soul, every part of my body, and every part of my life is dedicated exclusively to the Lord. I belong entirely to Him, because I have been bought by the shed blood of the Lord Jesus Christ. Amen.

CURSES OF GENDER, IDENTITY, AND DESTINY

Curses of gender, identity, and destiny are extremely common and harmful. A curse is a wish, proclamation, prayer, or invocation for harm or injury, intended to cause torment. Cursing often involves using profanity or insolent language designed to denigrate. It could also be to call upon divine or supernatural powers to send injury, to cause evil, or afflict. (Merriam-Webster) All of these dictionary definitions highlight the **power of the tongue**.

There is ample evidence the Bible credits blessings and curses as having powerful consequences. For the purpose of this discussion, we are looking at evidences that curses have power. One example is that of Balak, king of the Moabites, who called upon a man named Balaam to curse the children of Israel. His reason was because they had defeated the Amorites and were now camped in Moab. (Numbers 22-24)

There are a number of words used for curse common in both the Old and New Testaments. The primary words share general meanings that include: to bitterly curse, to malign, to stab with words, to bring into contempt, to despise, vilify, to doom, to speak evil of, or to swear or proclaim an oath. (Strong's)

The way we express ourselves is very important. Proverbs 18:21 proclaims, *"Death and life are in the **power of the tongue**."* The writer is not speaking to Christians because there weren't any. He is speaking of normal people in clay bodies.

Throughout the Bible there are proclamations concerning the power of the tongue. We need to remember that God gave people dominion in the physical realm. We use words to communicate with one another, to express our feelings, and to cause things to happen. (James 3:6-10; Matthew 12:34-37, 15:18-19) Words can also be used to produce beneficial or sinful reactions and emotions in others. (1Timothy 6:3-5)

Curses can be specific formulas intended to cause misfortune, harm or evil, or they can be thoughtless words spoken seriously, or in jest. The results can be equally devastating. Because they are based in sin, **curses bring consequences**. We will now explore different kinds of curses, how we have been cursed, and how we have cursed others or ourselves.

Curses Through The Family Line

As noted earlier, God the Father and Jesus **proclaimed** and described the consequences for various forms of rebellion against the Laws of God. They singled out specific bloodlines, **people groups**, cities, and nations. In the Old Testament, God used His prophets to warn of these consequences and describe the form they would take.

Curses can affect us because of something spoken or done generations ago. Noah cursed his grandson, Canaan. From the loins of Canaan came a number of people groups. We believe that the curse Noah put on these nations has affected many people throughout the centuries. (Genesis 9:25-27)

A good example of the importance of the spoken word is found in the story of Esau and Jacob. (Genesis 27:14-41) In this case, it wasn't a curse that was being spoken; it was a blessing. We see how important both of these boys perceived the blessing to be, once the time actually came for it to be imparted.

Esau received a blessing of sorts, but it wasn't the blessing **he wanted**. He had sold his birthright to his brother for a bowl of food. He cheated himself out of what should have been his, because he gave away his rightful inheritance as the elder son. (Genesis 25:29-34) The **perceived curse** Esau received was in the form of a lesser blessing. As a result, all the generations that came from his bloodline have received *the curse*.

Words are important. How words are received and what the receiver does with them are equally important. How a **person perceives** and acts upon what they hear can be the key to discovering the root of a problem.

Curses of Names

God placed great importance on **names** and their declaration of **identity** and **destiny**. (See Genesis 17:5, 15, 19; 32:27-28) The Hebrew word most often used for *name* means an appellation, as a mark or memorial of individuality, honor, authority, character, fame, renown, or report. (Strong's, 8034)

Several people described in biblical accounts receive one name at birth and another name, with a different identity and destiny, at a later time. Lucifer received the new identity of Satan because of his rebellion. Based on what God said to the serpent, we conclude this name is a curse.

Usually, **new names** were given by God as **a blessing**. This is similar to the process of being **born again** as a child of God. At birth, we receive one identity and destiny as a child of darkness; later we receive the **new identity** and **destiny** as a child of light.

Although names are supposed to bless our identity and destiny, they can also be a curse.

A name given a **baby in the womb** can be a curse. It could define the baby as **unwanted**, an **accident**, or a **mistake**. Children, who knew they were unwanted, grew up with a nagging feeling that they should have died, instead of being born.

Because they were given the message they shouldn't have been conceived or born, they have lived with the **curse of abortion**. Although the body was allowed to survive, they have experienced abortion in their relationships, education, marriages, careers, hopes, and dreams.

Women have told us that their parents were hoping for another boy because of their culture, because they needed laborers for their farm, or they already had four girls and wanted a boy. Men have reported their parents already had three boys and wanted a girl; or mommy hated men and boys and only wanted girls. There are many reasons a child's gender is not acceptable to parents or other family members.

The name given **to a child** can also **defile** true gender, identity, and destiny. Regardless of the reason, the effect on the children is the same. Children are filled with self-hatred when they believe they are the **wrong gender.** When they receive the message there is something wrong with them, and nothing they can do will change it, their true identity and destiny **are cursed**.

In the days of the Bible, when a child was born, the parents spent eight days in fasting and prayer to determine the child's name. They knew the importance of the name for proclaiming identity and destiny.

Unfortunately, we've ministered with people whose parents apparently had no understanding. One man had been named after *weird Uncle Harold*. His parents had felt bad for the uncle, because no one really liked him. They thought naming their son Harold would be a blessing for the uncle. Sadly, they didn't consider the effect on their son's heart when he discovered how and why he received his name.

Other parents named their child for a much-loved family dog. The dog was big, hairy, sloppy, and drooled all the time. They knew the dog would die someday, so using its name would give it a measure of immortality during their lives. When the child was old enough to understand, they told her why she received her name.

This was all very well for the parents and the dog, but what does it say to the heart of the child? She received the message that her reason for existence, and her destiny, was as a replacement for the beloved dog. She grew up feeling that she never really had an identity of her own. This message was reinforced each time the name was spoken.

Curses of Nicknames

When we were born, the name written on our birth certificate became our legal identity. As we grow up, other names may replace it. We can be given nicknames or pet names by family members, children in school, teachers, coaches, business associates, medical experts, pastors, and other authority figures.

A nickname is a name added to, or substituted for, the proper name. This can be done for purposes of affection, ridicule, or familiarity. For example, other children can give names such as *string bean, fatso,* or *big-ears*. Children are capable of being amazingly cruel when they want, or feel the need, to put someone else down. There are also family nicknames such as *stupid, retard,* or *ugly*. Any of these names can be used to defile, or curse, true identity and destiny.

These *new* names can seem funny at the time. Most often, they represent a curse of identity and/or destiny, because they seldom agree with the name the Lord has chosen for us. When other people use these names, the impact on us is dependent upon their authority or significance. When we accept and use these names, the impact is much greater.

One woman's family called her *frog*. She was obviously affected by this name and identity. Although she was a very attractive, middle-aged woman, she perceived herself to be fat and ugly. She didn't know she could reject this identity others gave her. She accepted and believed it, unable to see the truth because of the power of the lie. The result of this curse in her life was a string of painful marriages and relationships.

One young man told us he was considering suicide because his career, his marriage, and his life in general, had no meaning. We interviewed him at length, trying to find the reason. The only clue we received was that his mother seemed to have a great deal of influence in his life. When we asked what his mother called him, he began to cry.

The name, *my little worthless one*, seemed cute when he was small, but it shamed and humiliated him. While telling the story, he was overcome with emotion. The feelings associated with that name were like daggers thrust deep into his heart.

For a time, we kept a book on the coffee table that gave definitions of names. Often, after ministry, we would look up the name of the person to see what its biblical interpretation was. In every case, the work Satan had done in the person's life was designed to convince them they were the opposite of what their name meant. He used family, friends, and authority figures in the person's life to accomplish this.

Curses from Others

For many, the word *curse* conjures the image of an old hag hovering over a boiling cauldron, muttering incantations. A witch can wear a long black dress, have long black hair, and wear a silver pentagram on a chain. In spite of this stereotype, a witch can dress like any normal, working person; or wear designer clothes, drive a luxury car, and move in the highest stratum of society.

We can be cursed without being aware of it. These curses can range from the incantation of a witch, to the casual or mindless, angry curse of a stranger we may have offended while driving our car. Someone might request or pay for someone to put a curse on us, our family, our church, or our business.

There are occult stores in which we can buy things to use for magical spells. We can consult professional witches. We could, almost certainly, find one in any town or city. They sincerely believe in the powers of witchcraft. If we were to pay them enough money, and hand them a picture, many would be willing to put a curse on that person.

In ministering to people involved in the occult, we have been told someone can walk through a department store touching the clothing, imparting spiritual influences; or that a satanist can sprinkle a powder blessed with spiritual stuff into food in a restaurant. There are also alleged accounts of satanists working in hospitals, using their position to afflict or even kill.

These things have been described to us and seemed credible. From the perspective of someone serving Satan, pain, suffering, sickness, or death inflicted on others, represent sacrifices to Satan, and serve his kingdom. The people providing the sacrifice believe they will receive power from Satan in return, so they are highly motivated.

Well-meaning parents may take their children to a spiritist, or a shaman, for *healing* and *blessings*. These practitioners might impart the spiritual by giving them something to drink, smearing concoctions on their bodies, blowing a liquid on them with the mouth, rubbing them with ashes, or blowing smoke on them. There are many ways they might subject children to spiritual powers.

We believe it is possible to take a child to a witch for physical healing and see them experience some relief from the physical symptoms. We also believe the relief will be temporary. In these situations, evil spirits have been given legal claim to the child's body.

There are religious groups and churches that either endorse or allow this type of activity among their attendees; and yet, Deuteronomy 18:10-12, proclaims these things to be abominations. Satan and his servants cannot give any good thing, no matter how beneficial these practices appear to be. Their purpose is to afflict, not heal, and they will use any deception to accomplish this purpose.

We are given many opportunities to accept curses by things presented to us through various types of media, from governmental entities, the medical establishment, schools, and churches. TV commercials tell us it is flu or allergy season, and we need to buy certain drugs to treat the afflictions. If we accept these predictions and associated curses, we may hurry to purchase our drugs so we will have them when we are afflicted.

Glenna and I realized the influence of this type of suggested curse and began using the mute button on the remote, refusing to listen to those commercials. Now, when the initial thought of sickness flashes into our heads, we reject it. Scripture tells us to take every thought into captivity, and it's our job to do so. (2 Corinthians 10:5)

Even in church, people say and do things that can be curses. They might be acting out of genuine concern. Consciously, they may want to bless, but subconsciously, they may hold a grudge because of an earlier slight. The head wants to do one thing, the heart, another. There is much going on in the heart we don't understand.

There **are** people in church whose prayers we don't want. We have heard them pray and don't want any curses, mindless or otherwise. However, we are careful not to cause hurt. We also have to be careful about what we receive. Frequently people come to us offering a word, *from the Lord*. We have learned to say, "We gladly receive all Holy Spirit inspired words."

People may say, "The Lord has been putting you on my heart a lot lately. Is it okay if I pray for you?" If we say yes, we are giving authority by giving them permission to pray. They could use our authority to serve another lord, knowingly or unknowingly. Our authority could be used against us.

Some years ago, we went through a time of heavy oppression. In response to our *prayerful* complaints, the Lord suggested we nullify all permission we had given to those whose purpose was harm. The results were amazing. Now, when someone wants to pray for us, we say, "We gladly receive all Holy Spirit-inspired prayers."

When some people say, "The Lord bless you." We reply, "Thank you. We gladly receive all blessings from our Lord," because we don't know to which lord they are referring. We feel no paranoia, fear, or anger; nor do we desire to offend. However, we must be aware of reality. We are supposed to be wise as serpents and, at the same time, harmless as doves (Matthew 10:16).

If someone else uses foul or abusive language toward us, we don't have to get angry or fearful. We can simply say, "That's not what my Lord says about me, and His opinion is the only one that matters."

Curses From Family Members

The curses that come from family spread across all the categories of curses. They frequently take root when we are very young and hang on longest. Because people were given dominion, our words are powerful. When we use them to criticize, condemn, or blame, we do great harm. When these words are stabbed into the heart, they can have long-lasting effects.

God proclaims, *"There is none who does good, no, not one. Their **throat** is an open **tomb**; with their **tongues** they have practiced **deceit**, the **poison of asps** is under their **lips**, whose **mouth** is full of **cursing** and **bitterness**"* (Romans 3:12-14). [Emphasis ours]

This is a description of fallen mankind. (See, also, Psalms 14:1-3; 53:1-3; 5:9; 140:1-3; 10:7; Romans 3:10-18) It is no wonder that this general description applies to families. We believe it is **normal** for parents and other adult authority figures, through their own brokenness, to say hurtful things that function as curses. There are cases in which children curse their parents, but much more frequently parents curse their children.

Many years ago, I saw a woman dragging her five-year-old boy through a restaurant by his wrist. As they passed my booth, I heard him ask, "Why are you holding me like this, Mommy?" She responded, "Because, every time I let you go, you get into trouble!" This is another wonderful message to plant in a child's heart.

Children don't know they can say *no* to the curses. The voices of parents, grandparents, aunts, uncles, and older siblings, all represent God to the heart of a child. Imagine a child telling their parents, "I'm not going to receive that curse because it's not what God says about me." Can you picture the parent's response?

Children are careful when there is a prospect of any form of violence. In order to survive, they probably wouldn't make inflammatory remarks. Verbal attacks from family members are often unprovoked, and children receive them as curses. The attacks come from those who should love and protect the children and speak blessings into their hearts.

The curse words may also be intended as helpful or conciliatory. We are reminded of a little girl having trouble with her math homework. After a time of seeing her daughter flounder and frustrate, the well-meaning mom tried to console her by offering, "I never was any good in math. I guess you're just like me."

The girl is given the message that she might as well give up, because she will never succeed in math. PHOOEY! Mom didn't know she was serving as an agent of mankind's greatest enemy by voicing the lie.

The little girl wasn't the property of her parents or family. They were given the responsibility to act as stewards over her life. God expected them to take care of her, provide for her, protect her, and represent Him well, so she could establish a good relationship with Him one day. Planting a curse in her heart did not represent Him well.

When parents discipline children by telling them they are *bad* girls or boys, or say, *shame on you*, they are cursing them. They may say, "If you're not good, God won't love you anymore." Can you see how this **defiles the image of God** in the heart of a child? Besides, it is a lie. God gives all of us unconditional love.

Parents frequently don't tell the child **what they did** was bad. They tell them **they** are bad, stupid, or ugly, and there's nothing they can do about it. These things, proclaimed by voices of authority, become **spiritual daggers** thrust deep into the **hearts** of children.

Suppose a child, who knows they have been naughty, walks through the room where dad is sitting. As they walk by, dad looks disapprovingly over the top of his glasses. It is the look that says, "You're not welcome here. Go to your room." He doesn't have to say anything. The *look*, the expression of **condemnation**, and the **cold treatment** tell the child there is something wrong with them, or dad wouldn't treat them this way. They identify themselves as *bad*. They don't know they can refuse that identity.

Often, a child who believes he is bad, decides, "If I am bad, I may as well act bad." Adults wonder at the child's abrupt change in behavior. He or she is simply responding logically to the false identity of the curse lodged in his or her heart.

Another example is the boy who goes to school and daydreams during class. At the end of the semester, he brings home his report card and apathetically gives it to his father. After his father has studied the card, he begins his customary tirade, shouting: "IS THIS THE BEST YOU CAN DO? AFTER ALL WE'VE DONE FOR YOU; AFTER ALL THE ADVANTAGES YOU'VE BEEN GIVEN; AFTER ALL WE'VE GIVEN UP SO YOU CAN HAVE A GOOD EDUCATION; AND THIS IS THE BEST YOU CAN DO? YOU DISGUST ME! YOU'RE JUST LIKE YOUR UNCLE! HE HAS ALWAYS BEEN A BUM, A FAILURE, AND A LOSER AND YOU'RE JUST LIKE HIM! GET OUT OF MY SIGHT. I DON'T EVEN WANT TO LOOK AT YOUR FACE!"

As the years go by, all these proclamations are manifest. Dad drinks coffee with his friends and laments, "I just don't know what happened to that boy. He had all the advantages and opportunities. He's smart enough and has ability, but now he just runs with that gang committing crimes and doing drugs. Society must have ruined him. I don't know what else it could be."

When we were children, we used to defend ourselves from the hurtful words of others. We would say, "Sticks and stones may break my bones, but words will never hurt me." Massive phooey! If someone is hit with a stick, the physical damage will usually heal in a relatively short time. When someone is stabbed with words, the emotional damage could last a lifetime. That is why we need a Healer.

With the wisdom we expect to find in Scripture, we are told not to take everything people say to heart, because we may hear curses. (Ecclesiastes 7:20-21) We have been given a choice. We have permission to *just say no*! In this case, the expression applies to curses as well as to drugs.

We have all been cursed, whether we are aware of it or not. When family members torment one another in curse-producing ways, the person, their identity, and destiny are cursed and defiled.

This process of contamination and defilement begins very early in our lives. The enemy of our souls chooses every opportunity to torment mankind. Because his greatest weapons are deception and intimidation, he selects the most innocent and defenseless as targets.

As an example, perhaps a child has wet the bed and been forced to lie in the wet as punishment. They may have been spanked, had their faces rubbed in the bedding, been verbally abused, or ridiculed and humiliated, all in the name of training. This **defiles** their identity and forecasts their destiny.

Consider a baby in a dirty diaper, experiencing the physical discomfort of itching and burning, crying for help. Imagine the emotional effects produced when he believes no one cares because his needs are not being met. Imagine the sense of outrage and injustice, and the curse received as a result.

We've been told some family members force children to eat or drink body wastes as a part of ritual or systematic abuse. How pure and clean could the thoughts of such victims possibly be? Victims of systematic sexual, emotional, and physical abuses will certainly have attitudes and beliefs about themselves that are curses of their identities and destinies. These beliefs frequently trigger **self-defiling** behaviors that are the fruit of the curses.

Regardless of our skill at masking these traumas and burying them deep in our souls, their effects are profound. They become powerful curses affecting our health, physically, emotionally, and spiritually. They also impair our ability to relate to other people, our Creator, and ourselves. They affect the way we act, speak, and respond to the events of life.

In these cases, the curses were invoked with **trauma inducing actions** as well as with words. Over time, these activities generate **expectations** of further defilement and abuse. Victims frequently verbalize these expectations to themselves and others, **perpetuating** the curses. This is not a theory. We have met many people who have come to believe that these abuses and the defilement are normal.

Purchasing Curses for Ourselves

As described above, there are many different kinds of curses that may have affected us at some time. However, they represent a small percentage of the total. A greater percentage is represented by curses we pay to have put on us, through various forms of **witchcraft**.

Talking to spirits of dead people, seeking secret knowledge or wisdom, or entreating them to influence events, is called **necromancy**. When we engage in these practices, we allow spirits associated with these practices to have influence in our lives.

King Saul knew he was rebelling against God's Word and engaging in an abomination when he went to the medium at Endor to communicate with the dead prophet, Samuel.

The medium described an old man, covered with a mantle, she identified as Samuel. The spirit prophesied that Saul and Israel would be delivered into the hands of the Philistines and said, "Tomorrow you and your sons will be with me." This work of necromancy was successful and its result was a curse. The army was defeated and Saul and his sons were killed. (1 Samuel 28:5-19; 31:1-6)

Young people sometimes play a game called Bloody Mary, or Mary Worth, at parties. They have been deceived into believing this is *just fun*, the way Halloween is *just fun*. They light a candle in a dark room, hold it up to a mirror, and summon Mary. Sometimes, a being does appear in the mirror, and the young person is so frightened they never do it again.

At other times, an alliance is established between the young person and the spirit. Because the spirit's presence was requested, it takes full advantage of the opportunity. If it can establish a place in the young person's life, it will remain until forced to leave. Functioning as a **medium** or **spiritist** subjects the youngster to the control of that spirit.

Anytime we ask spirits to tell us things about hidden knowledge or the future, it is **divination**. Many of us, including Christians, have gone to witches to have the cards read, or have consulted astrological charts.

In Bulgaria, we ministered with Turkish gypsies who attended church regularly on Sunday morning. These same "Christians" went to the city square in the afternoon, put up their tables, and read the cards and crystal balls.

There are many forms, instruments, and practices of divination. Among other things, one can use cards, crystal balls, or pendulums. Some claim to *read* the bumps on our heads, the lines of our palms, tea leaves, coffee grounds, and astrological charts. In the game section of a typical American toy store, we might find Ouija boards, the Eight Ball, and other divination *games*. They are all practices of witchcraft and magic and, as such, are abominations, according to God.

A slave girl, possessed by a spirit of divination and known for her fortune telling, followed Paul through the streets for days, shouting the truth concerning his identity and that of his companions.

After many days, Paul was greatly annoyed and turned to the spirit and said, "I command you in the name of Jesus Christ to come out of her."

The Bible says the spirit came out of her that very hour. Doesn't it seem a little odd that a spirit telling the truth would provoke Paul? (Acts 16:16-18)

Paul knew the nature of his enemy. He knew that Satan and his servants were incapable of doing something good. Though the words were true, the motivation was for evil. Many people are confused about this. They seem to believe that Satan can be bad, yet do good things.

Some people call *Madame Zelda*, on her 900-phone line. They are reluctant to give offerings in church, but are willing to pay four dollars per minute to receive a curse from a spiritual reader or practitioner of astrology.

All forms of divination represent curses, no matter how good they sound. The witch employs a divination spirit. When the witch tells you something is going to happen, and you choose to believe it, the minions of the divination spirit are assigned to cause it to happen. The fortune may sound good, but neither Satan nor his kingdom is capable of giving a good gift.

Suppose a young woman is told she is going to meet and marry a tall, dark, handsome stranger. It sounds great, but after she marries him, she discovers he has a basement full of torture implements. Satan never gives anything without a stinger attached.

People also use witchcraft and magic in an attempt to take control. They rebel against the authority of God and bring curses upon themselves and others. In Section 4, we will discuss the issues of control, rebellion, and witchcraft in more detail.

The Lord has some hard things to say concerning all such activities. *"You shall not learn to follow the **abominations** of those nations. There shall not be found among you anyone who...practices **witchcraft**, or a **soothsayer**, or one who **interprets omens**, or a **sorcerer**, or one who **conjures spells**, or a **medium**, or a **spiritist**, or one who **calls up the dead**. For **all** who do these things are **an abomination** to the LORD, and because of these abominations the LORD your God drives them out from before you"* (Deuteronomy 18:9-12). [Emphasis ours]

When the Law was given, God commanded that anyone found practicing or using works of magic and witchcraft should be killed. This is another great opportunity for God's critics to proclaim how bloodthirsty He is. To the contrary, His actions and commands are based in love. He knew, better than anyone else, the terrible consequences people would experience as a result of using spiritual or demonic powers.

Cursing Ourselves

What about our own **attitudes, beliefs, perceptions,** and **expectations**? They have been formed by the things described above and have a profound affect on our souls and lives. How did we develop them; where did they begin; and how do they now manifest in our lives?

Our own voice is the **most powerful voice** in the world **for our soul**. We can make a silent proclamation in our heart or proclaim loudly with our mouth. We can invoke harm, injury, torment, or great evil upon ourselves. We are cursed when we despise our God-given identity. Many of us hold ourselves in contempt, and our hearts are filled with self-judgment and condemnation.

The **most powerful curses** are those we place upon ourselves. These could include vows, oaths, and proclamations we may have made at any time in our lives. We have heard people speak curses upon themselves in a clearly conscious way, and we have heard these curses proclaimed thoughtlessly, or in jest. It doesn't matter. Whether they are deliberate or mindless, the results can be equally devastating.

We refer to this phenomenon as *self talk*. We give hopelessness and negative expectations much more power when we combine them with our faith. When we engage in worry and dread concerning the future, we are mingling our faith with the anticipation of bad things. Not only is this a sin, because we're not trusting in God, but it is also a curse. The Bible confirms that we are greatly affected by the beliefs of the heart, because they are made manifest. (Proverbs 23:7)

Jesus, in confronting the Pharisees, proclaimed that we are cursed and blessed by our own words. (Matthew 12:34-37) When we employ our own words to agree with God's word concerning our identity and destiny, **we are blessed**. When we employ our own words to agree with the world or Satan concerning our identity and destiny, **we are cursed**. (James 3:2-10)

This is illustrated by the accounts given of the Exodus from Egypt. Because the children of Israel were functioning in rebellion in their hearts and with their mouths, God honored their proclamations that they would die in the wilderness. It is as though He said, "Thy will be done."

There is no indication that this was God's will for them. It does seem to us, instead, that He was manifesting sadness when He responded to their proclamations. (Numbers 14:28-29; Hebrews 3:17-19) God accepts people's choices because He loves us too much to impose His will on our lives, even if it would be good for us.

Have you ever heard people after a church service **compete** to see who is the most miserable? Sister so-and-so tells everybody about her diseases, all the drugs she's taking, her miserable family, and her miserable life. In response, brother so-and-so assures her she doesn't know what pain really is. He describes, in detail, all his diseases and the drugs he's required to take, along with all their side effects. He tells her about his job, how miserable he is, about his family members, and all the ways they cause him to suffer.

As a result of the troubles he enumerates, brother so-and-so wins the prize for being the most miserable person at church. We suspect that in the spiritual, he receives a badge with a big, bright M for miserable. Then, he goes to his miserable home, sits in his miserable kitchen, drinks some miserable coffee, and wonders what is wrong with God. "Why does God allow these bad things to happen in my life? Why doesn't He show me His love and provision, the way He does for other people?" Once again, the Lord proclaims, "So be it unto you according to your words."

In a crowded space, someone next to us sneezes. Almost immediately, we feel tickling sensations in our sinuses or tenderness in our throat. The thought flashes through our head that we have *caught* the flu. When we accept the thought, we increase our chances to be afflicted, even though the common flu virus takes days to start producing symptoms in our bodies.

This brings up another issue. Some people don't understand the difference between testimony and reality. If we are not feeling well, we can affirm what our Creator says about us. Without lying, we can say, "I'm feeling under the weather today, but by Jesus' stripes I've been healed. I'm sure I'll be okay, because that is the truth on which I'm going to stand." (1 Peter 2:24) We don't have to say, "I'm fine; everything is fine; it's lovely" when it's not.

It is a very serious thing to have a curse placed on you, or to place a curse on someone else. Because of the **programming** we have received from the world around us, our soul *computer* has been filled with old, non-beneficial software. We need to replace that *curse* software with the Word of God, so we can **reprogram** our computer with **life**.

Cursing Others

Another way we can **curse ourselves** is **by cursing others**. Earlier, we quoted from Ecclesiastes concerning curses people offer you with their words. The same writer also says our hearts know that **we** have **cursed others,** as well. (Ecclesiastes 7:22)

Because of the dysfunctional environments in which most of us are raised, it is common for us to say disagreeable things about our parents. In our minds at the time, much of what we say may be well founded. However, these things present a spiritual problem. Jesus took this kind of curse very seriously. (Mark 7:10)

All of us have cursed others with our words or actions at some time in our lives. We may have been critical or judgmental, used nicknames that were not complimentary, or put down a sibling, friend, co-worker, or fellow church member. We might think we're being cute or clever by saying things that are sarcastic to put others down. We may decide this person really needs to be taken down a notch.

The consequences of having done so are not always readily apparent. However, we should ask ourselves, "Is this really how God sees this person? Is this the way Jesus would respond?" If not, we should renounce our words. We believe they do have an effect on our lives spiritually, because of what God said about **receiving back** what **we have given** out. (Luke 6:37-38; Malachi 3:10) We are assured we will receive good, for good, and bad, for bad.

We thoughtlessly proclaim curses into our families, cities, governmental institutions, and schools. Our words have great power. (Proverbs 18:21) It is our responsibility to use those words in agreement with Christ. (I Timothy 6:3-5) Scripture tells us we have the power. (Revelation 12:11) The Word also says we are responsible for every word that comes out of our mouths. (Matthew 12:36-37)

Since realizing the importance of our words, one of us will ask the other, "Is that really what you meant to say," or, "Is that what you really want to happen?" We know we had better review what we said. Usually, we say a short prayer like, "Lord, I renounce these words; I ask you to cause them to fall to the ground with no power. I speak the power of the blood of Jesus over all my words and over all the curses I've proclaimed on my family, my church, my community, or myself."

Because we are the ones who speak the words, we are the ones who will stand judgment. If I say to someone, "Oh, sister, you're looking so pretty today," I had better mean it. If I'm thinking, "That old headache, I had to *butter her up* because I want something;" I have a problem, because it is recorded in heaven. I will someday stand before the Lord and account for every motivation, and everything said or thought. Nothing will slip by.

Not only must we live with the effects of curses here, but we will also deal with the consequences in eternity.

We Have an Alternative

Death and life are in the power of the tongue. (Proverbs 18:21) We can speak death; or we can speak life. The weapons of our warfare are not temporal. (2 Corinthians 10:4) We **are** to bring every thought into captivity to the obedience of Christ, and speak accordingly. (2 Corinthians 10:5) We should be the voice of our God here on earth. We need to be sure our prayers are not waging war against God's will, and our voices are not being used by Satan to further his kingdom.

We are told that we are to speak psalms, songs, and spiritual blessings to one another, to our towns and cities, and to our governmental leaders. (Colossians 3:16; Matthew 5:44; Luke 6:28; I Peter 2:17) We are to speak blessings and not curses. We may need to get on our knees before the Lord and repent of the idle words of our mouths. We should begin to speak blessings into existence for our country.

The Lord appointed our President and government. We may not agree with everything they say or do. They are there because God places authorities over us. There are Scriptures that tell us not to touch the anointed of God. (I Samuel 24:6; I Chronicles 16:22) Who are we to speak against what God has put in place? We should honor God for what He is doing, by doing our part.

We don't have to agree with the pastor on television, or the one down the street. If we think they are in error, we should be petitioning God to flood their hearts with light, life, and truth. We should be asking the Lord to fill churches with the Holy Spirit, causing His will to be done there. We must choose to speak life rather than death.

We may not know how to pray for a certain situation, but it is our responsibility, as Christians, to pray. The Lord has chosen to use our prayers to further His will on this earth. If we don't know how to pray for our President, our city leaders, a church body, or our own church, we can tell the Lord we want His will to be done.

Some people might choose, "Lord, I don't know what to pray, so I'm going to pray in accordance with Your Spirit. I ask You to pray through me for Your will to be done in this situation, for this person, or concerning this group of people."

Using the model Jesus gave us, we can pray, "Heavenly Father...I want Your kingdom to come and Your will to be done on earth just as it is in heaven; in my heart and life, in my family, in my church, in my community, in my country, in my government, in the White House, Congress, the schools, the courts, the police departments, the news media, and the entertainment industry!" (Matthew 6:9; Luke 11:2) It is not complicated. Imagine what would happen if every Christian prayed this prayer once every day.

We can't fail if we ask that God's will be done. We don't have to know what His will is. We aren't qualified to wear the *God badge*, so we can trust Him to decide what is best. When we ask that His will be done in every strata of life, we are empowering Him to send angels to cause those things to occur.

Curses of Physical and Emotional Trauma

There is an issue relevant in all our lives concerning **physical and emotional trauma**. While we view this as another form of curse, we have segregated it from the section above in order to look at cursing, and its consequences, from another perspective.

Our lives are punctuated by **normal issues** such as rejection, abandonment, violence, accidents, and disease. We can begin to experience these things in the womb and continue to experience them to the present. These experiences are, technically, not curses. However, they affect our lives in much the same way, by establishing beliefs and expectations.

We would like to look at this from the best-case scenario. We begin life in a relatively safe and comfortable place, mommy's womb. Our *world starts to change* when it is time for the **birthing process** to begin. Mommy's body does strange things. It starts pushing and squeezing, forcing us out of that familiar place. We probably sense fear and urgency in the unusual activity and hear unfamiliar voices along with the sounds of mommy's distress.

This is confusing and traumatizing spiritually, emotionally, and physically. While we don't consciously remember the events, it is inevitable that, as babies, we experienced the fears and discomforts associated with the birthing process.

If all goes well, **after we are born** and breathe air for the first time, we may be placed in a little plastic crib. Being separated from mom, who was our world, could instill rejection and abandonment in the heart of a newborn.

In difficult births, we might feel bruised and battered. As adults, some of us may still have indentations in our skulls from the forceps used to assist our birth. We believe these experiences create traumatic body memories that have long-term emotional and spiritual consequences.

Normal **growing-up** experiences guarantee more bumps and bruises. Sometimes they are physical, sometimes emotional, and sometimes both. These normal experiences can include violence associated with victimization and abuse. They could be severe enough to require hospitalization.

The years of **adolescence** can be particularly hard for most of us, when we are faced with the pressure to succeed. Then, of course, there are organized sports activities, the process of establishing dominance, and the dating ritual. All these things produce pain and associated traumas. Times of great physical and emotional stress seem to have a lasting effect on us spiritually, as well.

When we react to these experiences in fear, for example, we open the door for spiritual forces to torment us. (1 John 4:18) When our expectations are based upon all these fears, the expectations become negative, faith-driven, **self-fulfilling prophecies**. As such, they become curses functioning in our lives.

We can be free of all manifestations, symptoms, illusions, body memories, and everything serving Satan's kingdom received into our body or soul. We can be free of all the thoughts, feelings, emotions, attitudes, beliefs, perceptions, and expectations that have become curses in our hearts and lives.

We can also be free of any **negative spiritual effects** of hospitalizations, surgeries, medical procedures, dental procedures, all associated medications, narcotics, inoculations, drugs, alcohol, or any other physical substances that have gained access to our bodies.

Substance Abuse, Escape, and Counterfeit Healing

We are convinced that **all sin reactions** to pain and trauma give the enemy of our soul the legal right to afflict us. We all **want to survive** and **have our needs met**, so we find creative ways to meet them. We believe **all sin** is based on these primal needs and **our perception** of what it takes to provide them.

As a result, many of us have used, or abused, drugs, alcohol, or other chemical substances in an **attempt to escape** physical or emotional pain. These substances affect our spiritual, emotional, and physical health.

When we relinquish control of our mind and nervous system through the use of such substances, we open the door for tormenters.

We may use **daydreaming** and other **methods of escape** to avoid dealing with our problems. This fairly common form of escape is called dissociation. We have all seen children and adults sitting in the midst of activity, with eyes glazed over, totally removed from what is going on around them. Their consciousness is somewhere else. Calvin, in the comic strip, *Calvin and Hobbs*, is a good example of a daydreamer, obviously preferring his imaginary world to reality.

This pattern of behavior probably begins very early in life. **This doesn't make us bad; it makes us normal**. We believe God gave us the ability to escape in this way because He knew how hard life would be. Before we accepted Jesus as our Savior, our options were limited, but now Scripture gives us an alternative to dissociation. The Lord provides our place of escape. (Psalm 91:1-3)

Some of us, as children, were taken to witches, shamans, or spiritists, for counterfeit healing or benefits. As we've said before, all forms of witchcraft and magic produce demonic infestation affecting our bodies and souls. As Christians, we have the dominion and authority to declare our freedom from all the things done to us.

In Conclusion

We have all had many opportunities to receive curses, and yet we can be free of the effects of these curses by not giving them a place. *A curse without cause shall not alight* (Proverbs 26:2).

The word alight creates a word picture of a curse flying around **like a bat**, looking for a place to land. It is, of course, some kind of a spiritual thing and can only land if it finds cause. If there is no legal claim or reason to land and no door open, it simply flies away.

If I tell Glenna how crummy or sickly she looks, she can choose to receive my words, in which case, she will provide a landing place for that little bat; or she can decide not to receive it. She may say, "Thank you for your concern, John, but I'm feeling fine. The Lord is in charge of my life." In this case, nothing happens because she hasn't provided a place for the curse to land. She doesn't respond in fear or anger, but chooses to disregard it.

Many of us are so easily offended. We tell others about all that was said, as well as the things not said, that offended us. We describe how we have been treated with disrespect. From our perspective, the other people are at fault. From God's perspective, **we decide** to produce sin responses that open our door to **receive the curse**.

Cursing is constantly going on all around us, but we don't have to accept it. We don't have to put curses on other people. We can **listen** to our own words, **monitor** the thoughts being processed in our heads, and **reject** those that are not from God.

The things we have heard and accepted as truth can keep us in bondage until we realize all curses are lies, because they do not agree with what God says about us. As we believe in our heart, so are we. (Proverbs 23:7) Since our attitudes, beliefs, perceptions, and expectations can function as curses, **we can reject** those that are non-beneficial.

When we discover the truth, reject the curses, and renounce accepting them, we take away Satan's legal claim. When the legal claim is removed, the **spiritual bat** no longer has a right to land or remain. The eviction notice is served against it, and the curse it represents.

In the following prayer, we have included many of the different issues described above. If some don't pertain to you, praying about them will have no effect. We trust that some will apply, and the prayer will be beneficial. If you agree, it is time to pray.

Sample Proclamation:

In the name of the Lord Jesus Christ, I renounce all the lies of Satan's kingdom and all names and nicknames I've received from any source that are not in agreement with my true gender, identity, and destiny as a child of God.

I also renounce all curses I have received from, or through, ancestors, family members, authority figures, friends, or anyone else. I renounce all familiar spirits representing any of these people, all their words, and their influence.

I renounce and proclaim the destruction of all curses associated with ungodly or counterfeit healing, witchcraft, and magic placed upon my life or being at any time, by any means, including by my own words, actions, or beliefs. I renounce and nullify all curses I've placed on anyone else's life or being by my words or actions. I also renounce all curses I have received through these sins.

I renounce all the curses I have placed upon myself through my words, actions, or beliefs. I renounce giving control over

any of my soul or humanity to Satan's kingdom as a result of pronouncing or receiving these curses.

I now proclaim the destruction of all curses resulting from spiritual, emotional, and physical traumas I have experienced, and all the spiritual components of these traumas. I command the destruction of all the effects of abandonment, betrayal, victimization, and abuse. I renounce all forms of dissociation and sinful escape, and command all their effects to be destroyed.

I command the destruction of all curses associated with ungodly healing and spiritual infestation, affecting my body or soul, as a result of hospitalizations, surgeries, medical procedures, dental procedures, medications, narcotics, inoculations, drugs, alcohol, or through other physical substances that have gained access to my body.

I proclaim the destruction of all thoughts, feelings, emotions, attitudes, beliefs, perceptions, and expectations that have become curses in my heart or in my life. I now renounce and command the destruction of all manifestations, symptoms, illusions, pain, and body memories, along with all triggers, such as sights, sounds, smells, tastes, sensations, and stimulations, by the power of the shed blood of the Lord Jesus Christ.

I claim the power of the blood of Jesus Christ over all these curses and bind everything serving Satan's kingdom that has been attached or assigned to me, in any way, by these curses.

I command everything serving Satan's kingdom to leave every part of my life and being, as well as the lives and beings of any others I have cursed, and go where the Lord Jesus Christ sends them.

I claim back every part of my soul and humanity: everything I've lost or given away, and everything that has been killed, stolen, or destroyed.

I proclaim that everything I received from Satan's kingdom is now replaced with healing, restoration, light, and life, by the power of the shed blood of the Lord Jesus Christ. Amen.

SPIRIT OF ANTICHRIST

Jesus, the Christ, is the only One **chosen** before the foundation of the world and **anointed** for the special task of providing salvation. He is the only One qualified to define our identity and destiny, and fill our hearts with perfect love, acceptance, approval, significance, satisfaction, confidence, fulfillment, comfort, security, happiness, peace, and joy.

What does a Christian have to do with antichrist? If we seek these things described above from anyone or anything else, we are going to an antichrist. We will explore some of the ways antichrist spirits affect us directly and indirectly.

An antichrist can be an **opponent** denying the existence of a Messiah altogether, an **alternate** diminishing the true Christ, or a **counterfeit** or replacement for Christ.

In the book of Revelation, chapter 13, two beasts are described. The first beast is the one frequently referred to as the Antichrist. He is the one who will receive the spirit of Satan in the end times. (See 2 Thessalonians 2) However, according to the Apostle John, **many antichrists** have come, and many deceivers. (1 John 2:18; 2 John 7)

Notice that the comings and goings of antichrists are stated in the past tense. They have come into the world, they have gone out into the world, and they are many.

Satan and all the spiritual entities serving him oppose God, His master plan for salvation, and His Anointed One. We conclude **all of them** are spirits of antichrist.

Antichrist Denies Messiah

Do any of these statements, inspired by antichrist, sound familiar? "There is no God, no heaven or hell, no Christ. It is all just mythology. I'm too smart to believe in that stuff. I plan to eat, drink, and be merry, because tomorrow I may die. When you're dead, you're just worm-food. I am an atheist!"

In two of his Psalms, King David refers to **fools** who say there is no God. Therefore, when we hear someone make remarks like the ones above, we know we are dealing with a fool. (Psalm 14:1; 53:1)

This simplifies things, because we are told in Proverbs not to argue with a fool. (Proverbs 23:9, 26:4) God tells us not to offer our pearls to someone like this, because they will stomp our pearls into the mud and turn to attack us. (Matthew 7:6)

Furthermore, we don't believe there is any such thing as an atheist. We all know in our hearts there is a God. He says the entire creation declares His existence. He also makes it clear that man has no excuse for denying His existence. (Romans 1: 18-21, 10:18; Psalm 19:1-4)

However, there are many people who are opponents of God, who *hate* Him for various reasons, or *reject* God and everything for which they think He stands. Many are convinced they *can't* afford to *trust* God because He might be like others they have known. We do not believe there is anyone living who does not know there truly is a God, the Creator.

People say Christians have *blind faith* and ridiculed them for it. However, to believe the entire universe came from nothing as a result of an accidental *big bang*, is not collapsing into chaos, but is now functioning with perfect order, requires **massive faith**. When we look at the heavens, the stars in the sky, the clouds in the air, the plants, the animals, and the miracle of the human body, we marvel at that level of *blind faith*.

Humanism is idolatry based upon the **worship of self**. This belief system is a nontheistic religion, antagonistic to traditional religion, while stressing an individual's capacity for self-realization through reason. Please note that **self** is the operative word. If we claim to be an atheist, or humanist, we simply place ourselves on the throne that belongs to the Creator.

This religion includes worship of, or preoccupation with, all aspects of self: physical appearance, needs, wants, and accomplishments. If we worship our intelligence, our abilities, our independence, or the talents God has given us; if we trust in our strength, rather than in God and His ability; if we worship faith and our ability to have faith, rather than the Author of all faith; we are worshiping antichrist.

People worship and serve this antichrist in the hope that they can find some goodness about themselves. They don't have time to worship the Creator, because they're too busy worshiping themselves and their ability to do important things. In a movie we once saw, one of the characters proclaimed, "Glory to man." These worshipers are too busy establishing their own counterfeit salvation to be interested in the true salvation and the true Christ.

Antichrist Diminishes the Work of Jesus

Earlier in this book, we discussed what is necessary to accept the **gift** of salvation and be spiritually reborn. We accept these things based on our understanding of the Bible. There are others who seem determined to believe in different ideas. An antichrist can propose these other ideas in order to **diminish** the **completed work** of Christ.

This religious spirit can acknowledge the Christ, but requires **works** by the believer and imposes **laws** for them to achieve complete salvation. Some would say, "Sure, I believe in God. I believe in heaven and hell, and I believe that Jesus made it **possible** for us to be saved. Now that He has done His part, we have to **do our part**."

This is to propose an **alternative** to the Scriptures and diminishes what Jesus, the Christ, accomplished! Paul warned about perverting the Gospel of Christ. (Galatians 1:6-9)

A woman confused about a number of issues came to us for ministry. In our effort to understand the problem, we asked how she was saved. She told us that she had always been saved. When we asked her what *always* meant, she told us it had been for as long she could remember.

John asked, "Do you remember how you were saved?"

She answered, "I've always attended church, since I was a little girl."

John asked her if her salvation was based on attending church and she said yes. To that, John asked, "Does that mean that if a dog attended church, it would be saved?"

"Yes," she replied. She believed that by attending church she earned the right to go to heaven. (Romans 10:2-4, 11:6)

There was no reason to believe she was saved, because she had no concept of what salvation was. After an explanation to help her understand what *being saved* meant, she eagerly received the **gift** of salvation.

One person reported joining a procession at Easter; crawling up a hill, bloodying hands, elbows, knees, and feet; and kissing the feet of a statue of a dead Jesus hanging on the cross. John suggested, "Next year you need to crawl up that hill, being sure to scuff your elbows and knees, so you can bleed and suffer as much as possible. Then, when you get to the top of the hill, stand to your feet, slap that statue across the face, and proclaim, 'You failed! I have to suffer and bleed to earn my salvation, because you are a failure!'"

This person was greatly offended, got red in the face, and looked ready to fight. We didn't understand why, because all the actions described, were proclaiming Jesus' failure. He had been **diminished** and was viewed as an impotent, dead man, still hanging on the cross. While grateful for His sacrifice, this person saw Him as weak and powerless, and had no concept of Him, raised, glorified, and sitting at the right hand of the Power on high.

Like so many others, this person decided it was necessary to earn, or somehow deserve, salvation, not depending on the righteousness of God, but on **their own ability** to establish righteousness. This spirit of antichrist offers a salvation of works as an alternate for true salvation, based on the righteousness of God, His finished work, and **nothing more**.

The Bible is filled with proclamations concerning the true Source of salvation. Throughout the New Testament, salvation is defined as **a gift** purchased by Jesus. Among these are many places in Romans, chapters 3-11, that state salvation and righteousness are **gifts of God**! Our part is simply to accept the gift. (Romans, 3:21-24,26,28,30; 4:2-3,5,16,23; 5:15-16,18-21; 6:22-23; 8:9-11)

Antichrist Attempts to Replace Christ

An antichrist spirit can also function as the **replacement** for, or **imitation** of, the Messiah. Only Christ can provide for the salvation of our souls. Antichrist may agree, "Yes, of course there is a God and a Heaven, there is a Hell, and Jesus is the Savior who did die for you. You will go to Heaven someday, but you need to be *reasonable* and *understand* that He is very busy.

"He is running the entire universe. He is taking care of mankind and guaranteeing that His master plan will be fulfilled. He is overseeing the activities of, perhaps, billions of angels and other created beings.

"It is not reasonable to expect Him to take an active role in your life and fill your heart with everything you need. He is occupied with many important things. If you want to have your heart filled, you need to go to the others He has provided for you."

This spirit could speak through a well-meaning mouth, and offer **replacement** methods for having our heart needs met.

This spirit would **suppress the truth** and those who agree with it would gladly accept the replacements. Professing to be wise, they become fools and exchange the incorruptible God for images in the likeness of corruptible man, birds, animals, and creeping things. Those who exchange the truth for the lie, worship and serve the **created** rather than the Creator. (Romans 1:18-25) [Author's paraphrase]

What About Created Ones?

Because we are normal people, we grow up with heart needs that are also normal. These needs include **love, acceptance, approval, peace, joy, significance, satisfaction, security, comfort,** and **assurance.** When we don't believe we can receive these things from an invisible God, we find an alternative.

Who, in your life, has become too important to you? Are your parents more important than Christ because they represent **love, comfort, or security**? Are your children more important than Jesus because they represent **approval and significance**? Is your family more important than the gift of salvation because it represents **peace and joy**?

What about your friends and those with whom you work? Do they even know you are a Christian? Are you too afraid to tell them because you desperately need **acceptance,** and they might reject you? In public, do you laugh at crude jokes, talk, and act like a pagan, in order to be accepted? Is there any noticeable difference between you and non-believers?

Do these others represent **comfort or assurance** that you really are OK? Do you find comfort and security going to a place where everyone knows your name? Can you see that many of us hope to receive from other people the **recognition** we desperately need?

We believe it is a problem when the approval and acceptance of those around us is more important to us than our Creator. The Bible says that God will give us up to the uncleanness brought about by our own **idolatry** of people or things. (Romans 1:24-25)

When Jesus was on earth, He proclaimed that a person is not worthy to be His disciple if they love family, their own life, or others more than Him. (Luke 14:26) [Author's paraphrase] When we make others a higher priority than Him, we give them priority in our lives. It is as though He is standing at a distance and we place them between Him and ourselves. We claim to want a relationship with Him even though we have placed **these others** between.

Idolatry is also the worship of a physical object as though it were a God. Many people worship ancestors and still consider them to be a part of the family. In some cases these ancestors are viewed as divine beings who are consulted by family members in prayer.

Other people revere their parents or other family members in an unhealthy way. We meet people who are very much into hero worship and give extraordinary honor and devotion to other people. Fans worshipping a celebrity illustrate this. It is amazing to see people scream, yell, cry, swoon, and carry on as they do.

If we worship a movie star, a sports hero, a president, an industrialist, a great inventor, a wife, our parents, our children, or anyone other than our Creator, we are worshiping antichrist. We allow those people to become too important to us because we desire to receive acceptance, love, and affirmation from them. Being a *groupie* makes us a part of something.

If we have posters, paintings, photographs, albums, paraphernalia, and a statue of Elvis, wearing his favorite jacket, in a corner, is it hard to determine the identity of our god?

Do we look to pastors to be our intermediaries, to hear from God for us? Do we hold them up on a pedestal and make them responsible for our spiritual growth and well-being, because we have no intention of being responsible ourselves? If so, we have made that man, woman, or those people, antichrist in our lives.

What Is Love?

Today the term, *I love you*, is used to describe a great many things that don't have anything to do with the love described in Scripture. Too often, "I love you," means "I lust you," "I want to possess you," "I need you," "I need you to need me," or "I want to control you," (all of which are prescribed by the gospel of Hollywood). These indicate sicknesses of the soul, emotional starvation, cravings, and yearnings.

When we interact with other people, we are often striving to have these needs met. However, no other human being can possibly fill our hearts with all the things we so desperately need. Seeking these things from people is futile idolatry. Only our Creator, and the Father of our spirits, is big enough to provide them.

Suppose someone sits in a cowboy bar and wails, "If you ever leave me, I'm gonna die!" We would say this person is worshiping antichrist. If he means what he is saying, the *love* he is singing about is based on sick dependency. We would not interpret this as love for someone else; because it's based in the singer's desire to have his needs met. How pathetic does that sound?

People make, or identify with, that kind of declaration because they are fouled up and are desperate for someone's attention and acceptance. They are willing to give their own soul or life, in order to receive that acceptance. That is idolatry. There are many songs that express the same kind of destructive attitudes and declarations.

Holding offense because of a hurt from the past represents another form of idolatry associated with normal dysfunctional relationships. Perhaps someone we *loved* ran off with the mailman or our best friend. Even after so many years, our perceptions, attitudes, and behaviors toward other people are based on that old experience.

We may be angry with God because He allowed bad things to happen to us. We feel rejected, abandoned, and betrayed because He will not force them to return to us. We focus our anger on people, in general, and on those who represent the offender, in particular. This particular brand of *love* could be based in the fear of failure, or, maybe, the need to win.

They may have long since forgotten us. Yet, we have allowed our identity and destiny to be defined and controlled by what *they* did to us. They may be happily married and living in Tasmania, but **we** have allowed them to control our emotions and attitudes, making our lives miserable! Can you see whom we are worshiping?

We have placed another person on a pedestal between God and us. We tell God, "I want to love and serve You." At the same time, we are harboring bitterness and anger. We need to give up all that garbage, so we can truly worship and serve Him. The way to be free of this particular idolatry is to forgive and turn all judgment over to God.

What if the person who was wronged marries again, and projects onto their new spouse what the previous spouse did? The new relationship and spouse will suffer as well. Everything seems to fall apart because of the tendency to project the old emotional debt on other people. It is all idolatry.

It is vital we not allow our **hatred** or **bitterness** to rule our lives and the lives of others in this way. If we are allowing someone, or something, other than God, to define who we are, it is time to be free from that **perverted form of worship**.

What About Created Things?

We are told to flee from idolatry. (1 Corinthians 10:14) The worship of false gods is idolatry. It doesn't matter what, or who, the god is. The sovereign God is the Creator. Anything, or anyone, that has become of primary importance in our lives, can become a god for us. Often we measure our worth or establish our significance by the things we idolize.

Suppose you came into our home and found all the rooms filled with tables of all sizes, shapes, and descriptions. On the tables you found photo albums filled with photos of tables. On the walls were paintings of tables.

If you were one of our best friends, we would invite you into our *secret* room, where we kept all the most valuable tables. Would you think us a little strange?

In the book of Matthew, there is an account of a man who came to Jesus and asked, *"What good things **shall I do** that I may have eternal life?"*

Notice, this man's perception was that he could do good deeds to earn eternal life. Jesus told him to keep the commandments. The man was quick to say he had never committed murder or adultery, never stolen, or given false witness, had always honored his father and mother, and loved his neighbor as himself.

It was a fine testimony, but there was no mention of the First Commandment, *"You shall have no other gods before Me"* (Exodus 20:3). Jesus told the man to sell everything and follow Him. When the young man heard this, he sadly went away, because he had many possessions. Jesus obviously knew which of the Commandments the young man had not followed. For this man, the **accumulation of things** had become more important than God and he was in idolatry. (Matthew 19: 16-24)

Some of us still have all our high school clothes. We can't get into any of them, but we can't bring ourselves to give them away. They represent past glory, memories, and emotional attachments we believe define our identity.

Others of us still have all the stuffed animals from our childhood and teen years. We couldn't bear to be rid of them because they represent something we've lost as adults. We can snuggle into the fake fur and re-experience some of the feelings from earlier days. In our hearts, we become the child who could find comfort, security, and protection from all the monsters through our furry friends. Who needs God?

Still others have an extra room stuffed full of things we don't even remember. We don't need to remember what they are, since that isn't the motivation for keeping them. Dusty old pieces of aluminum foil, rolls of string, greeting cards, and useless stuff, have become a **source of security**. In our hearts, these things may have replaced the security offered by the Lord.

People have told us if their houses were burned down and they lost everything, they would commit suicide. There would be no more reason for living. For them, the things are more important than the life given them by God. This indicates they are worshiping and trusting in the created things, rather than the Creator.

Do any of these situations seem familiar? Are we holding on to things because they are our preferred source of security? Is it easier to believe in a room full of stuffed animals, old clothes, or dusty junk, than a God we can't see and don't really know? Is it possible we are hanging on to the tangible because we can't totally trust in a spiritual, loving, faithful God?

A spirit representing Satan's kingdom might tell you it is unreasonable to expect Jesus to provide complete salvation. Your significance, satisfaction, security, or fulfillment should come from the **accumulation of things**. To agree with this spirit of antichrist is to function in idolatry.

We can also enjoy the accumulation of things if we look to the government for healthcare and a retirement income. This is *guaranteed security*, because we know we can trust in our government. We *know* it *always* protects us, provides for us, and does what is best for us.

If we want to experience **satisfaction** through experiencing wonderful **emotions** we can go to a great movie. We know of people who went to see the movie, *Titanic,* seventeen times. They laughed, cried, produced an abundance of emotional energy, and left the theater feeling satisfied. Who needs God when you can get so much good from a movie?

If movies aren't our thing, we can go to a football game, paint our face purple and gold, put our hair in spikes, and scream and yell ourselves hoarse for our team. Once again, we can experience the excitement and energy of these wonderful emotions. (Isn't it interesting that many people who do these things think Christians are strange and overly emotional if they weep, dance, or raise their hands in church?)

For some, a job, or career, is their reason for existence. They proudly admit they are workaholics. When they are not at their job, they are thinking about their job. In this case, the motivation isn't money, although the accumulation of wealth represents security. Their **significance** and **value** are based upon the work they do. In this case, **work is their idol** and represents antichrist in their lives.

People sometimes **establish their significance** and **identity** through their association with a **game**. It is simply a competition designed to entertain. Yet, to many people it is important to wear a jacket with the team emblem on it, or the uniform number of their favorite player. These people represent a distinct *nation*, within the general population, that has its own language, cultural distinctiveness, and set of values, all based upon a game.

If someone's house contains all kinds of football paraphernalia, models of the Heisman Trophy, autographed footballs in glass cases, other assorted sports items and pictures of football heroes, is it hard to figure out what or who they are worshipping?

I grew up in a family of six that was very much into games. Over the years we played board games such as Monopoly and Risk, card games like canasta or gin rummy, and badminton and croquet in the yard. At different times, everyone in the family, visiting members of the extended family, and neighbors played. **The spirit** of competition was functioning powerfully.

I remember many emotional outbursts, anger, frustration, and name-calling. When someone was doing poorly, they were called denigrating names. Other unpleasant names and remarks were reserved for someone doing very well in a game, like Monopoly. Having fun and just enjoying a game in such an environment was inconceivable.

At home and at school we were told to be good sports, but I learned that it didn't matter what people said. What mattered much more was how people acted and reacted. This whole situation represented a double bind. I could do poorly, and receive degrading names and identities; or I could do well, and receive degrading names and identities. There wasn't much of a choice.

I saw this principle in operation at home and at school. Since those days, I have seen it repeated in all walks of life. These experiences colored my view about such things. I have attended parties where it was announced we were going to play Trivial Pursuit. I may have played, grudgingly, or just watched the interactions, arguments, and emotional outbursts, as others played. It reminded me of my childhood and it was not fun or enjoyable. I can't help but view someone, who **establishes their significance** by the accumulation of trivial information, with sadness.

There are also people who have memorized thousands of Scriptures. They have a great deal of philosophical knowledge *about* God, but they don't *know* Him. They have a relationship **with a book** called the Bible. You can see them protecting and pampering the book that has become so important to them. Our concern is that the **created thing** called a book has become a replacement *god*. They don't have a relationship with the living God.

We are reminded of a Scripture in which Jesus described what would come in the judgment. Apparently, there will be those who come to Him and proclaim all the good works they have done, *in His name*. Jesus will tell them He never knew them. (Matthew 7:23)

These people may have believed they were doing good works. We don't know if they were deceived into believing they were saved, when they were not. They did know enough about Scripture to pray, prophesy, cast out demons, and do other things in His name.

Assuming they were not, knowingly, agents of Satan's kingdom, these were people with head knowledge but no heart knowledge of Jesus. They were defined as people who *practice lawlessness*, so we conclude they were worshiping the antichrist, or **counterfeit**, instead of the Christ.

What About Spirits That Imitate the Holy Spirit?

At a meeting in a large church, we heard a pastor proclaim that he had come to this meeting desperately seeking God, and determined to receive *anything* supernatural. We were concerned because, with that attitude, we are convinced he could receive *anything*, without being aware it wasn't from the true Holy Spirit.

If we worship **supernatural manifestations** rather than the God of Creation, we are worshiping antichrist. We need to proclaim that we will only receive what comes from the God of Creation. Otherwise, we could receive **spiritual** *gifts* from spirits of antichrist rather than from the Holy Spirit.

Broken people, desperate to receive significance, importance, or something special, are willing to take whatever they can get. In this way, it is possible for the **counterfeit** to be spread from person to person. Some might say, "I received something really powerful last night. I felt this heat in my heart, like I was going to burn up from the inside. I have also found that anyone I touch gets that heat now." Unfortunately, many people will say, "Give me what you have," without thinking, discerning, or judging the spirit, as we are told to do. (I John 4:1-6)

There are deceiving spirits that imitate the manifestations and gifts of the Holy Spirit, such as those functioning through the slave girl in Acts 16:16-18. We conclude that there will be many deceivers like the slave girl. We expect to see false prophets and ministers pretending to be Christians. These people can function in their roles as a humble minister in a small church, or in a highly exalted position.

We've been told not to be surprised if deceivers come as ministers of God performing signs and wonders. We've been told that even Satan transforms himself into an angel of light, to deceive. (2 Corinthians

11:13-15) The Bible speaks a great deal about those who practice lawlessness, and there are Scriptures that describe lawlessness. (2 Thessalonians 2:9; Mark 13:22) Jesus spoke about a time when His followers, the elect, would have opportunities to be deceived.

Remember what we said earlier about receiving prayer or ministry from those who claim to represent Christ? People have reported they had prayed for many believers while they were functioning Satanists. They imparted spiritual *blessings* that had nothing to do with Christ. They seemed pleased because they had deceived the *stupid, Disneyland Christians*. Those who received the *blessings* seemed willing to receive prayer without question.

Christians have an obligation to be discerning, to be wise as serpents and gentle as doves. We have an obligation to judge the spirits by the fruit because the spirits of antichrist are already in the world. Christians must be aware enough to discern the difference between the **counterfeit** and the real Christ.

It doesn't matter whether a spirit of antichrist comes as the **opponent**, the **alternative**, or the **counterfeit** of the real Christ. Any time we worship anything, or anyone, other than the true God of creation, we are worshiping antichrist and we are functioning in **idolatry**. Here is another opportunity to pray.

Sample Proclamation:

In the name of the Lord Jesus Christ, I now renounce all the false gods of humanism and any other religious organization serving Satan's kingdom. I renounce the Antichrist, the False Prophet, Hades, Death, and the Dragon.

I renounce the dead Jesus still hanging on the cross, the angry father in heaven who would reject me, the voice of the accuser pretending to be the true Holy Spirit, all unclean religious spirits, all the religious people, and all familiar spirits.

I renounce all the deceiving spirits that represent ancestors or any dead person. I renounce all the lies, deceptions, and illusions of any religious organization or training I have received.

I renounce all attitudes, beliefs, perceptions, expectations, and programming I received due to my involvement with any religious organization.

I renounce all the rituals, ceremonies, oaths, proclamations, laws, requirements, and obligations connecting any part of my being to Satan's kingdom. I renounce all responsibilities placed upon me by any religious system.

I also renounce all forms of witchcraft, magic, manipulation, control, intimidation, violence, guilt, condemnation, and the need to perform, or to do things, in order to receive acceptance and approval.

I renounce everything associated with any religious belief system that defiled my true identity, destiny, or gender, including all spirits, attitudes, perceptions, strengths, and competition.

I renounce all forms of spiritual armor, protection, powers, strengths, abilities, weapons, and everything else I have received from Satan's kingdom in order to survive, protect myself, or provide for my own needs.

I renounce all spirits that imitate the true Holy Spirit, and His manifestations or gifts; and I renounce anything else I have received which would deceive me or draw me away from fellowship with my heavenly Father and the Lord Jesus Christ.

I renounce receiving any spiritual energy, from Satan's kingdom, into any part of my body or being, through deception or as an act of my will. I renounce giving worship, idolatry or sacrifice to anything, or anyone, other than my God, the Creator and Father of all things, and the Lord Jesus Christ. I renounce giving any of my spiritual, emotional, or physical energies, by any means, to serve Satan's kingdom.

The Lord Jesus Christ has paid for all the sins of the world, including my sins; therefore, I command all these sacrifices be given to Him, as He is the only One worthy to receive them.

I command everything associated with these prayers, serving Satan's kingdom, to release everything belonging to me, leave every part of my life and being, and go, now, where the Lord Jesus Christ sends it. Amen!

SECTION THREE: THE SOUL

God has told us that He is the Father of our spirits; therefore, our spirit must be created whole and complete. God has told us, in His word, that He owns all the souls, so we originally received a complete and properly constructed soul. However, there are many Scriptures that indicate the soul can be damaged.

A baby in the womb possesses a whole soul, but it already has sustained damage and received programming we can't quantify or fully understand. As we will see in our analysis of the soul, damage is done to the soul as a result of sin. We believe we begin sinning as babies in the womb, because we receive messages that cause us to react in fear, anxiety, anger, or other sinful ways.

At birth, we have already been affected by damage to our soul as a consequence of sin. We are born needy and vulnerable to emotional injury into families that don't know how to fully provide for our needs.

As children, we require constant care and nurturing from our parents and families. When they fail to understand and provide for those needs, our souls continue to be damaged. We go through childhood with some needs that are never met. Normally, we respond in a sinful way, with fear and insecurity that produce even more brokenness of soul.

DEFINING THE SOUL

When we were first introduced to this ministry, the Lord put us on a very steep learning curve. We had been invited to join a deliverance ministry team, but had little knowledge and no experience to enable us to minister in this arena. The resources we had available to us were very limited. We read books, listened to tapes, and attended seminars that helped, to some extent. For the most part, we learned in the school of hard knocks.

During the first couple of years we experienced a phenomenon that seemed totally incredible. We would be ministering to a person who seemed like a normal adult; then, in a moment, we were talking to someone different. This someone spoke and had the mannerisms of a five-year-old. The expressions on the face, the inflections in the voice, and the body language all seemed to be those of a child.

I can't possibly express the level of frustration I experienced during these encounters. As a *logical* engineer, I knew it couldn't be real, because a person could not *switch* from adult to child so quickly. If this was just deception, we were dealing with someone who should have been working in Hollywood. However, I *knew* it must be all demonic and dealt with it accordingly.

Out of ignorance and fear, I shouted and yelled, bound and cast. One day, in the midst of such a tirade, I was confronted. The person to whom I was *ministering* was sobbing pitifully and asked me a terrible question. "Do you know how it makes me feel, when you call me a demon?" I didn't know what to do. This was a huge challenge to my *logical* belief system.

As those first few years went by we studied as many sources as we could find, and concluded this phenomenon might he something other than demons. The more we studied and tried different methods of ministry, the more comfortable we became with this new paradigm. We finally accepted the belief that the people who had experienced extraordinarily terrible childhoods could *possibly* be suffering from multiple personality disorder, or MPD.

Later, while attending a conference, we discovered this phenomenon had been renamed and was now called dissociative identity disorder, or DID. Along with this discovery, we read and heard a great deal concerning what is called satanic ritual abuse, or SRA. We believed that such things happened only to *the few* people involved in formal satanism.

When we left the States for a particularly long trip to South America, our belief system was reasonably solid. We had our paradigm in place; we had classifications for different types of people; and we had balanced it all with *logic*. This offered some sense of security that what we were doing made sense, so we could apply it to a broader spectrum of people. Then, the unexplainable occurred.

In every city and church, we met people who had never been a part of a satanic coven or been subjected to what the experts called satanic ritual abuse. Yet, there were individuals in every group who responded to ministry the way those who had been involved in satanism responded. They would switch back and forth, from one personality to another, providing us a wonderful opportunity for frustration. This didn't seem to be a rare condition, at all, but one that appeared to affect many people, to some degree.

By the end of the trip, the frustration level had become almost unbearable. We were experiencing all this turmoil concerning something we couldn't control or explain. I would lie in bed at the end of the day and voice my frustrations to Glenna. Finally, when we were in our hotel room in Lima, preparing to leave for the States, I unloaded. I did what any normal husband would do, and vented my frustration by yelling at my wife.

I told her how frustrated I was. I told her that I was giving God an ultimatum. We were going to study this thoroughly when we returned home. We needed to find at least **two or three** Scriptures validating this phenomenon, or I was through with this ministry. I would go back to engineering, where I had equations that always gave the right answer.

After returning to the States, we spent a few weeks seeking Scriptures to validate the manifestations we had seen. Since the issue pertained to identity and identity disorder, we started looking for things that would relate to the identity. We studied the primary definitions related to the soul. We knew that each person was given only one soul, so this phenomenon must somehow involve the soul.

We did find many words that can be used to apply to the soul, many words that apply to the heart, and other words that apply to the mind. The **primary** words are defined, in part, as follows.

Soul, in Hebrew - in Greek

In Hebrew, the word is *nephesh*. (Strong's H 5315)

"The language of Hebrews 4:12 suggests the extreme difficulty of distinguishing between the soul and the spirit, alike in their nature and in their activities. Generally speaking, the spirit is the higher, the soul the lower element. The spirit may be recognized as the life-principle bestowed on man by God, the soul as the resulting life constituted in the individual, the body being the material organism animated by soul and spirit." (Vine's Complete Expository Dictionary, OT pp 237-38)

The Greek word is *psuche*. (Strong's G 5590) It denotes...the immaterial, invisible part of man...the seat of many things...'the inward man.' (Vine's, NT pp 588-89)

Heart, in Hebrew - in Greek

Heart in Hebrew is *leb* (Strong's H 3820), and it means "'heart; mind; midst'...[It] may refer to the organ of the body...or it may also refer to the inner part or **middle** of a thing...It can be used of the man himself or his personality...The seat of desire, inclination, or will can be indicated by 'heart.' The 'heart' is regarded as a synonym of 'mind.' The heart is the fountain of all he does, all his thoughts, desires, words, and actions that flow from deep within him." (Vine's, OT pp 108-9)

Heart in Greek is *kardia* (Strong's G 2588), "'the heart'...the chief organ of physical life. By an easy transition the word came to stand for man's entire mental and moral activity, both the rational and the emotional elements. In the New Testament it denotes the seat of many things including physical life." (Vine's, NT p 297)

Definition of Mind

The word "mind" in Matthew 22:37, *dianoia* in Greek, means deep thought, imagination, understanding. (Strong's, G 1271) "meditation, reflecting'...knowing, understanding, or moral reflection." (Vine's, NT p 408) (Also see Mark 12:30; Luke 10:27 and Acts 8:37)

"When renewed by the Holy Spirit, the whole mind set changes from the fearful, negative of the carnal mind to the vibrant, positive thinking of the quickened spiritual mind." (*Spirit Filled Life Bible*, NKJV in Word Wealth, Mark 12:30)

Planting Seeds in the Soul

As previously discussed, the Bible mentions seeds, vines, trees, branches, and fruit. Jesus spoke specifically concerning the seeds of the mustard plant. Although the seeds can be very small, they can produce a very large plant. This plant would produce leaves, fruit and seeds, which are used in many ways. (Matthew 13:31-32, 17:20; Mark 4:31-32; Luke 13:18-19)

When any seed is planted, it lies in the ground awaiting the germination process. Seeds can also be planted *in your soul* the same way they can be planted in the dirt of the earth. We believe this is the context of the analogy being presented by Jesus concerning the mustard seed. He is speaking of the kingdom of heaven in this analogy. A seed of the kingdom of heaven cannot be planted in the earth, but instead, is planted in the soul. He also speaks of a seed of faith, which cannot be planted in the dirt but can be planted in the soul.

Jesus compared people to trees by proclaiming that a good tree bears good fruit and a bad tree bears bad fruit. A **good man** produces **good fruit** from his heart and an **evil man** produces **evil fruit** from his heart. In these verses, the seeds planted in the soul produce good and bad treasures **of the heart**. (Luke 6:43-45; Matthew 7:17-18)

Even though we were created in the image of God, people can do evil things. This is because, due to the fall, we were all born as children of darkness. Seeds of iniquity were planted, as generational iniquity, through the father. For this to be, the evil seeds must have been planted in the heart of the person being described as a tree. If we received death, fear, rejection, rebellion, and lawlessness through our fathers, all these things would naturally manifest in our hearts, even as babies in the womb.

During ministry, it is not unusual for people to describe events that occurred while they were in their mother's womb. When the parents have been asked to verify what the Holy Spirit had shown, they were amazed at the accuracy of the information. This seems to invalidate the position that the baby is just a fetus without consciousness.

If so, the seeds could be affecting the person at all three levels of their being and producing fruit from the moment of conception. On the other hand, we believe we could also experience the planting of the seeds of joy, peace, patience, and other positive attributes.

We believe it is normal for both kinds of seeds to be planted in the same soul. We also believe it is normal for people to produce good and bad plant structures. These opposing plant structures would be produced from roots which developed from the different seeds. These opposing plant structures would produce fruit, some good and some bad. We become **double-minded trees**.

Germination and Growth

External pressures produce internal pressures, stimulating the original seeds to grow and develop. These stimuli, both good and bad, serve as spiritual nutrients causing germination and growth of seeds. They can come in a variety of ways.

In elementary school we placed beans between a piece of felt and a piece of glass in a dish of water that wicked up through the felt. The seeds had plenty of *nutrients in them* to start the process of growth. In that moist environment the little plants grew each day. The root appeared on the bottom side of the seed and a little sprig of growth appeared at the top.

In people, we believe the seeds also have nutrients within. The seed is nurtured, watered, and fed by normal life events. When words, experiences, and interactions with other people occur, the seed sprouts, producing a small plant. This small plant eventually produces fruit. For example, when a mother and father fight about the baby, the baby naturally responds.

If the response is based in fear, the seeds are stimulated to germinate. In response to harsh words, the plant develops further. With additional negative stimuli, the plant might produce fruit, such as angry outbursts or fearful withdrawal. When we react in any sinful way, the process of germination, growth, and fruit production will eventually be the result.

We have met people who knew their parents were planning to have them aborted, or were planning to kill them when they were born. At these times, the voice of death would speak lies to the babies, with the purpose of defiling their identities and destinies. It would tell them they should not have been conceived, they were unwanted, and unloved. The seeds stimulated by this voice could include anything associated with sin or even a form of abortion.

The mothers' feelings such as fear, anger, rejection, or betrayal can stimulate similar sin responses in babies. The baby perceives and shares the emotions generated in mom. This can later stimulate automatic reactions, perceptions, beliefs, and expectations that may affect the baby's entire life.

On the other hand, some people remember being aware of their mother humming or singing contentedly. They recall experiencing a sense of well-being and security. This is an example of external stimuli that serve as spiritual nutrients causing germination and growth of good seeds. This can also stimulate automatic responses affecting the person's entire life.

Fruit Development

We believe the Lord has shown us, through the physical creation, how things occur in the spiritual realm. Spiritual seeds, planted deep within our being, develop plants producing fruit that will affect every aspect of our lives. Fruit development can begin in immature trees, producing only a little fruit in proportion to its size.

On the other hand, some plants can develop roots and plant infrastructure for a long time before the fruit becomes evident. Then suddenly, the plant can produce massive amounts of growth and fruit. In the case of a person, the fruit could include manifestations of fear, rage, hatred, shame, or any other strong negative emotion. People have told us their lives were great, until suddenly these things appeared *from nowhere*.

Do you remember seeing the old, hand-operated water pumps in cowboy movies? Typically, this pump has a metal body, a handle on the backside, a flared opening on top, and the spout through which the water flows. There was often a cup of water sitting next to the pump that was used to *prime the pump*.

Before starting to pump the handle, it was necessary to poor the cup of water down the well. This wet a circle of leather down in the mechanism, which expanded to cause suction. When the handle was pumped, the suction engaged and the water was pulled up the pipe and out the spout.

A person's *emotional well* might work in somewhat the same way. When particular words are spoken, or an unpleasant or traumatic event occurs, the spiritual components of iniquity *prime the pump*. They pour a small amount of emotional energy, with which they are associated, into the emotional well. Then our sin response generates enough pumping energy to produce a strong flow of emotion, which manifests as fruit. This can elicit negative reactions from others. More harsh words could be spoken resulting in an argument.

This process of sin-based fruit production would have a snowball effect, with each party continuing to produce the energies of sin, nurturing the sin based plants. The plants would grow and produce even more fruit. This is normal in family units dealing with issues in a **normal, dysfunctional way**.

The escalating process can be derailed at any time by the influence of the Holy Spirit. The energies representing the Holy Spirit are another form of nutrient. They stimulate a different type of seed, and produce healthier kinds of fruit. These fruits of love, peace, joy, and righteousness are in conflict with the fruits of normal dysfunction. Once again, we see the manifestation of normal double-minded trees.

The type of fruit produced is dependent upon our environment, our nurturing specific seeds, and **our choice of response**. Unfortunately, our responses are usually stimulated by the iniquity dwelling in our hearts. Until we are free of the power of iniquity, we will function, to some extent, as slaves to that power. Until we destroy the roots of the bad plants, stopping production of bad fruit, there is no reason to expect change. A definition of insanity is to expect different results when we continue to do the same things.

Our goal is to remove the roots of the bad plants. If we, as *ministers*, were to **attack the fruiting tree** with our swords, we could do a great deal of damage **to the person,** who is infinitely loved by our heavenly Father. Instead, we ask Him to show the person involved, and us, the real issues needing ministry. We expect Him to know *how* the seeds of sin were planted and *where* the roots are located. We trust Him to find the most efficient and merciful way to deal with the problem tree.

Jesus proclaimed that His Father **removes every branch** that does not bear good fruit. He also **prunes every branch** that does bear good fruit so it will **bear even more** good fruit. (John 15:1-2) This process of removal and pruning eliminates damaged, diseased, or infested parts. This gives a tree the ability to produce good quality fruit more consistently.

God Commands

Jesus commanded us to love the Lord our God with **all our heart**, all our **soul** and all our **mind**. (Matthew 22:37) During our study, this particular Scripture was a source of frustration. Our first impulse was to view this as a case when the Lord was being painfully redundant.

It was only after we found the definitions shown above, that some light of understanding was shed. After looking at the definitions, we saw many commonalities and some subtle distinctions. It occurred to us that Jesus knows how we are constructed and how we think. He was preventing us from finding some loophole in the command.

With this as our basis of understanding, we could look at all the definitions and Scriptures to find some logic. We determined that the word **heart** could be the most complicated. If a Scripture stated that a javelin was thrown by one man and pierced another man's heart, the word probably referred to the physical organ. If a Scripture were to state that the heart of God communes with the heart of man, it's more likely to mean the spirit.

In most cases, when the word **heart** is used, it is referring to the intangible, **middle part** of our being, functioning somehow between the spirit and the body.

This cleared up some of the confusion. We understand that when we read Scriptures in context, our ability to understand a particular verse is much better. We find in most places the words, **heart**, **soul**, and **mind**, all apply to the part of our being we commonly refer to as our soul. We believe Jesus used all three in order to be thorough.

Many times in Scripture, there are commands to **love**, **serve**, or **praise** the Lord with all our heart, soul, mind, will, and strength. There are many, in both Old and New Testaments, which refer to these commands. We selected **more than thirty** that make the commands specifically.

(Deuteronomy 4:29; 6:5; 10:12; 13:3; 26:16; 30:2,6,10; Joshua 22:5; 1 Samuel 12:20,24; 1 Kings 2:4; 8:23,48; 2 Kings 23:3; 2 Chronicles 6:38; 15:12,15; 34:31; Psalms 9:1; 111:1; 119:2,34,58,69,145; 138:1; Proverbs 3:5; Jeremiah 24:7; Joel 2:12; Zephaniah 3:14)

Conflict in Our Soul

When we look at these commands, we have another opportunity for frustration. If we are told to do something thirty times, **it must be possible not to** do it. It must be possible to love, serve, or praise Him with **only part** of our heart, soul, or mind. **Different parts** of the soul may actually be **in conflict** with one another.

We could go to church, sing, dance, raise our hands, and ask the Lord to fill our lives with His presence. Simultaneously, a part of our soul **hidden** deep inside, could be commanding, "You stay out of my life! I don't know You! I don't trust You, and I don't want You around me! You're probably just like all those others who hurt me!"

Now we have a conflict. The head part of the soul is pleading for God to come, and the heart part of the soul is commanding God to go away. Which one will He listen to? According to the Bible He listens to the heart.

This brings up a question. Are DID and MPD identified biblically? We believe they are. I wanted to find one or two Scriptures to validate the phenomenon. Here are just a few of the ones we found: *"With flattering lips and a **double heart** they speak"* (Psalm 12:2). *"Purify your hearts, you **double-minded**"* (James 4:8). [Judah has] *"...committed adultery with stones and trees...Judah has not turned to Me with **her whole heart**, but in pretense,"* says the LORD (Jeremiah 3:8-10).

These Scriptures speak to the fact that we have hearts or souls that can respond in *at least* two ways concerning God. If this is true, we are capable of responding in more than one way to other things, also. In our opinion, the Scriptures validate the existence of the phenomenon called dissociation. There is still one soul, but it is responding in multiple ways. We believe this is the source of much conflict in our hearts.

How does the soul respond in different ways? Have you ever heard someone say, "A part of me wants to go out for pizza, but another part of me wants to stay home and relax?" If you were to ask why, they might give you a silly look and say they don't know. Apparently, we don't know why we respond the way we do, or how our own soul works.

We know that hands, feet, ears, and eyes are created for specific purposes. Is it *possible* our soul is segmented in some way, with different parts created for different purposes? The Bible tells us we are supposed to experience love, joy, peace, all the fruit of the spirit. Could there be specific parts of our soul somehow associated with all these things?

Perhaps our souls have some parts doing one thing while other parts are doing something else. Consider the expression mentioned above, that people so frequently use. How real is it? Could it be that some parts of our soul are engaged in conscious activities; while other parts are engaged in unconscious activities, such as breathing?

Maybe we do have things going on in our hearts of which we are not consciously aware. Is the Bible referring to dissociation in this verse? *"The **heart** is **deceitful** above all things, and desperately **wicked**, and who can know it"* (Jeremiah 17:9)?

Is it possible we could be motivated to respond to God, people, situations, stimuli, challenges, and tests because of things we don't even remember? We not only think it is possible, we also think we can demonstrate that it is. The verse from Jeremiah may give us a clue.

We could be responding because of old programming, old beliefs, or understandings. At one time we may have believed our survival was dependent upon a specific set of actions. Now, we continue to function according to this programming because it has been established *in our computer*.

There is another, even more interesting, Scripture. *"If anyone among you...**deceives his own heart**...this one's religion is useless"* (James 1:26). We find this tantalizing because it tells us we can even deceive our conscious selves. When we are doing religious things for the wrong reasons, with the wrong motivation of heart, these things are useless. They are nothing but *dirty rags*, in God's eyes. This is not good news.

The Psalmist pleaded, *"Search me, oh God, and know my heart"* (Psalm 139:23). He was aware he didn't know what was going on in his own heart. Very wisely, he asked God to judge his heart, so the light of truth would shine. God's judgments aren't bad. They are good, because they are motivated by **love**, and His knowledge of what is best for us. Our job is to ask Him for help, as the psalmist did.

What happens if we perceive God says no, or if He doesn't help **when** we want or **the way** we want? God promises He will help us to get to the right place, as long as we call on Him and follow what He says. So, what if He allows us to march through some of the tough stuff and won't take us out of the trials? Could our idea of help and His idea of help be so different that, when He does help, we can't see it?

Perhaps when we were seven years old, our puppy was run over by a car. We prayed, but He didn't save the puppy. We, then, decided, "No way am I going to trust You again!"

What if we prayed when our little brother, our grandfather, or a good friend was dying; or we had to move to a new town and didn't want to; and the bad things happened anyway? As a result of experiences like these, our head might say, "Come," while our heart might be saying, "Stay away." There is a conflict in our soul, with *different parts* of our being trying to impose their will and control our mind and our actions.

Meanwhile, God is watching us struggle through the consequences of our double mindedness. He will not take control against our will, solve the problems against our will, or make us do things we don't want to do. He is only going to help if we ask Him.

Sin Causes Damage to the Soul

How many times have you heard people say things like these? "**She** made me mad." "**He** made me sad." "**They** offended me." "**He** broke my heart." "**Someone** hurt my feelings." "**That** tickled me to death." "**You** scared me to death." "I'm just looking for someone to **make me** happy." Notice that it's always someone **else** doing it. Someone else, whom we have allowed to function as God in our life, is responsible. That we could be responsible is an unacceptable option. This is a problem.

If we spent the same amount of energy dealing with problems instead of trying to blame them on others, we would be much healthier. Our responses, emotions, and decisions can't possibly be someone else's responsibility. This reminds us of a movie in which the bad guy has a gun to someone's head and shouts, "If you don't do what I say, I will shoot, and it will be **your** fault!"

Can you see the irrationality of this statement? The decision and actions of the gunman cannot possibly be someone else's fault. The same attitude seems to be held by people worldwide. Watch the daily news reports. Does any of this make sense? Are perpetrators not responsible for their own actions? Are individuals not accountable for making bad decisions?

Let's make it more personal. Sister so-and-so tells everybody she has been offended, because someone else did something she thought was inappropriate. It cannot be someone else's responsibility when sister so-and-so **decides** to be offended.

Brother so-and-so calls everybody he knows and proclaims his outrage at what someone said. It cannot be someone else's responsibility when brother so-and-so **decides** to be outraged.

This is the same as saying someone else *made* me a Volkswagen. One person can't make another person into anything; nor can one person make another of us feel anything. Each of us is responsible for having control of our emotions, our reactions, and our decisions for how we respond to any situation.

We need to get it straight. Who is responsible for our sins? We read, *"Lord, be merciful to me,* **heal my soul** *for* **I have sinned** *against you"* (Psalm 41:4). [Emphasis ours] The word, heal, is literally: to **mend, repair** or **make whole.** (Strong's, 7495) His own sin was the problem. Can you imagine him telling everybody he was doing sinful things because someone else **made him** do them?

The psalmist was *tuned in* to God, and was aware the problem wasn't someone else's sin. He was taking responsibility for his own reactions and sins. The other key words are, **heal my soul**. This is a plea that can only be answered when we acknowledge our own sin.

God says He forgives our sins when we confess our sins, **not** when we blame someone else for them. We have to be as courageous and humble as the writer of the Psalms, if we really want to be whole.

How many times have you heard someone proclaim they have a *broken heart* and assumed it was just a figure of speech? We don't think it is just a figure of speech. We believe the psalmist was either speaking from personal knowledge, or was inspired by the Holy Spirit. Scripture confirms it is possible to have a broken heart. *"The LORD is near to those who have a* **broken heart.***"* (Psalm 34:18). (Psalm 51:17, 69:20)

The word *broken* in the above Scripture can literally mean: to burst, break down, break in pieces, broken, destroy, hurt, quench, shatter, smash, crush. (Strong's H 7665) "Sometimes it is used figuratively to describe a 'shattered' heart...(Psalm 69:20; Ezekiel 6:9)." (Vine's pp. OT 24-25)

The words in this biblical definition are generally the same used by the *secular* psychological community to describe the effects of dissociation. When I sought two or three verses, I had no idea we were going to find so many.

This brings to mind the picture of a clay pot, thrown to the ground, with shards going in every direction. Can you imagine our intangible soul being shattered, broken in pieces, or crushed? This is not a pretty thought, and yet, we believe this could describe the normal condition for most people. The good news is that there is good news. We have another promise to hold onto, *"He heals the **brokenhearted** and binds up their wounds"* (Psalm 147:3).

Is it possible the Lord created us with abilities of which He wasn't aware, and our ability to dissociate came as a surprise to Him? We don't think so. We think He created us with the ability to survive, in spite of all the challenges of living on this earth.

Can We Lose Control of Our Soul?

We are told that we should be vigilant because Satan, like a lion, is seeking whom **he may devour**. (1 Peter 5:8) What does Satan want to devour? Is it our flesh? He is a spirit being and would have no use for flesh. We believe it is energy he seeks, and as much control of our soul and humanity as we give him through our sin.

It is interesting to note that Peter is not talking to pagans; he's talking to Christians. We conclude that through sin and deception, control of parts of **our soul** can be *lost* to us. The one receiving control is Satan, or a representative of his kingdom.

Jesus even warned that it would be possible for a man to lose his own soul while gaining the whole world. (Mark 8:36) How are we to read this? Does the statement suggest that we would cease to have a soul as a part of our being? We don't believe so. This word *lose* includes the concepts of damage, to suffer loss, or to be **cast away**. (Strong's G 2210) In our view, casting away control of the soul is a function of free will.

Let's consider an example. We were ministering to a woman who was thrashing around on the floor. We had bound the spirits, so we knew this wasn't entirely a spiritual issue. We knew the soul was involved, so there must be a good reason for the thrashing. We decided that our activities were in conflict with her will, and we needed to discover why. Since we believed she wanted to be free, we asked questions to find the reason for the manifestations.

She told us she had been involved in Satanism and had signed a contract, in blood, agreeing to sell her soul in order to receive things from Satan. She was terrified because she was convinced she couldn't be saved. The voices in her head kept reminding her of what she had done.

We stopped, prayed for guidance, and I received a flash of insight. I was reminded of a Scripture in which God proclaimed that **all the souls** belong to him. (Ezekiel 18:4) This shed new light on the woman's problem.

I asked her if she would sign a contract, in blood, to sell me her country. She looked at me as if I were crazy, and informed me she couldn't sell her country because she didn't own it. I asked her if it would matter that the contract was signed in blood. She told me the contract would be meaningless because she couldn't sell what she didn't own.

We then quoted the Scripture to her and explained that she could not have sold her soul. The contract she signed was not valid. She was quiet for a time, processing this new information. Finally, she looked up at us with new hope, and we were able to proceed with ministry.

None of us can sell, or give away, something that doesn't belong to us. Jesus knew who owns the souls. He must have been referring to the loss of control of the soul. If it weren't for what Jesus did, we would not have the ability to reclaim control of our soul after we have given the control away. This is another example of why we need a Savior.

Satan seldom comes to us with a contract asking us to sign away our soul for riches, fame, and fortune. He uses lies, deceptions, and the effects of our own sins, to take control of parts of our soul, one piece at a time. We believe it pleases him to steal those things of value without having to pay anything for them. We believe it is true that Satan strives to swallow up that which has been given to us by our heavenly Daddy.

Let's look at some examples. We regularly hear comments like, "I just feel dry and empty, as though there are things inside of me that are asleep. I don't know how to wake them up. I can remember when I could cry and feel normal emotions, but at some time in my life, that part of me just died." We hear about the apparent loss of parts of humanity or soul, and the conflict that comes when all our soul parts aren't in agreement.

We don't believe these are clichés, but statements of a person's reality. We believe there are specific gifts, abilities, and talents we have been given by the Lord. These could include music, art, dance, cooking, praise, and worship. Perhaps, when we were very young, making our first attempts to display those gifts, someone said, "Oh, that is so stupid. You're never going to do it right. You might as well quit now."

We might have said, "I give up." It is possible we gave up precious gifts from God at a very early age. Now, the gift or talent is on a shelf, in a dark corner of our heart, and possibly under the *protection* of our enemy.

For example, a little boy decided to draw an elephant. He went to the back bedroom where he wouldn't be disturbed and worked very hard on the picture. When he was finished, he took it into the living room where his father was working on his racing forms. To his father, the racing forms were more important than almost anything else.

When the boy showed him the picture, his response was, "What is that mess?" The little boy told him it was an elephant. Dad dismissed him with a sour look and told him to go outside and play. I was that little boy. There have been many who told me I should pursue art as a career. I suppose I'll never know how good I could have been, because I didn't want to experience that kind of reaction ever again.

Lest you think this is unique, Glenna remembers the time when someone looked at a picture she had drawn, and said, "Oh, that's pretty. Did your brother do it?" Everyone knew that her brother was *the artist* in the family. Glenna just wanted to receive the message that she was valuable and important as an artist, also.

How often do you think she drew pictures after that? She let the artist do it. She decided she would have to do something else. She gave away the possibility of developing this gift to the *voice* that told her, "Why bother; you'll never be as good as him."

Many of us have chosen to give up gifts and abilities that made us the unique person God created. We do so because we believe the lies spoken through the mouths of people around us or in our own minds. They tell us we aren't really talented, gifted, or especially capable in an area of interest to us. Often, they make a joke of the cutting remarks but it isn't a joke.

God gives these gifts to us for a reason. They may be part of His master plan for all eternity. If we have *lost* them in a corner of our heart, we cannot contribute our part to the plan.

People have asked the Holy Spirit to show them what they gave up, and why. One woman remembered a time her mom watched her at dance class and said, "You'd better study and learn to be a scientist." As soon as she remembered this, she began to cry because she understood why she gave up her dream.

We ministered with a lady to whom the Lord had given a gift of poetry. Although she never studied poetry, or how to write it, there was a time in her life she had been able to sit down and the Lord would start writing poetry through her. In spite of this fact, something happened along the way and she decided she was a failure. She put her poetry away and forgot it.

Years later, we had a wonderful ministry session with her, and she decided to take it up again. In the evening service, she read a poem she had written that afternoon following our session. It was awesome! It was glorious and prophetic poetry. We were so blessed!

We have found that when we ask the Lord to restore all that seems lost, we discover it was never really lost. It was just put in hibernation somewhere.

Soul Damage Affects the Body

We are convinced that damage to the soul affects the body also. Not only have we seen an abundance of evidence, but we also have some great Scriptures from the Proverbs. Please note that these Proverbs are designed to produce a contrast between one condition and another.

In Proverbs 14:30, the contrast is focused on the sin of envy, but we believe it would be appropriate to expand it. James tells us that under the law, when we are guilty of one sin, we are guilty of all. (James 2:10) Our paraphrase would be, a sound heart is life to the body, and the heart, which is not sound, is death to the body. This particular statement is *rottenness to the bones* which could manifest in the body in a variety of ways.

We are told that sorrow of the heart breaks the spirit. (Proverbs 15:13) We do not believe the spirit is broken in the same way as the soul. When our heart experiences these things, it affects our spirit adversely. In this case, the word *broken* would be more accurately defined as smitten, afflicted, or stricken. (Merriam Webster's) Broken could apply, but these other definitions are, seemingly, more applicable to the spirit. Do things that affect our spirit also affect our body? To answer this, we look at more Scripture.

The Proverbs tell us that a merry heart is like medicine to our body, but a broken spirit dries the bones. (Proverbs 17:22) Remember, a *broken spirit* is defined as afflicted or smitten, not as the soul being broken into pieces. The word *merry* suggests generally good feelings.

Some studies have suggested that those who consistently manifest unhappiness, fear, anger and an unwillingness to forgive, are doing damage to their own bodies. Because of these emotions, toxins are produced. These toxins attack the body in general, causing infirmity, disease, and a slow, painful suicide.

On the other hand, good emotions produce the opposite effect. Studies have shown that people in the hospital with cheerful, positive outlooks heal significantly faster than those who don't. Reports also demonstrate that these positive responses cause the body to produce endorphins. These are natural drugs that benefit the body and the soul. *God was right.* A merry heart does stimulate the process of healing.

We have now been told that a sound heart is life to the body; that envy, sin associated with the soul, is rottenness to the body. Something that wounds the heart, or soul, also causes the spirit to be afflicted. When the spirit is afflicted, there are adverse effects in the body. We see that damage in our soul can affect our body directly or affect our spirit directly, and that affects our body adversely. Problems in the soul seem to be the root of problems in both the spirit and the body.

We conclude that a soul functioning in sin will generate effects that are detrimental to the body, such as sickness and disease. The soul that is restored produces the emotions and responses of righteousness. These will generate effects that are good for the body and promote health.

We have ministered with people concerning issues of their souls and had them later tell us that manifestations in their bodies just faded away. Pain and discomfort they had experienced for years diminished over a period of time. We have received cards and letters expressing gratitude to the Lord for what He has done in their bodies, as well as in their souls.

We have read that we *should expect* to **prosper** in all things and be in **health** just **as our soul prospers**. (3 John 2) Since we are sure Apostle John was praying in accordance with the Holy Spirit, we believe this prayer applies to anyone who is a member of the body of Christ. The words, **in all things** and **be in health**, cover a wide spectrum of possibilities.

It is reasonable to believe the prospering of the soul will help heal the spirit of the crushing and bruising it has experienced. It also seems reasonable to believe that our healing and prosperity will be inhibited if our soul does not prosper.

The Lord will give life **to our mortal bodies** through His Spirit dwelling in us. (Romans 8:11) In this case, life includes strength and vitality, so it is reasonable to expect this for all of us who are parts of His body. As we give up the old programming producing sickness and death, we should experience benefits in our bodies.

Hasn't the Work Already Been Done?

We are occasionally asked why it is necessary for us to go through soul cleansing and restoration, if all things have become new as a result of our salvation. If we all died with Christ, were raised with Christ, and are now seated in heavenly places, what is the need?

To this question, we respond with a question. Why don't normal Christians manifest the nature of God and live in perfect victory the way Jesus did?

From an **eternal perspective**, we are a new creation. However, we have always seen life through dark spiritual glasses that caused us to perceive everything in a distorted way. As a result, it is normal for us to respond in ways that can be destructive to others as well as to ourselves. Our soul is still motivated by the same thought patterns, attitudes, beliefs, feelings, and desires it had before we were saved. The Scriptures make many references concerning the sad condition of the soul before salvation. (2 Corinthians 3:14; 4:4)

We only know for sure about our own sinful inclinations, but we believe the same is likely to be true for those around us. We respond to people, situations, life, and even God, in ways that must be the product of old programming. We see the truth of this in our own lives and from observing people.

We know these things did not come from our heavenly Father. We've heard so many references to the self-righteous hypocrites who attend churches. In all fairness, we suspect that the people being referred to are merely deceived. The beliefs and perceptions of the past are **so normal** they don't see the truth.

It is apparent that our view of sin and God's view are totally different. God often sees sin in those things we believe are good. Remember the Scripture that states even our best works are like dirty, smelly rags to Him? (Isaiah 64:6) Our views are often based upon old, non-beneficial programming. When we do *good* things with the **wrong motivation**, He looks upon them and *holds His nose*.

Old Programming Versus God's Truth

Most of our old programming is not in keeping with God's truth. Much of it dwells in our hearts. The heart is the center of physical function as well as moral and spiritual function. There appear to be levels of consciousness of which we are not aware. As we discussed earlier, Scripture indicates that most of us don't know what is going on in our own hearts. (Jeremiah 17:9; Mark 7:21-23; Proverbs 23:7)

As a result, we respond to other people, events in life, and even God, in ways we don't understand. The things we believe about ourselves, other people, and God represent the worldview within which we operate. These concepts and expectations, planted in the heart and expressed in our words and actions, often become self-fulfilling prophecies.

We might respond explosively to seemingly unimportant events and are then surprised at the fervor of our outburst. We proclaim, "Gee, I don't know where that came from." Programming, put in place many years ago, could be stimulating automatic responses. We might react in a way we believe is necessary for our protection, our survival, or to have our needs met. In every case, we are convinced that **no response is accidental**. There is always a reason.

Often, when we receive salvation and join a church, we discover we are supposed to conform to a new set of rules. We are a *new creation* so we should act as though we never did bad things or lived through terrible experiences. We have been told that everything has been made new, so we should now function as though *everything is new*.

In some churches we are told to *just move on*. This attitude represents a source of serious concern. We are to *believe* that we are seated in heavenly places and be at peace. If we have enough faith, we shouldn't have problems. We are told that the problems are *of the flesh* and we should crucify the flesh. Practically, what does that mean?

Does this mean we are not allowed to have problems? If we do, are we demonstrating a lack of faith? If we still experience sickness and disease have we failed, and are we functioning in sin? What if we haven't found victory over the normal bondages of life? Does this mean we really weren't saved, but are only deceived?

We believe the voice of *the blackmailer* is controlling the lives of many of us. We want to be approved by other Christians who *seem* to have it together. The voice insists that if we allow others to suspect we have problems, or if we become a nuisance to them, **we will be rejected**. If they discover the truth of who, and what, we really are, **we will be cast out**.

After receiving these messages, any rational person would construct a good *church mask* with a plastic smile. When we are asked how we're doing, our response becomes, "I'm blessed, and everything is fine." At this point, it would seem that we are manifesting *church programming*. Does wearing a good church mask represent real Christianity?

We try to put it all under the blood, as we were told, but it doesn't make the pain, shame, and manifestations of sin disappear. We ask, "What's wrong with me? Am I really saved?" We might decide Christianity is too hard, or we're not capable of being a *good* Christian. We might become discouraged, and simply drift away.

Through His prophet, Jeremiah, God proclaimed that the prophets and priests had healed the hurt of his people slightly. They said, "Peace, peace," when there **was no peace**. (Jeremiah 6:14) In this case, God was proclaiming that the prophets and priests had failed to properly minister to His people. Maybe it was just too much trouble or represented too much time. As a result, the pain and suffering continued.

It would be wonderful if we could find all the disenfranchised Christians and help them discover they are not so bad, after all. Instead of proclaiming, "Peace, peace, when there is no peace," we could assure them they can find peace, as a process, if they really want it. They might discover they are normal and all they need is time to work out the process of gaining their freedom. (Philippians 2:12)

The things that cause difficulties in our lives cannot simply be covered over and forgotten. There may still be painful memories, old hurts, fears, and destructive life patterns that need to be healed. They represent spiritual strongholds influencing our hearts, souls, minds and lives. They should not be lightly dismissed.

Work out Our Own Salvation?

We've never found the Scripture verse telling us to *just put it under the blood and move on*. We do remember a proclamation concerning renouncing the **hidden things** of shame. (2 Corinthians 4:2) This sounds like the opposite of what is so commonly quoted. Instead of hiding those *things of shame*, we are to **bring them out** into the light. (Also see John 8:32)

This is a command to take an active part in the process of achieving a greater level of freedom for our souls and bodies. Paul states that if anyone **cleanses himself,** he will be sanctified and prepared for every good work. (2 Timothy 2:20-21)

We have crossed the Jordan, into the Promised Land, and now face our enemies. God has promised that all we have to do is fight the battles for **our** Promised Land, and He will guarantee our victory. He has already defeated our enemies and caused us to be more than conquerors. Now we are to *go forth* and demonstrate that we are His children.

We are instructed to, *"**Work out your own salvation** with fear and trembling"* (Philippians 2:12) [Emphasis ours] Even though this seems to contradict previous statements concerning salvation, we are certain that

God has done a completed work in the part of our being known as the spirit. (1 Corinthians 1:30) We are also certain that our souls and bodies are works in progress. The Lord expects us to take an active role in the cleansing of these parts of our Temple.

We are not able to accomplish these things in our own strength. We are being opposed by evil spirit beings. In order for us to succeed in this exercise, we need the full and active participation of the Holy Spirit. This *spiritual war* is a process of rooting out spiritual strongholds in our own souls with His guidance and power.

It is not reasonable to expect to win the war with just one battle. This is not the biblical precedent we have found. When the Lord sent His people across the river into the Promised Land, He warned them that they would **not** be given the land all at one time. He told them He would give them only part of the land until they were able to occupy it.

This process would continue, piece-by-piece, until, eventually, they would have possession of all the Promised Land. He explained that if He gave them too much territory at one time, wild beasts would increase among them. (Deuteronomy 7:22; Exodus 23:29)

We see the parallel when we view this as a shadow, or type, of the New Covenant. God restores to us all of our *Promised Land*, all of our *soul* and *humanity*, everything He created us to be, in the process of salvation. It is necessary to clear out all the wild beasts, *the creatures* that have invaded our land, so we can possess everything.

If it were to occur all at one time, it might be more than we could bear. Not only do we see this model in Scripture, but we also see it functioning in our lives. It is the most loving and gracious way He can restore us. As the process takes place, we see the construction of the **inner court**, the second phase of the temple, being completed as a part of His master plan. With our **willing participation**, the process can be **accelerated**.

Confess and Be Cleansed

Is it necessary to remember *all the events* of our lives and confess *each individual sin*, in order to be forgiven? We don't believe so. None of us can remember all our sins, nor can we understand the depth of sin existing in our lives and hearts. It is only necessary to acknowledge and confess those things the Lord shows us.

The Word of God tells us wonderful things will occur if we confess our sins. (1 John 1:9) When we confess our sins, we acknowledge that we are desperately wicked. We admit we have no hope of salvation, if it's based upon our abilities. We confess that our only hope is to depend on His mercy, grace, and **finished work** of salvation. (1 Peter 1:13-15) When we stop depending on our own abilities, and depend on Him entirely, He will do everything He promised.

God is able to restore our souls (Psalms 23:3). If we have given control over parts of our soul or humanity to our enemy, it is time to renounce the contract. That is how we take away our accuser's power and control over parts of our soul. The gifts and the calling of God are irrevocable; therefore, the authority we were given over our soul is still ours. (Romans 11:29) We renounce giving him access and evict him. This is not complicated.

Our willingness to face difficult issues associated with the hurt, anger, and pain we have experienced, enables the Lord to accomplish this task so we can experience the freedom and victory in our lives today. As we walk through the steps of restoration and cleansing, we are sanctified, or set apart, made holy, and freed from sin. (Hebrews 2:11)

The Lord has made Himself responsible to complete that work He has begun in us. (Philippians 1:6) The Bible doesn't specify just when that process will be complete. Therefore, we believe the salvation of our soul requires us to take an active role if we want to **speed up the process**, **minimize the discomfort**, and **walk in a greater degree of victory** now.

Our loving, heavenly Father has given us the opportunity to work together with Him to accomplish it, and we help choose how and when the process will proceed. In doing so, we can be doers, not just hearers of the word. (James 1:21-22) His Word is Life and Truth and is able to renew our souls and fill us with light. (John 17:17)

He will enable us to do as He instructed. It is encouraging to know He would never give us a command that we couldn't fulfill. That would be unrighteous and unjust. (Matthew 22:37) Will we wait until we're in heaven, at the judgment seat of Christ, or will we accomplish this work here on earth, in this clay body?

Sample Prayer:

In the name of the Lord Jesus Christ, I confess and renounce the sins that have broken and shattered my heart. I confess and renounce the hidden things of shame that have given Satan's kingdom legal rights against me. I renounce all forms of demonic goodness; self-righteousness, self-

justification, self-deception, religious observances, and the light which is really darkness.

I renounce the mind of the flesh, which is hostile to God. I renounce believing or proclaiming that others are responsible for making me sin. I am responsible for all my sinful words, actions, and reactions. I renounce giving anyone power over me by proclaiming they are responsible for me.

I claim the power of the shed blood of the Lord Jesus Christ as payment for all the sins that Satan would claim over any part of my soul or humanity. I command everything serving Satan's kingdom, all its influence and control, and all its effects in my life to go, now, where the Lord Jesus Christ sends it.

I renounce giving any sacrifice, including any spiritual, emotional, or physical energies, as well as any part of my soul or humanity, over to Satan's kingdom.

I command everything serving Satan's kingdom to give the Lord Jesus Christ everything received from me as a sacrifice, because the Lord Jesus Christ is the one who paid for all my sins, and He alone is worthy to receive these things.

Heavenly Father, I ask You to shine your light of truth and search my heart, so I will know where I have deceived myself. I ask You to resolve the conflict in my soul, so I can be free of double mindedness. I ask You to restore health, lost as a result of my sins, to my spirit, soul, and body. I ask You to make me prosper and be in good health as my soul prospers.

I ask You to help me perceive, react, and respond to myself, to others, to events of life, and to You the way I should. I ask You to heal, to make whole, my broken heart. I ask you to reclaim everything belonging to me that has been devoured by Satan and his kingdom.

I ask You to restore everything associated with my true identity and destiny, and everything I lost or gave away, as well as everything that has been killed, stolen, or destroyed because of my sins.

I ask You, Heavenly Father, to do whatever it takes to make me whole, so I can love, worship, and serve You with all my heart, all my soul, all my mind, and all my strength; so I can be all You created me to be and be raised up to the highest and best place You have created for me. I want nothing less, and I give you permission to do this work in my life. Thank You. Amen.

METHODS OF DISSOCIATION

Many of us have used, or abused, drugs, alcohol, food, or other substances, in order to escape physical or emotional pain and abuse. These not only affect our physical and emotional health, but they also affect our spiritual health. When we give up control of our mind or nervous system, through the use of such substances, we open the door for tormenters.

In order to cope with the distresses of our lives, we can also resort to dissociation. We discussed this issue briefly in the section concerning physical and emotional trauma. We have studied information regarding this phenomenon from various sources. We offer a brief description taken from a group called the Sidran Foundation:

"Dissociation is a mental process that produces a lack of connection in a person's thoughts, memories, feelings, actions, or sense of identity. During the period of time when a person is dissociating, certain information is not associated with other information as it normally would be.

"For example, during a traumatic experience, a person may dissociate the memory of the place and circumstances of the trauma from his ongoing memory, resulting in a temporary mental escape from the fear and pain of the trauma and, in some cases, a memory gap surrounding the experience. Because this process can produce changes in memory, people who frequently dissociate often find their senses of personal history and identity are affected.

"Most clinicians believe that dissociation exists on a continuum of severity. This continuum reflects a wide range of experiences and/or symptoms. At one end are mild dissociative experiences common to most people, such as daydreaming, highway hypnosis, or 'getting lost' in a book or movie, all of which involve 'losing touch' with conscious awareness of one's immediate surroundings. At the other extreme is complex, chronic dissociation such as in cases of Dissociative Identity Disorder (DID), Multiple Personality Disorder (MPD), and other dissociative disorders, which may result in serious impairment or inability to function."

Many of us have grown up using **daydreaming** and other methods of escape to deal with life. Picture a little boy in a classroom, totally bored with what is going on, and watching the clouds float by. He is daydreaming about adventures on some distant land or maybe even somewhere out in space. After failing to get his attention, the teacher impatiently pounds on his desk demanding, "What is the answer to that question?"

The boy's reaction is, "What question?" The boy isn't giving the teacher a hard time. He didn't hear the question. His body was sitting at the desk, but his mind, or consciousness, was somewhere else.

I remember many times I was required to do homework. I could *read* whole chapters in my textbook. My eyes would look at every word as I turned the pages. All that time I would be thinking of other things. As a result, I could finish the entire reading assignment and realize I had no conscious memory of anything I had read. I didn't want to read all that meaningless stuff, so I left my body there and *I went somewhere else.*

We've all known occasions while driving a car when our consciousness was *somewhere else*, engaged in other mental activities or conversations. We arrive at our destination without remembering how we got there. Some of us can go to the shopping mall, walk around for hours, and, later, have *no conscious memory* of what we did or saw. We can engage in a variety of activities and later not be able to recall them.

We learn to dissociate as children in order to deal with boring, unpleasant, or traumatic events. Because of hurtful experiences, fear, trauma, and even burdensome responsibilities, we seek sources of salvation (**escape**) such as fantasies, imaginations, sleeping, movies, books, TV, music, videos, magazines, pornography, computers, video games, virtual reality, sex, sports, or shopping. We believe God gave us the ability to dissociate because He knew how hard life would be. He knew we would sometimes need to escape in order to survive.

For most of us, the problem isn't with our ability to escape, but rather in our choice of where, with whom, and how often we escape. We don't believe we are *bad* for doing so, just normal. However, we often continue to dissociate as adults.

Someone might think that these choices of escape represent harmless pastimes, but we don't think that conclusion fits with Scripture. Before we became Christians, our options were limited, but now we have the Lord. He has told us to come to Him. (Psalms 18:1-3) He is our refuge, strong tower, and our **best place of escape**. When we choose to go someplace else, we are rejecting the help He would offer.

Dreams, Fantasies, and Imaginations

For many of us, living in a world of dreams, fantasies, and imagination is very appealing and greatly preferable to real life. Most of us begin to use the ability to create *idealized situations* and *people* in *our minds* when we are children. It is our way of coping with difficult situations and people. Using our **imagination** as an **escape mechanism** can continue into adult life.

Just as stated above, this represents potential problems. These idealized creations stimulate us to have *unrealistic expectations* of things and people around us, even ourselves. When anyone fails to measure up to the *idealized images* we have created, we become disappointed and frustrated. Our expectations, both spoken and unspoken, are not being fulfilled. This could apply to our spouses, families, churches, or any other people or entities.

When these expectations are not fulfilled we can respond with a sense of betrayal, anger or despair because we conclude there is *no hope*. The only way we will again find hope, and get past the phenomenon, is to give up everything pertaining to our *idealized life*.

We often spend much of our conscious life dwelling on the things of the past. *Past problems or past glories* occupy our thoughts. We prefer to *live in the past* because it frees us from the challenges of the present. We may also be controlled by experiences of the past and project them into events and circumstances of the present through **our dreams**.

We can give you an example of how this works. One morning, early in our marriage, we woke up and began preparing for the day's activities. As Glenna began her preparations, she noticed that I was very unfriendly and glared at her each time she looked my way. After a few minutes of this, she demanded to know what my problem was.

I had a dream just before waking, in which I caught her with another man. Because this was something associated with my past, I was furious at her and was manifesting my anger. Then, when faced with having to tell her what was going on, I was embarrassed. It seemed so ridiculous when I spoke the words, but those feelings were real and very powerful, all due to a dream!

We can just as easily use pleasant dreams or daydreams in an attempt to compensate for unpleasant life events. We can escape by thinking about *the future* and all its *possible problems and potential glories*. We can use all these methods of escape in an attempt to free us from current responsibilities and difficulties.

Scriptures tell us that what is real is better than the cravings of *wandering desire*. These are described as *emptiness* and *striving after the wind*. (Ecclesiastes 6:9, AB)

Is trying to live in the past or the future like grasping for the wind? The past is gone and there's nothing we can do to change it. The best we can do is get healing for those things that are inhibiting our growth and development as whole, victorious children of God. We can plan for the future, but we cannot live in it.

Fantasizing about the future saps our energies for living in the present. When we live in the **realm of fantasy**, we are *trying to be the creator*. We don't listen to the Lord because we want to do things our way. We need to let our God be the Creator and follow His lead

Jesus told us not to worry about tomorrow because tomorrow will have its own problems to deal with. (Matthew 6:34) It is enough to deal with the problems of today. Jesus also told us to pray for *our daily bread*. (Matthew 6:11; Luke 11:3) He instructed us to **live in today** and to seek His kingdom today, so He can provide for our tomorrows.

We can imagine ourselves as being many things. Through our **imaginations** and **scenarios**, we can imagine being a victim or a conqueror. We can imagine living in yesterday, or living in tomorrow, and we can **create** whatever circumstances we want. God has given us the ability to function in very creative ways. We can use these abilities to function righteously, or we can use these abilities to function in sin. It is our decision.

Consequences of Dissociation

Our problem isn't in using an ability given by God, but in using that ability badly. When we go anywhere else, except to the Lord, we give the enemy an opening to our souls. God is the almighty Creator. When we try to assume His role in our lives, we are attempting to **compete with Him**.

When we try to be an almighty creator, we are trying to replace God in one of the roles only He can fill. Anytime we try to be like God, we are functioning in idolatry according to the religion of humanism. This is sin and guarantees our failure. (1 Corinthians 10:14)

Because God is the source of infinite light, it is reasonable to believe that His enemy is the source of darkness. Before we open our door to God's enemy (and ours), we should consider this Scripture, *"Therefore take heed that the **light** which is in you is not **darkness**"* (Luke 11:35). Can you see that *some light, or apparent reality,* is actually deceptive? (2 Corinthians 11:14)

When used in sinful ways, our fantasies, imaginations, and scenarios can give Satan's servants opportunities to deceive us. They *appear* to become whatever we want, seeming to assist us in our effort to be like God. Many of us have spent more of our waking hours living in our fantasy world than the real world. Some of us are embarrassed when we talk about our habits; others of us consider these activities normal, not realizing their danger.

In this process, we deceive our own souls. After all, we aren't really doing all these things, we are only thinking and lusting about them. We say in our hearts, "Nobody knows but me; I'm not hurting anyone." While this is a nice rationalization, it doesn't necessarily *line up with reality.*

These imaginary activities are described in Scripture. We remember Jesus saying, *"... whoever looks at a woman, **to lust** for her, has **already committed adultery** with her in his heart"* (Matthew 5:28). When we give a seminar, there are usually more women present than men. As I teach and look at the women, have I committed adultery? The verse says if I look at a woman, *to **lust** for her*, I have committed adultery. So, from a practical perspective, what does this mean?

I could look at the women attending a seminar and experience no reaction. I could also look at one particular woman, notice the way she has her legs crossed, and see a vivid image in my mind. I could use that image to produce **imaginations** and **scenarios** that would definitely be sinful. I could choose to *produce emotional and physical energies* of sin and become hot with lust. At this point, it would seem that I *lust for her* and I would be guilty of adultery.

So, the problem isn't in looking; the problem is in **responding sinfully**. We can use fantasies and imaginations or scenarios, and it is all happening inside. We are reminded that from the hearts of men proceed **evil thoughts,** and all these **evil things** coming from within **defile a man**. (Mark 7:21-23)

Let's say we rent a James Bond movie. We could set up our *theater* with drinks and chips, and feel secure because we're just going to watch a video. Early in the action, Bond gets involved with one of the many women in the movie. As they go to the bedroom, the camera shows a suggestive silhouette on the wall. If we produce the emotional and physical energies of lust, the little door opens, and the creature associated with lust comes in to occupy its place.

In another scene, Bond attends a séance held in a castle on top of a cliff. It is night and there's a thunderstorm raging and wind howling. Several people are seated around a table, holding hands. Candles are burning in strategic locations. The primary witch is muttering incantations when, suddenly, the window flies open with an explosive WHOOOOOSSH! Everyone jumps, and we experience chill bumps on our arms and on the back of our neck. We enjoy the excitement and energy of the supernatural. The door opens again, and something associated with witchcraft comes in to occupy its place.

As the movie progresses, we have come to despise the villain. We are outraged at the terrible things he has done. Late in the movie he comes around the corner of the building with a machine gun. Bond appears at another corner of the same building with a bazooka. At first we see a close-up of Bond's finger; then the camera pulls back, as we see an explosion. We stand up and cheer, feeling that warm sense of satisfaction, as we see the villain's arms and legs flying through the air. We are glad he is dead. Once again, the little door opens and **we receive** the consequence of sin.

As an engineer, I think this is a wonderfully efficient process. We sit at home watching a movie and the little door opens over and over again. We can receive the consequences of many sinful activities without even leaving our sofa. There is nothing inherently evil about a piece of plastic with pictures on it. The problem is in the hearts and minds of those responding in sin. The body is sitting on the sofa; the mind is engaged in sinful activities and *giving place* to our enemy.

Does this principle **only** apply to a movie or video we watch on the screen? Let's explore that question. Suppose we are driving down the road and an *idiot* comes in from a side road and cuts us off. We stomp on our brakes. We bring our car under control and the effects of adrenaline start fading. Then we notice the idiot hasn't even slowed down. He sped down the road, totally forgetting us, but we haven't forgotten him.

We are still experiencing the emotional turmoil **he *made* us feel**. It is entirely **his** fault. We start running a scenario in our mind, in which we don't hit our brakes. We chase him down and ram him with our car, so he goes into a ditch. We get out of our car, grab a tire iron, go to his car, and beat in his windows. Then we stand, with our tire iron, threatening to beat in his face, giving us the opportunity to vent our fear and anger.

But that isn't satisfying enough, so we rewind our mental video and start running it over again. This time we chase him down, ramming him into the ditch. We continue to ram his car until it explodes in flames. This time we stand at the top of the embankment, watching his car burn and telling him all the things we have always wanted to say to the idiots of this world. This is much more satisfying.

We could continue running this scenario, over and over again, as long as we want. We could run it on the way to work and spend the whole day re-running it. We could open that little door as many times as we choose and receive into us as much of the *demonic energy* as we want. After all, *we're just thinking*; we are not really *doing* anything bad.

At the end of the day we could go home to our family and vent all the *demonic energy* we have received on our unsuspecting loved ones, spewing forth the venom we would like to have spewed onto the idiot. Does this seem familiar? All these things fall into the category of **unreality**. We receive the demonic energies into us when we open the little door, and we produce an abundance of sinful energies in response.

Then, we ask, "I wonder what's wrong with God? Why does He allow all these bad things to happen in my life?" It wasn't God's decision for us to engage in sinful activities. God simply says, "Your will be done," but that isn't the end of the matter. Even though the Lord is obligated to honor our free will, He is able to **motivate us** to change our minds.

If you remember the discussion concerning fiery serpents, you'll understand why we believe **pain can be used for good**.

Familiar Spirits

As previously discussed, our fantasies, imaginations, and scenarios can give Satan's servants opportunities to **deceive us**. Based on our ministry experience, if we respond to any person or entity in a sinful way, we give opening for **a deceiver**. As real-life events or sinful imaginations, fantasies, and scenarios produce sinful responses; we give more power and control to **them**.

They *appear* to become **whatever** will serve **our purposes**, seeming to assist us in our effort to be like God. We've met people who have a variety of fantasy lovers. In some cases, these *normal people* have told us they had a great deal more sexual activity with their fantasy lovers than with their spouse. From our perspective, each time they engage in these activities they are giving more power and control to the familiar spirits *hiding behind the mask*.

Based on testimonies we've received from many people, familiar spirits can also produce a voice, in the mind, like the one represented by the mask. When the mind *sees* the image, it also *hears* the appropriate voice.

These spirits might *appear* to be **whatever** will serve **their purposes** the best. They can apparently wear a spiritual mask, which is designed to elicit the maximum sinful response. One woman had a terrible fear of dogs. She remembered an event in her life when a big, black dog chased her home from school. In the real-life event, she barely got into her yard ahead of the snarling, barking dog.

In this case, the familiar spirit could look like that big, menacing dog that repeatedly barked and lunged against the fence. That image and the associated emotional trauma had existed in this woman's heart for many years. The familiar spirit associated with that dog had been given an important place in her life.

When we minister with people, we find examples of dysfunctional and abusive relationships with parents, other family members, or anyone else. When these relationships are **based in sin**, or have sinful components, familiar spirits can represent the people involved. They put on a mask and use the appropriate voice. Once in place, they function through the mind **of their host** to produce sinful responses.

We offer these simple examples to answer the question and illustrate a phenomenon that seems to be common to most people. Another way to illustrate this issue is with the following:

Several years ago, we were with our pastors in a jungle city in Peru. One evening, we went to a little video parlor with our pastor's wife and rented a video called *Bogus*. The word, "bogus" means something that is not genuine, a counterfeit, or a sham. The word "sham" means a trick that deludes, a hoax, a cheap falseness, or hypocrisy. (Merriam Webster's) We believe this movie was very appropriately named.

The story was about a little boy whose mother was killed. She had named an old friend as guardian for the boy if anything should happen to her. On the way to meet his mother's friend, the little boy met a man who introduced himself as Bogus. They established a friendship of sorts, and the little boy discovered Bogus would come whenever he was wanted.

We soon discovered that Bogus wasn't a real person, but was a familiar spirit who came to the little boy *in his time of emotional need*. As a result, the little boy and Bogus established a deeper and deeper relationship. In response to the little boy's actions, mom's friend became very concerned, because she felt he was living in his fantasy world, and needed to face real life.

Eventually, this woman also met Bogus and discovered that he was a *friend* from her childhood. He had *helped* her through hard times in her life. In one of the closing scenes, he and she danced together romantically, after they were reacquainted. She had rediscovered something that had been, and still was, very important to her.

The message of the movie is clear. It doesn't matter how young or old we are. We can always use familiar spirits to *provide* comfort, support, or *whatever we might need*. This seems to be the theology of Hollywood being fed to a very gullible audience.

This theology teaches that Christianity is bad, but everything associated with the occult, witchcraft, and the New Age is good. It teaches that spirit guides are good. It doesn't bother to consider that these spirits could be sent from hell and their assignment is to destroy us. (See John 10:10) In this case these Hollywood prophets have chosen a religion for themselves and are trying to draw in others who are willing.

Parents have told us that their children were required to participate in New Age or occult activities in public schools. In one instance, the children were told to lie on the floor and listen to some special sounds, or music, that would help them relax. After they were relaxed, they were instructed to imagine someone they would like to have as their friend. Their new friend could look like anything they wanted and would help them when they were feeling stressed, lonely, or afraid. The friend would also help with schoolwork.

These children were advised not to tell their parents about these exercises, because their parents *wouldn't understand*. The parents asked us if we thought their concerns were valid. We agreed, sharing their concerns. I told them about some of my experiences with the occult. These parents instructed the school administration to remove their children from that exercise or that class. The children were given something else to do while others in the class were spending time with their familiar spirits.

That brings us to children who watch movies about the *X - Men*, *The Power Rangers*, *The Captain Planet Kids*, *Pokémon*, *Harry Potter*, and other programs about witchcraft or the supernatural. According to these TV programs, witchcraft and familiar spirits can be used for good. The children involved think, "This is cool. I can have my crystal power wand and destroy all the powers of evil, because my heroes on TV do it." It is a good thing to destroy evil, isn't it?

Can you see our concern here? Parents are allowing the television to function as a babysitting service. That babysitting service is programming children to believe that witchcraft and magic is a good thing. Our heavenly Daddy has proclaimed that all forms of witchcraft and magic are abominations. That little heart door is wide open to receive familiar spirits of witchcraft.

Many years ago, I saw a cartoon in which a little, pink girl-bunny was floating above the floor in the hallway at school. She was in lotus position, murmuring, "Uuummm."

A little boy-bunny came running up to her and said, "You have to help me. I have a math test today and I didn't study for it." After he begged sufficiently, she gave in and touched him on the third-eye position, in the middle of his forehead. He started going through all kinds of contortions and manifestations, finally ending up with an enlarged head. He proclaimed, "I just received the spirit of Einstein."

Later in the cartoon he experienced some negative consequences, but the message was clear. You don't really have to study. Just receive the right spirit guide or familiar spirit and you can do anything. Can you see how seductive this would be for a normal child?

We may engage in fantasy porn and, in our minds, form images of those with whom we would interact. We call that mental image *a construct*. It is composed of some combination of sinful energies. This construct functions as a mask that hides the true identity of a familiar spirit. When we give that spirit a place, it has legal access to our mind, soul, and body.

When we imagine that sexy image of our fantasy lover, we are seeing the disguise **we created** for that creature to deceive us. When we mentally engage in sinful activities with the image, we are actually engaging in those activities with the creature.

Some of us may regularly have sex with fantasy lovers. Some may go into a hypnotic state, travel to some other universe, and be involved in many different types of activities. We might run a vivid scenario in our head and masturbate. Some of us may have a more active sex life in our fantasies, than with our spouses.

It doesn't matter whether the mask is hiding the image of a thing associated with sexual sin or some other sin. We can engage in sins of anger, rebellion, the supernatural, witchcraft, magic, violence, or death. These ambassadors for Satan's kingdom don't really care which sins we choose to commit. Their job is to deceive, motivate, and stimulate us to commit sin and to bring defilement to us in every way they can. They present us with something like a menu and invite us to take anything we want from the menu. Once again, *our will be done*.

This is very seductive and many people, not just children, buy into it, thinking it is good to receive help from the spirits. However, that it is not what the *Owners Manual* says. God tells us these activities, and the people who practice them, are abominations to Him. (Deuteronomy 18:10-12) We are told that Satan disguises himself as an angel of light. (2 Corinthians 11:14) The Lord warns us to beware that the light **in us** is not darkness. (Luke 11:35; Matthew 6:23)

The things that come as a result of occult activities are not sent from God. They aren't really pink ponies, amber unicorns, purple dinosaurs, space aliens, fairy princesses, or good mommies and daddies. They are unclean spirits sent specifically to deceive us and take control of our souls. Your children may not know this, but now you do.

Resorting to any form of escape other than to Jesus Christ will subject us to the control of Satan and his kingdom. If we have allowed ourselves to become *subject to* those familiar spirits, they will influence our thoughts, perceptions, beliefs, and attitudes, through *their* interpretation and translation of what we see and hear. Once again, we remind you that **pain can be used for good.**

Familiar Spirits of Death

Through Adam's sin, **death** is the **first of our enemies** to have come into the world. In other sections of this book, we discuss the fact that sin dwells in our flesh. Sin is defined as an action and it is also the **spiritual entity** that becomes our master when we let it in. We hear its voice when it is outside wanting to come in, and we hear its voice after it has entered.

The apostle Paul wrote that ***death** is actively at work in us*. As we discussed previously, Paul was proclaiming that when he did things that were evil, it was not he that did them. It was the sin (**death**), that ever-present evil, which **dwelt within him**. It was **the voice**, within him, constantly prodding and insisting he do its will. (Genesis 2:17, 4:7; Romans 5:13-14; 1 John 3:8; John 10:10; Hebrews 2:14-15; Colossians 2:11-15; 1 Corinthians 15:26, 56-57)

Because death still has a place in the flesh and souls of Christians, it is necessary to discover its effect in our lives and remove its influence. When we see people controlled by fear, we pity them, because, from our human perspective, they need help. Here, the voice of fear is equivalent to the voice of death. The fact that a person allows the **voice of death** to rule, condemns them.

The conflict is in the head. Paul said that the *mind of the flesh* does not submit itself to God's law. He said it *could not* submit. The creature, in this case death, is controlling the mind of the flesh. That creature is hostile to God; therefore, the mind of the flesh is going to be **hostile to God**. (Romans 8:7-8)

In ministry sessions, people have told us they have conflicting thoughts, or voices, in their minds. We are convinced the thoughts we have are not always our own thoughts. We believe they may be from the voice of death dwelling in our hearts. There can sometimes be a great deal of commotion, with all the voices vying for control in our minds.

When we have thoughts, or hear words of fear, condemnation, shame, worthlessness, rejection, or inadequacy spoken by other people; it is the voice of death using the voices of those we know and love. They may be unaware they are allowing death to speak through their mouths, but the messages still bring a form of death.

We have seen the influence of death in the lives of many people with whom we have ministered. A man in his thirties complained that when he goes to church, he doesn't experience anything good. He told us how frustrated he was. He didn't understand why other people seemed to receive so much joy and satisfaction from the services. He didn't understand the love of God and couldn't experience it, although he desperately wanted to.

We asked the Holy Spirit to show this man why he was having so much trouble. Suddenly, he looked up and proclaimed, "Well, this is ridiculous. I just remembered something from a long time ago, but it doesn't make any sense." We asked him to tell us anyway. He told us he remembered a time when he was about seven years old. He and his puppy were playing in the street. A big truck came around the corner and ran over his little dog.

After he prayed, "Please, God, fix my puppy," the boy sat waiting but nothing happened. Finally, he went home, and as he walked, he remembers having these thoughts: "God doesn't care about you. He doesn't care about your puppy. He doesn't care about your prayers, but I do. I want to be your friend. We can go to a quiet place where we can always be together. I'll never leave you."

There were hot, angry tears streaming down this man's face as he told us the story. For the first time in thirty years he had discovered the pain buried deep inside. He also discovered how angry he was at God, because He didn't *fix his puppy*! A part of his soul went to that quiet place. We suspect it was the part of his soul that could experience a relationship with God.

We led the man through some prayers. In them, he gave all the pain, unhappiness, and anger to Jesus, Who paid for all these things on the cross. He renounced the **comfort** and **friendship** of death. He forgave God and asked Him to heal his heart. Later, we received a testimony that many things had changed in his life. He was able to worship and feel the presence of God. He was even getting along with his boss at work. This was a major miracle.

In another example, a little girl, about four years old, loved spending time with her daddy. One evening he told her that the following week he would be going on a business trip. When he returned they would have time to play together. She didn't have a concept of the time involved, but she agreed.

On Monday morning, she told daddy goodbye and went about her normal, busy day. In the early evening she went to mommy and asked why daddy wasn't home yet. Her mom reminded her that daddy would be gone five days. She told her this was Monday, and daddy would be gone until Friday. The girl still didn't understand, but accepted it.

That week went by very slowly. Every day the little girl asked her mother if this was the day daddy would be home. Every day mommy patiently told her it would be on Friday. Finally, Friday came. In the mid-afternoon, the little girl positioned herself in a front window, where she could see the driveway. She propped her head on her hands and waited for daddy.

At last she saw the car pull into the driveway. Daddy climbed out and headed for the front door. The little girl was almost overcome with emotion and excitement. As he came up the sidewalk, she ran for the front door.

As it opened, she cried, "Daaaddeeee!" At that moment, mom came from the kitchen to tell him his boss had just called about a crisis at work, and dad needed to call back immediately. His daughter came running toward him, with arms outstretched, but he just patted her on the head and said, "Just a minute, honey, I'll be right back." She was left there totally deflated.

As she slowly walked to her bedroom, a voice spoke into her heart telling her that daddy hadn't missed her and didn't really care about her. No one ever really cared about her. It offered to take her to a quiet place, promised always to be her friend, and said it would never go away or ignore her.

Many years later, we met a woman who wondered why she couldn't experience a relationship with God. She wondered why she had suffered through five marriages, five divorces, and couldn't seem to have a good relationship with any man. She wondered out loud as she sobbed quietly. When we asked the Holy Spirit to show her the reason, she reluctantly told us the story about the little girl.

During ministry, she renounced **familiar spirits of death**, all the **attributes of death**, the **place of death,** and her **fear of life**. After we had a chance to minister to the anger, outrage, rejection, abandonment, and the fear of being rejected, she told us she felt a sense of freedom. Later, we heard that she, too, had experienced many changes in her life, including a growing relationship with God. We could describe other similar scenarios, we've heard, in which the voice of death played a very important role.

Based on all these reports from normal people, we have concluded that death is multifaceted. It fills our life with the **haunting fear of death** in many different forms: physical death, emotional death, the apparent death parts of our soul, death and abortion of marriage or relationships, loss of career or lifestyle, death of hopes and dreams, death of health and vitality, and death of confidence and security. The different manifestations of death can be as unique as the individuals involved.

Death has been here for a long time. The whole creation is impregnated with its influence and power. The creatures producing the **voice of death** never sleep or rest, but clamor for attention. Even so, we are told that Jesus came to destroy the power of death. That He might **deliver** and completely **set free** all those who had been held in **bondage** by the **fear of death** throughout their lives. (Hebrews 2:14-15) Once we understand that we are in bondage we can experience the freedom for which Jesus gave His life.

We Do Have Other Options

When we are tempted to wallow in shame, it is comforting to remember that it is God who has *justified us*. The voices of death have no right to condemn us. (Romans 8:33-34) We have already *been approved* and *accepted* by the only One whose opinion matters. When we *renounce the voices*, and the sin that has given them legal ground, **they must go.**

We are instructed to bring every thought into captivity by making note of what we are thinking and how we are responding. (2 Corinthians 10:5) Scripture tells us to turn away from unfruitful and, frequently, damaging pastimes, and turn toward things that are beneficial. We are advised to *meditate on things* that are true, noble, just, pure, lovely, and are of good report or praiseworthy. (Philippians 4:8) These things will edify our soul and spirit.

When we acknowledge the **first thought** that can turn into a scenario lasting for hours, we choose. We can accept that thought, engage our will, spend hours engaged in angry conversation with someone who is not even there, or we can reject it. It is amusing to think the *original thought* wasn't even ours but, instead, might have come from a demon.

We **cut it off** with authority and say, "No! I'm not going to receive this. devil, in the name of the Lord Jesus Christ, get out of my life, my head, my nervous system, and my ears. Jesus has paid for all my sins. I don't want to hear your slimy voice or listen to your garbage any more. Get out of here!" **We can take control and dominion**. We don't have to let him rule our lives, our minds, our thoughts, our nervous systems, or anything else!

This might be easier said than done. People have told us their lives are so dependent upon fantasies and habits of dissociation they wouldn't know how to get through the day without them. For these people, there doesn't seem to be any hope of finding freedom.

*"God is our **refuge** and **strength**, a very **present help** in trouble. Therefore we will not fear"* (Psalm 46:1-2). Rather than engaging in sinful scenarios, we can meditate on all the things that will be **good for our soul**. Instead of filling our hearts with demonic energies, we can fill our hearts with the energies of righteousness and power.

We need to go to the One who will protect us from all those who would bring our destruction. (Psalm 91:2) We can ask Him to show us when we are thinking destructive thoughts. We can ask Him to give us the ability to put down all those thoughts, fantasies, imaginations, and everything that exalts itself over Him. These are simple decisions for which we need to start taking responsibility.

We need to protect that which was given to us: our hearts, souls, and minds. (Proverbs 4:23) We are not required to give anything to the creatures that want to destroy us. The Lord has invested a great deal into our salvation, and He has given us commands for our good. He has even created the fiery serpents for our good. It seems appropriate to let Him help us to obey His commands.

Restoration of Our Soul

In a previous section we discussed restoration as a part of salvation. When Peter was in a prison, he followed the Angel's instructions and the chains fell off his hands. Although Peter was technically delivered, he was still in the prison, surrounded by his *demonic* guards. If he were to stay there long enough, they would wake up and put the chains back on. Instead, Peter followed the angel. They went out and immediately the angel departed from him. (Acts 12:6-10)

When the Lord gives us a command, His righteousness is on the line, so He obligates Himself. He can only command of us what He has made it possible for us to achieve. More importantly, He is obligated to help us if we will humble ourselves and ask. **There is good news**! The Psalmist wrote, *"He* **restores my soul***; He* **leads me** *in the paths of righteousness for* **His name's sake***"* (Psalms 23:3). [Emphasis ours]

There are two wonderful promises in this proclamation. First, He will **restore our souls**. If He is willing to do it for one, He is willing to do it for all. The second promise may be even more important. The promise is not dependent upon our ability to earn it. The covenant He has made with us obligates Him to do His part perfectly. Even when we fail to function perfectly, He will do His part **for His name's sake**.

We have heard teachings that suggest He will **refresh** the soul, but we need to look at all the other definitions. The predominant meanings of this word all speak of something being **brought back** from **somewhere**. The question, which seems obvious, is **from where**? We are talking about an intangible part of our being called the soul.

Where does it go, that it needs to return? Peter was in a physical prison but where does our soul go that it must be brought back? In accordance with our accumulated experience and understanding, parts of our soul are put in a non-physical prison.

People who have experienced ritual abuse have related amazing things *they could see* in their minds. They have described castles, caves, and dungeons with torture implements. They have also told us about places existing in other times, spaces, and dimensions. Based on their understanding, parts of their souls, associated with specific events or systems of events, were apparently imprisoned in many of these places.

*"You desire truth in the **inward parts**, and in the **hidden part** You will make me to know wisdom"* (Psalm 51:6). [Emphasis ours] In this verse, the words, inward parts, are self-explanatory. The word, hidden, means **kept secret, closed up**, shut out, or **shut up**. (Merriam-Webster's) This definition suggests there are **secret parts** of which we may not be consciously aware. They could be the hidden parts that dwell in these spiritual and emotional prison cells. These are the parts we want to rescue.

Satan is a thief who comes to steal, kill, and destroy. (John 10:10) We don't believe the thief esteems the physical body as having value, except as a generator of energy. We don't believe the thief has the ability to kill, steal, or destroy the spirit. Therefore, we believe his primary target would be our soul, and all it represents. Our object is to take back all that has been **killed**, **stolen**, and **destroyed**. This would include all soul and humanity.

Until we saw evidence to the contrary in South America, we were sure that such things couldn't apply to us. Then we started meeting many Christians who could tell us similar types of things, in spite of widely different backgrounds.

As an example, one little girl was naughty, so she was placed in a dark basement for days at a time. The only water she had was that which dripped out of an old, rusty faucet. Her only food was that which crawled across the floor. She was frequently sent to the *basement prison* as punishment and lived in her own private hell for many years.

The woman, who told us about her experiences as this little girl, could still see herself **closed up**, crawling around that basement floor, hoping to find something to eat. Then **the woman commanded** everything associated with Satan's kingdom to leave the little girl and every part of her own life and being. Finally, the woman asked the Lord to minister and bring restoration.

When the prayers were completed, she said the little girl was now in her heart with the Lord. We asked her if she still had those intense feelings and emotions that pertained to the little girl. She said they were all gone and were no longer afflicting her.

One man told us he couldn't remember the last time he had experienced emotions. We asked him to tell us what the Holy Spirit was showing him. After some time, he told us he saw an image of what looked like a dungeon with chains and torture implements hanging from the walls. He also saw a horrible-looking figure chained to the wall.

We thought this figure must **represent** a part of his soul. We explained to him that the image in his mind was probably created when he was very young. It was possible that emotions had become so dangerous, or painful, he decided to put them in a dungeon.

During this process it became apparent that the figure in the dungeon represented painful experiences and the emotions of self-hatred associated with them. Once these issues, and the fear associated with them, were uncovered, it was easy to proceed with ministry. The man renounced all the components of sin. He **commanded** everything associated with Satan's kingdom to go where the Lord Jesus would send it, and he asked the Lord Jesus to minister and bring restoration.

We really aren't sure how it works, but we've seen similar results many times. We were later told the man was learning how to experience and respond to normal emotions. The Lord had restored his emotions and his humanity associated with them. This man could now learn how to appreciate the things he gave away as a child.

Everyone wants to survive, have their needs met, and escape from painful things in life. As a result, we put those painful things in dark places, hoping they will go away. When we put away the memories associated with painful and unpleasant things, we apparently **shut up** the parts of our souls associated with those events. Then we **lock them up** so we don't have to remember, or deal with, those memories or emotions.

Unfortunately, this limits our ability to be everything the Lord has created us to be. We were created to function as whole and complete children of God. If we have parts of our souls hidden away, or scattered throughout the dimensions, we cannot function properly.

The key to healing is letting go of the **illusions** so we can discover the truth. *"You shall **know the truth**, and **the truth shall make you free**"* (John 8:32). [Emphasis ours]

Glenna and I have been given the privilege of helping many hundreds of people. When they discover the truth of who they really are, why they respond as they do, and their authority and dominion; they are set free. When they discover they can function as a rescuer for parts of their own soul; there have usually been amazing changes in their lives.

Now What?

We have the authority and dominion to pray effectively for the release of parts of our souls from prison. As we do so, we need to remember Who really is the minister of deliverance and restoration.

We read Scriptures in which the writer pleads with the Lord to heal his soul. (Psalm 41:4; 86:11) In both cases, the plea is that the Lord will **unite**, cure, repair, or **make whole**, the heart/soul. (Strong's H 7495)

Many times in the Gospels, Jesus used the word **peace**. (John 14:27; 16:33) Jesus proclaimed that He was leaving this peace so we may have peace. This word is from a primary verb meaning, **to join**, prosperity, one, quietness, rest, **set at one again**. (Strong's, G 1515) There are a number of words in the Old Testament that have the translation *peace*.

When we look at all these definitions, we see a concept associated with the word peace. We see that it applies to something being joined or set at one again. Peace causes that which is divided, to be completed, perfected, also to bring **restoration**. Peace also speaks of **being whole**, in perfect health and prosperity as applied to our mind or our body. [*shelem* (Strong's, H 8002) which comes from *shalam* (Strong's, H 7999)] This seems to fit together, perfectly, with the Scripture that says, "**He restores my soul**."

While on earth, Jesus proclaimed that the peace He gives is not the peace that the world would give. Do you see that this statement can be viewed as a proverb, contrasting what the world offers, to what He provides? The things the world gives usually are the opposite of peace.

Jesus told His followers that He would, through His work as Messiah, **set at one** again souls and bodies. He would cause completion and perfection as well as provide restoration. He is the Author of health and prosperity through salvation. He can also use us as **His tools** to accomplish His work.

You may be familiar with the children's nursery rhyme: "Humpty Dumpty sat on a wall. Humpty Dumpty had a great fall. All the king's horses and all the king's men couldn't put Humpty Dumpty together again."

We agree this is true, but **the King can**! The King can do those things that cannot be done by His horses and men. The King knows where all the pieces go. The King knows which pieces have to be preassembled, and He knows the perfect order of assembly. The King is the original manufacturer, the Creator, and He can.

The New Testament states, *"May the **God of peace** Himself **sanctify** you completely; and may your **whole spirit, soul, and body** be preserved blameless at the coming of our Lord Jesus Christ"* (1 Thessalonians 5:23). [Emphasis ours] (Also see Jeremiah 29:13-14)

We believe this prayer serves as a **promise** of what is **available** for us. People have told us this is impossible, but it must be possible. When Jesus commanded us to love the Lord our God with all our heart, all our soul, and all our mind, He put His righteousness on the line. If it were not possible, His righteousness would be forfeited. He can't command us to do something that is impossible, because that would not be righteous!

We have a promise from the One who knows our souls better than we may ever know them. If we will allow Him the opportunity, He is willing and able to heal and restore the souls. He is able to make it possible for us to love the Lord our God with all our hearts, all of our minds, and all our souls. He is the **only One** who can. It is time to pray.

<u>Sample Prayer:</u>

In the name of the Lord Jesus Christ, I renounce the voice of the accuser and its function in my mind or mouth. I command the destruction of all demonic goodness or badness I received by competing with my God, the true Creator.

I renounce everything serving Satan's kingdom associated with being a creator. I renounce all their power and control over any part of my life or being, and I renounce all contracts, vows, proclamations, and agreements I have made in my heart, or with my mouth, that have turned anything over to Satan or his kingdom.

I renounce the sinful use of dissociation and all forms of sinful escape. I renounce the use of daydreaming, dreams, fantasies, imaginations, drugs, alcohol, sex, food, shopping, movies, computer ventures and games, videos, books, sleep-- everything I have used to escape real life and the pain, fear, and unhappiness of life. I renounce everything associated with illusions and unreality.

I renounce all realms of sinful escape in any time, space, or dimension. I command the destruction of everything created by any form of dissociation in which I have engaged; everything that represents real life, dreams, fantasies, or imaginations associated with people, places, objects, events, sights, sounds, smells, tastes, feelings, emotions, body memories, sensations, and stimulations. I command the destruction of everything that would control, deceive, or hold any part of my soul captive.

I command all the spiritual components of these constructs to go where the Lord Jesus Christ sends them. I command the

destruction of all defilement and iniquity I have received through these activities.

I renounce all familiar spirits associated with family members, dead people, ancestors, authority figures, and other people or entities. I renounce being deceived by any familiar spirit or spirit guide. I renounce, and proclaim the destruction of all masks and illusions that hide the true identity of any familiar spirits, or spirit guides, that have ever deceived any part of my soul or humanity.

I renounce all familiar spirits of death, the voice of death, the friendship of death, the counsel of death, the comfort of death, the place of death, the haunting fear of death, and the fear of life.

I renounce all the powers, strengths, abilities, comfort, all real or perceived benefits, and everything else I have received from any spirit guide or familiar spirit, including the spirit of death, at any time during my life.

I renounce giving any idolatry or sacrifice, including any spiritual, emotional, or physical energies, as well as any part of my soul or humanity, over to anyone or anything serving Satan's kingdom.

I command everything serving Satan's kingdom to give the Lord Jesus Christ everything received from me as a sacrifice, because the Lord Jesus Christ paid for all my sins, and He alone is worthy to receive these things.

I claim the power of the shed blood of the Lord Jesus Christ as payment for all the sins that Satan would claim over any part of my soul or humanity. I command everything serving Satan's kingdom, all their influence, control, and all their effects in my life to go, now, where the Lord Jesus Christ sends them.

Heavenly Father, I now place into Your hands all the parts of my soul associated with my efforts to function as the Creator. I relinquish this job, and the weight of responsibility for this job.

I ask You to restore to me all my soul, humanity, and everything associated with my true identity and destiny;

everything I lost or gave away, as well as everything that has been killed, stolen, or destroyed.

My Lord, I ask You to cleanse my spiritual eyes, my mind, and my heart, of everything that would deceive me and prevent me from seeing and knowing You as You truly are, or from seeing and knowing myself as You created me to be.

I ask You to give me the revelation that You are my Father and I am your child. I ask You to fill my heart with the revelation of how different You are from any other person or being I have ever known.

I ask You to flood my heart with Your presence and power; with Your perfect love, acceptance, approval, peace, joy, satisfaction, and security. I ask You to fill me with everything I have never received, everything necessary for me to be free from emotional starvation and all associated cravings and yearnings.

I ask You, Heavenly Father, to teach me how to trust You and how to escape to You. I want to know You as my place of escape. Thank You. Amen.

Can You Be Like God?

Since the Garden of Eden, the iniquities of Adam have been passed down through all the fathers on the earth. The serpent told Adam and Eve they could receive the knowledge of good and evil and **be like God**. This promise of **being like God** seduced Adam and Eve. It is still seducing normal people who come from the seed of Adam.

We have not changed much in these few thousand years. We still want to be the *center of the universe*. We want everything now, in accordance with our will.

On more than one occasion, the Lord has shown His mercy by judging Glenna and me. He has shown us that we are spoiled, self-absorbed, nasty little kids, at heart. In His mercy and grace, He would simply say *stiff-necked*.

When God was leading the children of Israel through the desert, they were constantly complaining because **they wanted** the Promised Land with its milk and honey, **right then**! They didn't want to experience problems and testing. They were normal people and it cost them forty years.

When it was finally time for the people of God to enter the Promised Land, the Lord explained that He would not give it to them all at one time. He told them He would give them portions of the land. When they were able to occupy it, He would give them more. He promised to complete **this process** as long as they followed His rules. (Deuteronomy 7:22-24; Exodus 23:29)

When people tell us they have experienced complete deliverance, *all at one time*, we are concerned. This doesn't seem to fit the model we've seen represented in the Bible. We are told that the Lord is the same yesterday, today, and forever. (Hebrews 13:8) We believe He gives us the Promised Land of our soul **as a process**, also.

When He has taught us how to occupy what we've taken back from the enemy, He helps us to take more. We believe *restoration of the soul* is a process of being taken from glory to glory. As we occupy and possess all of **our** promised land, He is **transforming** us from glory to glory. (2 Corinthians 3:18) This process of possessing our souls must occur, because He has guaranteed that He will complete it. (Philippians 1:6) The only uncertainty is how quickly this process will take place in our individual lives.

Maybe we're still in the wilderness or maybe we're going through the Jordan before entering into our inheritance. God is not malicious. He doesn't do things just to see if we will fail. He does them for our good, as a part of His master plan. He wants us to be everything we can be. Fortunately, He gets to decide how best to accomplish it.

When Paul was imprisoned in Rome, he proclaimed that *everything was working for good*. Not only was it good for him, personally, but it also was good for the kingdom of God. (See Philippians 1:12–14) As people give the Lord permission to shine His light into the dark places in their souls, they will find greater measures of freedom. This requires cooperation because the Lord will not force this aspect of salvation on any of us.

We are also told to choose whom we will serve, and many people decide to *serve their own will*. When the Lord specifies His process for salvation and restoration, a normal person might respond with, "I think I'll do it **my** way. I know **when** I want it done – now. I know **how** I want it done – painlessly. I know **by whom** I want it done – **me**. I don't want to trust God, wait for Him, or be dependent upon Him. I want **my** will to be done, because **I want to be like God!**"

For Adam, wanting to be like God produced **death**. When we want to elevate ourselves to be like God, it will produce **death**. When the same tempter tells us we can be like God, his is the voice of **death**! When we want to assume the jobs of the Creator, the Father, the Son, or the Holy Spirit, we are inviting death to invade our lives and beings. As my old math professor would say, "It is intuitively obvious," **WE ARE NOT QUALIFIED TO DO ANY OF THESE JOBS!**

SECTION FOUR: SOUL FRUIT ISSUES

Based upon our studies, and experience with many people, we believe that children take on the job of being the judge very early in life. It seems as though they have a screen in their heart, labeled man, father, potential husband, (or Father God). At this time the child wants to know what the image of a man should be. The image of the earthly father is the one most likely to be on the screen. Without this image, the child would have a difficult time determining what kind of man they should be or what kind of man they should marry.

CAN YOU JUDGE LIKE THE FATHER?

Unwillingness to Forgive

This is a function of will, because a person is exhibiting **unwillingness** to give up **resentment**, or to grant **relief from payment**. This also implies there is a debt, or perceived debt, owed. One also chooses to feel **bitterness** against an offender. It doesn't matter whether the offense is real or imagined; the effects are the same. These responses are based upon judgments.

The offended party decides they have **the right** to hold onto the anger and resentment. They judge that the offense is such that they should keep the bitterness in their heart. They judge the motivations of the offender based upon their *infinite understanding*. This judgment gives them the right to establish value of the debt, which might be emotional or associated with something tangible.

Scripture tells us we are **poisoned** by bitterness and **bound** by iniquity when we are unforgiving. (Acts 8:22-23) The sin creature knocks on our door, and we open the door and invite it in. As a consequence, it dwells within us, giving us a greater inclination to sin. Imagine a hideous creature with chains, constructed one link at a time by our decisions, responses, and sins, in its hands. Our souls are poisoned and we are held in bondage by chains we forged.

While telling a parable about the kingdom of heaven, Jesus told of a king who was conducting his affairs. (Matthew 18:23-35) A man was brought to him who owed him a great debt. The man begged for mercy and promised to pay the entire debt if given the opportunity. As a result, the master was moved with compassion and forgave the debt.

Later this man, who owed so much, met another man who owed him very little. The other man begged him the same way he had begged his lord, but this man would not forgive. He had the other man thrown into prison.

When the king heard what had happened, he sent for the first man. The master was so angry he had the man delivered to **the torturers** until he should pay all that was due. Jesus concludes, *"So My heavenly Father also will do to you if each of you, **from his heart**, does not forgive his brother his trespasses"* (Matthew 18:35). [Emphasis ours] (Also see Mark 11:25)

This is worthy of some thought, because Jesus used words very specifically. Did you notice the words, *from his heart?* We don't believe being unforgiving will cost us our salvation. It is the same as any other sin and Jesus paid for it with His blood. We do believe *the torturers* we must deal with are those that poison, bind, and afflict us in this world. (Acts 8:23)

We are told we have to get rid of anger, rage, malice, slander, and all other emotions of sin, in order to be free. (Ephesians 4:31; Colossians 3:8; 1 Peter 2:1) We are told to see to it that no bitter root grows up in us. (Hebrews 12:15) We must forgive from the heart if we want to be granted relief from payment, and set free from the consequences of our own sin. (Matthew 6:14; Mark 11:25; Luke 6:37)

There are times in a ministry environment when a person proclaims sincerely that there is no bitterness in their heart. Then we ask them to describe an event for which they had forgiven someone. As they do so, their face may get red, they might begin to cry, and their tone of voice indicates intense emotion. When we ask where all the emotion is coming from, the typical response is, "I DON'T KNOW!"

God's law tells us that as we give, so shall we receive. The head may have decided to forgive, but the heart might still be holding on to pain, anger, and bitterness. Maybe our hearts can't forgive as long as these feelings and emotions are still boiling around in there. Remember, the head doesn't always know what's going on in the heart.

Effects on the Body

In the parable about the king and the unforgiving servant, Jesus said that God would treat us the same way we treat **our debtors**. This could include many kinds of debts, both real and perceived. It is possible that some people could use this as another accusation against God. We don't believe this defines God as angry or mean. This is another illustration of His love demonstrating His desire to free us from the control of sin.

As we discussed in section three, the Proverbs indicate that sinful reactions can manifest in our soul and body. The spiritual components of iniquity, we believe, have the ability to produce the physical consequences of iniquity. These supernatural creatures have been around for a long time and probably have the ability to affect our brain, organs, and nervous system. As we produce sinful reactions, these torturers may help to produce real emotional and physical afflictions.

Being angry with others doesn't hurt them; it hurts us. Our *fear- based* responses can stimulate our bodies to produce toxins that might cause great pain and damage and could, eventually, kill us. It is reasonable to believe that the reduction in fear-based responses will bring a reduction in real physical and emotional suffering.

Once again, we see God's perfect system for *motivating us* to do what is necessary to be free. From our earlier discussion of sin and its effect on the body, we know pain is used for good. The fiery serpents were good for the people in the wilderness, because they motivated the people to seek Him and keep moving forward. In that same way, physical and emotional pain produced by the torturers is good when it motivates us to truly forgive others and seek Him.

There are cards and letters in our file from people who tell us they have received physical healing as a result of their emotional healing. Their physical problems faded away after they dealt with the issues of their heart. Some have said they are no longer required to take antidepressants or medications to treat chronic pain.

Fearful Responses

*"Pursue **peace**...lest any root of bitterness springing up cause trouble, and by this many become defiled"* (Hebrews 12:14-15). [Emphasis ours] Responding in fear and pursuing peace are opposite actions.

Some people seem to believe that sin is only committed when we actively hurt someone else. Much more often, we sin in the way we respond to being hurt. Fear, bitterness, unwillingness to forgive, and many other negative feelings are produced as a result of what someone does to us. When we respond in these *normal ways*, we and those around us will be defiled.

When normal people grow up in normal dysfunctional environments, survival becomes a strong motivating factor. We believe *all sin is based in fear* and is associated with the *need for survival*. It could be the *fear of not having our needs met* or the *fear that we won't survive* unless we protect ourselves. The motivations for our *fear responses* are typically based upon our judgments and expectations produced by our judgmental heart.

There are times when people come to us requesting marriage counseling. Usually, each will accuse the other of being the source of the problem. If we meet with them, we assure them that the reason they need counseling is because both of them are contributing to the conflicts. We know the things troubling their relationship are not really based upon the actions of their partner.

Sometimes they try to blackmail us by threatening to divorce if we don't help them. This is meant to put the responsibility for their decisions on our shoulders. At this point we explain that, in our view, the marriage isn't of primary importance. Whether or not people decide to divorce is entirely their decision.

We care about two individual souls. We care that each one establishes a good relationship with our heavenly Father. When they do have a good relationship with our heavenly Father, working through problems in the relationship with one another will be much easier.

The real issues are buried deep in our hearts, embedded in the past, and empowered by fear and judgments. They concern dads and moms, dysfunctional families, ex-spouses, boyfriends or girlfriends, and normal trauma events. Normal people view others through spiritual glasses tinted by betrayal, victimization, and abuse.

Being normal people, we judge the words, actions, and motivations of everyone around us. When we see the slightest hint that our expectations are true, we respond in fear, which manifests as anger and rage. When these issues are resolved, today's concerns seem much less significant, because they are only fruit issues out on the tips of the branches of our soul tree.

The problems are always based upon what kind of relationship we have with our heavenly Father. Despite our fears, we hope other people will provide what we need. When we stop trusting in others to **protect us**, **provide for us**, and **assure our survival**, the power of fear will be nullified.

How do we know the problems aren't based in the here and now? The study of Scripture and the experience of hundreds of ministry sessions confirm our conclusions. As an example, a man with whom we have ministered gave us this account:

"Before I was married to my current wife, I had issues with women and with marriage in general. Many years earlier, I had been married and had children. One day, my wife and I planned a dinner party. I was working in the yard and she asked if I would watch the kids while she went to the store. I agreed and continued working.

"After a couple of hours, I began to feel concerned because she had not returned. I didn't know if I should cruise the neighborhood, thinking it was possible the car had broken down, or call the police. I decided to hope for the best and went in to take a shower. After showering I continued to stress.

"Finally, the phone rang. I anxiously picked it up and heard a familiar voice on the line. A man I thought was a friend told me, very matter-of-factly, 'Your wife is with me and she's not coming home.' There was no discussion. He wouldn't allow me to talk to her. I had been informed and that was the end of the conversation.

"When the company arrived for dinner, I was sitting in a puddle of tears. I don't remember a great deal about that evening. Someone helped take care of the kids and ordered pizza. My friends did everything in their power to console me and convince me that everything would work out.

"During the next year I went through a long and painful divorce. By the end of the process I felt betrayed by just about everyone: my wife, the man I thought was a friend, members of my family, and my attorney. As a result, I came to some conclusions I thought were reasonable: all women, and probably most men, were evil.

"I decided that a woman was like an octopus, having tentacles with suckers all over them and a terrible beak. This octopus would plant its beak in the center of a man's chest and suck out all his life energy. When she had sucked away everything of value, she would spit him out. His empty husk would float away on the current, and she would look for another victim.

"With this new understanding of the *true nature of women*, I began to make some changes in my lifestyle. I decided to protect myself from these evil creatures and *do* to them before they *did* to me. In truth, I wasn't completely successful. My desperate needs usually outweighed my good judgment. As a result, there were some good times, but overall, there were many years of pain and unhappiness.

"Finally, I decided to forsake relationships altogether. For several years I lived like a hermit. I went to work during the day, and during the evening I found solitary things to do. I read, watched TV, or went to a movie. I did many things to satisfy my needs that were not as dangerous as dealing with people.

"One day I was having a chat with the Lord and I told Him how lonely I was. It may have been my imagination, but I thought He told me He knew, and I needed to wait until He decided I was ready to deal with those, *evil creatures* again. Later, I was transferred to another city and met my current wife.

"When we were married, I hoped things would be much better. During the hermit years, I had received the gift of salvation. She was also a Christian, so I hoped we could *live happily ever after*.

"Soon after we were married, my wife announced she was going to the grocery store and wondered if there was anything she could get for me. I told her no and went on with what I was doing. As she went out the door, I checked my watch. I knew it took about six minutes to get to the store, about thirty minutes to do the grocery shopping, and about six minutes to get home. That meant she should be home in about forty-two minutes.

"At forty-five minutes I started feeling stress, wondering where she was, what she was doing, and with whom. When she arrived home, I was in a screaming rage. Finally, I found my composure and apologized for how I had treated her. The issue was now resolved *until the next time*.

"This occurred several times over the years before I finally sought some ministry help. When we asked the Lord to show me the real issue, it was terrible. In my mind was an image of my first wife, standing on a pedestal. She was wearing a goddess gown, and goddess light was beaming in every direction.

"The Lord told me that I had put her on that pedestal, clothed her in that gown, and given her the power to produce that light. He told me my idolatry was profound. I had given her control of my emotions, my feelings, my attitudes, and my reactions to other people by making her the god of my life. This was not what I wanted to hear.

"I wanted to hear Him comfort me for being a victim. I wanted Him to agree that she was evil. I wanted to be vindicated and justified, but He was having none of that. Instead, He informed me that her actions were, to a great degree, because of me. I had abandoned her by making her a low priority. In my heart, I had betrayed her, and my actions and attitudes helped her to feel unlovable and unwanted.

"He proclaimed that her sins were not my problem. Satan can't hold her sins against me. He can only hold my sins against me. If I was being afflicted in my soul, it was a consequence of my decisions. In making her the god of my life, I had allowed her to define my identity and destiny.

"Then, I judged her and all women, as being evil. I judged myself as being unlovable and undesirable, worthy only to be rejected, abandoned, and betrayed. I also judged God because He allowed these terrible things to happen to me.

"After I had been convicted of all these things, it was necessary for me to renounce all the judgments, fear, expectations, and idolatry that were ruling my life. After this event, my life didn't become a bed of roses, but it improved dramatically. The Lord is amazingly merciful."

This testimony *represents many* we have heard from people whose lives are filled with idolatry and the expectation of bad things. When we allow fear to rule, we can't be what God created us to be, because we are too busy becoming what Satan wants us to be. The **fear-based prejudice** illustrated in the example above could apply to any gender, race, social class, economic strata, or any other distinction we choose and judge.

The writer of Job 21:25, proclaims that a man can die in the bitterness of his soul, never having eaten with pleasure. We interpret this as meaning it is possible to have good things and not be able to enjoy them, because of **bitterness in our soul**. Can you see how Satan uses the sin of judgment, based in fear, to cheat people out of the good things of life?

We Assign Blame

The apostle Paul stated that we are **inexcusable** when we judge others. Because in **whatever we judge** we **condemn ourselves** inasmuch as **we who judge practice the same things**. (Romans 2:1) This proclamation speaks volumes. We hear someone complaining about someone else's activities, actions, or attitudes. A common expression in response to someone's words or actions is, "That person just drives me crazy."

We suspect we would find that same issue lurking in the labyrinth of the soul of the *complaining* person. The Scripture above indicates that we are looking at another person as though we were looking in a mirror. This is a classic case of attempted self-validation by blaming our own imperfections on someone else. We respond that way because we are seeing, reflected in someone else, the things we are ashamed of or dislike in ourselves.

We meet people regularly who complain they have been attending a specific church for years and they are considering relocating. In spite of *all they have invested* in that church, no one seems to care about them. They wander around without talking to anyone, and go home feeling rejected. They judge everybody else as being hypocritical or too uppity. They commonly ask, "Where is the Christian love I've heard so much about?"

There may be some validity to their opinions because Christians don't always demonstrate love. On the other hand, since these comments are based in judgment, Glenna has found a different way of dealing with this person. She asks the complainer, "When was the last time you offered an encouraging word to someone who looked lonely? When was the last time you did for others what you want them to do for you? Don't you know that as you give, you will receive?"

At this point, some people decide to be offended and others just quietly end the conversation. We have found that if we are not willing to sympathize with someone's judgments, they have no desire to talk to us anymore. These people are simply looking for someone to agree with them.

Anyone who has done bad things to us will deal with Jesus on their own. They will have to face judgment, the consequences of which will last for all eternity. By holding on to all the bad stuff we are not affecting them anyway. As long as we hold on to the ungodly connections between those who have hurt us and ourselves, all the bad stuff is ours.

Most of us have been told that we are selfish if we do things for our own benefit. It is time for a dramatic shift. It is time to do something that is good for us, so we can be free of torment and fear. Being selfish for the right reasons and dealing with our issues will free us of the judgments we have received, and those we have put on others.

If you have flown in a commercial airplane, you have been warned that the plane could experience a sudden loss in air pressure. You were instructed to put on your oxygen mask first and, only then, help others around you, because you can't properly help other people unless you are getting enough air.

The same applies with emotional health. If we are not experiencing a good measure of emotional health, we can't possibly help others. In this context, being selfish is not only good for us but for everyone around us. Being selfish can help us be better people.

Now is time to let the Holy Spirit show you the truth, and let the truth set you free. Bag up all the fear, pain, and torment garbage accumulated over the years. It is time to use your authority to be free of all the *yucky* stuff.

Jesus paid for all that stuff, so you can give it to Him. Let the Lord replace it with the good things He has always wanted to give you. His greatest desire is to help you be free. If you would like, it is time to pray.

Sample Prayer:

I renounce the unwillingness to forgive and all idolatry, bitterness, anger, and the underlying fear that produces these responses.

I renounce everything I have received from Satan's kingdom, and I renounce giving anything to Satan's kingdom that serves as a sacrifice.

I command Satan's kingdom to give the Lord Jesus Christ everything received from me as a sacrifice. He paid for all my sins and is the only one worthy to receive these things.

Father, I choose to forgive those who have hurt me in any way. I now place all these people in your hands. I choose to let you judge them, and I ask you to deal with them in accordance with your perfect will.

I ask You, by the power of the shed blood of the Lord Jesus Christ, to cleanse me of everything serving Satan's kingdom associated with unwillingness to forgive, idolatry, bitterness, anger, and underlying fear.

I bind and command everything serving Satan's kingdom to leave every part of my life and being and go where the Lord Jesus Christ sends them. Amen.

REJECTION AND ABANDONMENT

In the Garden of Eden, Adam was given only one law. Adam and Eve rejected it and, in doing so, **rejected God**. We understand that there are over-arching spiritual laws governing the universe. One of those laws states that as **we give** we shall **also receive**. As a result, Adam and Eve received rejection and were sent out of the garden. (Genesis 3:6-24).

When God told Adam he would surely die, the consequences included separation from God, **who is Life**. When Adam and Eve rebelled, the

Garden of Eden was closed to them, and God's presence was withdrawn. As a result, God's function in the earthly realm was greatly affected.

These two people, who had been given dominion in this realm, chose to reject God. They had, in a manner of speaking, evicted Him from **their domain**. (This is similar to what our culture has done, evicting Him from our government, our schools, and the public arena) They were left alone on the earth, which was being influenced by Satan and his minions.

This separation from God's presence must have been much more terrible than anything they could have imagined. Regardless of God's intention, it is reasonable to believe that Adam and Eve felt abandoned.

The definition of abandonment includes being *turned over* to the control or influence of another. In this case, they were turned over to the *control and influence* of the serpent, Satan, whose counsel they **had chosen** to follow. Their abandonment included the reality of *separation* and that of God's *protection being withdrawn*. They also had the sense of *being forsaken*. These results describe the spiritual, emotional and physical *impoverishment* for that which has *been forsaken*. (Merriam-Webster's)

Now, some thousands of years later, we respond naturally through our sin-based paradigm. Most people believe they have been abandoned by God. They believe He has forsaken them and left them under the control of one who hates them. They believe they are still being punished. They live a life of spiritual impoverishment, and bereavement, because they perceive themselves to be unlovable and unloved.

The lies and judgments of the accuser have been passed down in their spiritual genetics, through their fathers. The *voice* always interprets and translates everything that happens, giving it the spin of death. Living in this world influenced by death, everyone has experienced rejection.

For example, imagine a baby boy in mommy's womb. He has developed for roughly nine months while experiencing the comforts and security of a protected world. One day, mommy's body starts doing strange things. It starts pushing and squeezing, giving the baby a new message.

This message is that he must leave, or *die* to, this personal world. The process continues until the baby is ejected, or removed, from mommy's body. Then, a big person takes him away from mommy, cleans him up, and puts him into a plastic bin while others take care of mommy. Suddenly, mommy's body is not wrapped around him. He can't hear her heartbeat, feel her warmth, or experience her presence and comfort. The baby feels absolutely alone.

Eventually, he is put in mommy's arms. That is better, but there are still two layers of skin separating them. After a few days, mommy and the baby go home from the hospital.

Since this is a best-case scenario, we believe he will experience a great deal of mommy's time and attention for the next couple of years. This is good and comforting, for the most part, even though he is still separate.

One day, mommy disappears, and this very small child wonders where she went. He is left with dad, a relative, or maybe a friend. This is not nearly as comforting as being with mommy, so he experiences a new level of rejection and abandonment.

After a few days, mommy reappears holding a bundle of blankets in her arms. As she comes into the house, the little boy is very excited and wants to hug and snuggle because she has been gone so long. She says she can't, because this bundle of blankets is a new baby who needs her attention. The little boy wonders why they needed a new baby.

He continues to experience what he perceives to be rejection and abandonment. It seems to him that every time he goes to mommy for a hug, for closeness, or for security, she is busy with the baby. He might be allowed to watch mommy nursing the baby, stirring memories of security. Even so, he is not allowed to nurse any more because of the baby.

Since mommy came home with new baby, the boy has been wondering, "What did I do? What was wrong with me? Why did you replace me with that terrible baby? How am I going to get my needs met?" These questions gnaw at his heart and he knows it's the baby's fault. If it weren't around, everything would be okay. Resentment, based in fear, grows in the heart of the boy.

As the years go by, the child becomes more accustomed to separation from mommy. Then, one day, mommy tells him that the two of them are going for a drive. He is ecstatic. It has been so long since they've had some *quality* time for just the two of them. They get in the car and drive to a big building with a parking lot.

They enter the building and mommy speaks with a woman. Mommy encourages him to play with the other children while the grownups talk. He does so, but later thinks of something important he wants to tell her. When he looks around, she is gone. He asks the woman where his mommy is. He is told she had to go, but would be back later. He experiences a new level of rejection and abandonment, combined with betrayal of trust.

He doesn't know how to deal with all those other people, what the rules are, or how to get his needs met. He sees there is constant competition for attention and approval. Later, mommy does come back to pick him up, but the relationship is never the same. As the years go by, this normal child experiences many rejections from other children, from teachers, and from the world around him.

When he reaches adolescence, he begins to experience raging hormones and emotions with a new, magnified intensity. As if that weren't enough, there is a whole new dynamic called the *dating game*. He has gone from trying to survive in relationships with other boys, to establishing relationships with those scary, but desirable, girls. It is now necessary to compete for dominance in the hope of having his needs met.

In earlier years, he would innocently ask another child, "Would you like to be my friend?" Now, as a wise adolescent, he would get his friend to ask a girl, "Would you like to be the friend of my friend?" thinking he won't have to experience rejection if the girl declines. It doesn't work that way. His friend, the girl, and maybe the whole school, know the answer. He not only has to deal with rejection, but also humiliation.

He begins to assemble a form of spiritual protection we call *demonic armor*. This armor is designed to protect him from rejection, humiliation, embarrassment, and pain. It seems to have *pointy things* all over it, designed to keep others away. Sometimes the one getting too close will experience what feels like a mild electrical shock, and quickly move away.

The armor doesn't really work; it merely gives him the illusion of safety. Because many people wear the same kind of armor, the discomfort can be even more impacting. The pointy things exist on the inside as well as on the outside of the armor. Anytime the electrical discharge takes place, everyone involved feels it.

The expectation of rejection and abandonment is deeply planted in his heart. Eventually, this man meets a woman who has similar spiritual and emotional issues, making them compatible. He processes everything she does or says through his spiritual translator, looking for evidences of rejection.

When he perceives the slightest threat of rejection or abandonment, he goes on the offensive. Rather than wait to be rejected, he does or says something to give the message, "YOU CAN'T REJECT ME, BECAUSE I REJECT YOU FIRST!"

How many times have we heard someone say, "It's okay, because I dumped her?" He puts on his brave mask and pretends everything is fine, but inside he still feels wrenching pain at the confirmation that his worst expectations have been fulfilled.

This is a form of self-fulfilling prophecy that comes from deep in the heart. It is based on the fear that rejection and abandonment are normal–that everyone will always do what has been done so often before, because there's something wrong with him. There might also be the fear that God finds it all very amusing and enjoys tormenting him.

These beliefs and fears are based on the perceptions and judgments of a baby, a child, or an adolescent, and are projected into the life of an adult. For the skeptic, we do have another illustration of how powerful the fear of rejection and abandonment can be.

When we were married, we both had these issues. For several years, we spent a great deal of time ministering to each other concerning these issues and many others. In spite of this, my problem persisted.

One evening, the fear of abandonment manifested again, so we asked the Lord to show me the root of this torment. What I received didn't seem to make any sense. Glenna was determined to get to the bottom of this issue, so she insisted I tell her what I remembered.

Very reluctantly, I told her that when I was quite small, my mother sometimes sang a lullaby to my siblings and me before putting us to bed. I didn't see how this could be a significant factor in my life, so I wanted to forget it and move on. Glenna was curious so she asked me to recite the lullaby. The following is what I remembered:

> Three poor little children whose names I don't
> know…were stolen away, on a fine summer's day, and
> left in the woods I've heard people say;
>
> And when it came night, they sobbed and they cried, and
> these poor little children, they lay down and died;
>
> And when they were dead, the robins so red, brought
> strawberry leaves, and over them spread.

As I was reciting this lullaby, I was flooded with emotion and sobbed uncontrollably, with my head on Glenna's shoulder. When the well of emotion had been emptied, we were able to minister to the issue and ask the Lord for restoration. After the ministry, we came to the following conclusion.

Sometime after hearing the lullaby, I may have imagined myself as one of the children left in the woods to die. I don't remember the scenario, but I vividly remember the effects. Even after forty years, I experienced the strong feelings of desolation and fear I had associated with abandonment. Does this seem silly to you?

A little kid hears a lullaby, fantasizes about it, and desperate fears lodge in his heart. It is not a logical issue. This little boy heard a story and began functioning in *creator mode*. The fact that he never actually experienced those things is irrelevant. Because it occurred in his mind, and he experienced the feelings and fears in his heart, the emotional and spiritual consequences were very real.

As we discussed previously, from a ministry perspective, there is no difference between real events, imagined ones, or dreams. They seem to have the same impact on our soul. When we ministered to me concerning the lullaby, we did the same things we would do for any real-life event.

So, if something based on a fantasy can have such a profound effect in this little boy's heart, what about the issues of real life? How much more will they impact the heart of a normal person?

We tend to go through life looking for approval and acceptance from others. Usually, we only find what Satan's kingdom has to offer. If we're afraid that someone is going to reject us, we judge and reject them first. Usually, we do the same with God and His laws. Graciously, God accepts us in spite of our sin and rebellion.

For thousands of years, God has been working methodically to reestablish relationship with people. Even when His people rejected Him and turned to other gods, God continued to love them. When the consequences of their actions brought judgment and disaster upon them, God mourned. *"Oh that my head were waters, and my eyes a **fountain of tears**, that I might **weep day and night** for the slain of the daughter of my people"* (Jeremiah 9:1)! *"I would comfort myself **in sorrow**, my heart is faint in me"* (Jeremiah 8:18).

He assures us, just as He assured Joshua and the children of Israel as they were preparing to enter the Promised Land. He told them not to fear, but to be strong and of good courage. He promised **not to leave them or forsake them**. (Deuteronomy 31:6) Our only hope of receiving the acceptance and approval we long for is to **dive into His arms**. (2 Corinthians 5:21; Matthew 25:34; Luke 22:31-32; Galatians 4:4-7; Romans 15:7)

God didn't reject Adam and Eve. They rejected and abandoned Him. They forced the separation by willfully taking death and sin into themselves. He didn't want them to live forever in a state of spiritual death, so He removed them from His garden. He demonstrated His desire to reestablish relationship by sending His Son to pay for all our sins and free us from the power of death, in all its forms.

We have a formula, based on science, math, twenty years of teaching, and twenty-six years of engineering, to determine who needs ministry for rejection. We have used this formula many times, in many churches around the world, and it has never failed. According to our formula, *only the people wearing skin* have been affected by these things and need ministry.

Once again, it is time to be selfish and do what is best for you, your soul, your life, and your relationship with your heavenly Daddy. We ask the Lord to shine His light into your soul and minister to you so you can give Him all the fear and pain. Then He can set you free and change you forever. If you want this, it is time to pray.

Sample Prayer:

In the name of the Lord Jesus Christ, I renounce all the power of rejection and the fear of rejection. I renounce abandonment and the fear of abandonment.

I renounce believing the lies of Satan regarding my being rejected by God and my being unacceptable. I renounce every spirit or voice serving Satan's kingdom associated with rejection and abandonment, affecting my life in any way.

I renounce everything I have received from Satan's kingdom as a result of these sins. I command them to go where the Lord Jesus Christ sends them.

I renounce giving anything to Satan's kingdom in return. I command Satan's kingdom to give the Lord Jesus Christ everything received from me. He paid for all my sins and is the only one worthy to receive all these things.

My Lord, I ask you to restore to me everything I need to be whole and complete as you created me to be. I now proclaim that I am accepted and loved by my God and Father in Heaven forever. Amen.

SHAME, WORTHLESSNESS AND PRIDE

We have read that a cord with three strands is very hard to break. (Ecclesiastes 4:12) We believe this section describes just such a cord. Shame, worthlessness, and pride have much in common.

If I were to shout angrily at Glenna for something I thought she had done, and then discovered she hadn't, you might think I had committed a sin. You might be offended because I shouted at my wife. Some people get very upset at the thought of any form of spousal attack.

After my outburst, I could feel remorse for what I've done and ask for her forgiveness. I could ask those around who might have been offended for their forgiveness. I could even go before God and repent for what I had done. That is the beauty of the new covenant. When we **do something wrong** or commit sin, **we can repent** and it's blotted out.

Some of us have been told we **are something wrong**, we were a **mistake,** or we were an **accident.** We may feel shame as a result of experiencing abuse at the hands of bigger, stronger, or more powerful individuals, who were emotionally broken and fouled up. Abuse provokes feelings of degradation, guilt, betrayal, and rage in the victim. These feelings evolve to self-hatred, self-condemnation, self-judgment, self-defilement, and self-destruction.

We may judge ourselves and believe that it was our fault or that we deserved punishment. When we believe these lies, we also judge others, including our heavenly Father, based on those lies. We forget the truth of Scripture promising that if we believe on Him we will not be put to shame. (1 Peter 2:6)

We all have the same enemy who tells us there is something wrong with us. It may be something we can change, such as hair color, or the condition of our teeth; or it may be something we cannot change, such as our true gender, identity, destiny, or family.

What if my mother and father had agreed before my conception that they really wanted another girl? Throughout the pregnancy they verbalized their desire for a girl and suddenly, there was a little boy. In his heart, the baby knows he is not what they wanted.

Perhaps a father was so afraid of responsibility he didn't want any children? He didn't care whether it was a girl or boy; he didn't want to face the overwhelming responsibility. What if parents believed they couldn't afford to have children, and mom discovered she was pregnant?

What if a baby is the wrong color, the wrong shape, the wrong size, or the wrong anything? There are as many reasons for a baby to feel unwanted, as there are people. Everywhere we go, the normal shame issues exist and manifest in much the same way.

We've been to the Philippines, where people with enough money go to *bleaching parlors* to have their skin bleached. Their perception is that someone with light colored skin is more lovable, acceptable, or sexy. We come back to the States and many people go to *tanning parlors*. Their perception is that someone with dark colored skin is more lovable, acceptable, or sexy. Normal people everywhere strive to be something they are not.

People stress concerning their bodies. The size, shape, and proportions of specific body parts have all become obsessions. People have been convinced that **something is wrong with them.** Many believe it is necessary to change hair color in order to be lovable. They believe it is mandatory to have the right kind of athletic shoes, brand of jeans, antiperspirant, or mouthwash. Have you ever noticed the TV commercials are designed to convince us this is true?

We can't repent for something we **are**, even if we don't want to be that something. There is **nothing to repent** if our parents didn't want us, and don't know how to love or nurture us. Regardless of why our families are dysfunctional, the effects on us are the same. We cannot control these conditions, so we can't fix them. The people making decisions are not subject to our authority, so we have no responsibility for them.

When we are not receiving the blessings of our parents or other authority figures, we are more inclined to believe the lies of our enemy. When deciding how to deal with this dilemma, there are many options. We have selected two for discussion.

Worthlessness, or "The Tortoise"

The first option, in one extreme, is to decide there is no hope because we are worthless. No one will ever love us, care about us, or want to provide for our needs. Instead, people always want to use and feed upon us. Some of us decide that people are just too dangerous, so we protect ourselves. Some people have told us they had built a wall around themselves.

We imagine this wall to be a spiritual covering all around like a spiritual tortoise shell. It seems to have beneficial effects. In hallways at school, it functions as a force field that holds people at a distance, giving us a *safety zone*. At parties or public gatherings the shell enables us to stand against a wall and blend into the background, like camouflage. We are the wallflowers. We are motivated by the fear of being mistreated again.

We have judged other people, we have judged God, who created this painful life, and we have judged ourselves. The problem with our self-imposed shell, *or cell*, is that it also protects us from the only One who can help us find peace for our souls.

When we succumb to the **fear of worthlessness**, we may attempt to compensate for our hopeless state by being a *people pleaser*. We attempt to earn what we need. When people don't respond in a loving and accepting way, we assume it is because there is something wrong with us. We react in cycles of despair, hopelessness, and helplessness.

When we remove ourselves from social interaction, or become an emotional slave to other people, we are in **bondage to idolatry**! We allow other people, and their potential reactions, to control our lives and define our identity and destiny.

Pride, or "The Hare"

The second option, in the other extreme, is what we call pride, producing a **false sense** of our own **importance** or dignity, and **arrogance**. Pride generally leads to selfishness and opens wide the door through which the enemy can enter. It includes wrapping ourselves in a spiritual identity of *the hare*. Instead of hiding us from view, this shell demands attention. The hare dashes around performing, to prove to everyone how fast, wonderful, and powerful he is.

It may seem strange to equate pride with shame and worthlessness but we are sure this is scriptural. (Proverbs 11:2, 13:10, 16:18, 29:23). We view this as a circular pattern, with shame producing pride and pride producing shame. If we view this as the other side of the shame/worthlessness coin, it makes perfect sense.

Someone who feels shame is driven to find ways to compensate. We may attempt to compensate for our hopeless state by being oppressive or domineering. We might also claim superiority over others. In this case we have a desperate need for validation and justification. When we are motivated by these needs, our attitude is, *just be reasonable and agree with me*!

Arrogance is an attitude of superiority manifested in an overbearing manner or in presumptuous claims. For example, "I don't care if you don't like me! I don't care if my parents don't like me! I don't need blessings and approval from anybody! I'm going to be the most powerful and successful person in the world! God help you if you get in my way; I will crush you like a grape!"

The fear of being put down or disapproved causes us to **demand** honor. We demand that people acknowledge and praise our works. When they don't respond the way we want, we assume there is something wrong with them.

Some of us in the church function this way, if not with our words, with our actions. We work feverishly to accomplish good things to impress others. We desperately seek recognition for all the good things so we can feel good about ourselves. We may also be seeking recognition from God, because we think we are **essential** to His master plan.

In our opinion, much of what is being done *for God* is actually being done with this motivation. When we do good things for the wrong reasons (shame, fear, worthlessness, pride, or obligation), we are functioning in sin, and our good works will be of **no spiritual value**.

Our understanding of Scripture leads us to believe that these works, done for the wrong reasons, will all be burned up as hay, straw, and stubble at the Judgment. The only works that will be shown as gold, silver, and precious stones, will be those motivated by love. (1 Corinthians 3:11-15)

Boasting doesn't seem to impress God. He has saved us from death and given us the right to dwell with Him forever. He has bestowed his kindness upon us, not because of anything we have done, but as a gift **lest anyone should boast**. (Ephesians 2:4-9)

The apostle Paul presented it very clearly. When we speak for the wrong reasons, **we are like a clanging symbol**. Even when we understand great truths, without love **we are nothing**. If we give to the poor or even sacrifice ourselves, **so we may boast**, without love there is **no spiritual benefit**. (1 Corinthians 13:1-3)

Paul was speaking specifically about the gift of salvation, but the issue seems to be the same. When we are motivated by pride and the need to validate or exalt ourselves, we tend to boast. We draw attention to our good works and all the ways we facilitated the fulfillment of God's master plan. Everyone should be grateful for all we have done.

We would normally be called jerks or nuisances. We have enclosed ourselves in a spiritual shell for protection. We judge other people, the Creator of this painful life, and ourselves. We, too, are motivated by the fear of being mistreated and abused. We allow others, and their potential reactions, to control our lives and define our identity and destiny so we are in **bondage to idolatry**!

Someone at this end of the spectrum has a desperate need to be acknowledged publicly for good works. We seek the spotlight so everyone can see, and we can feel the radiance of **our glory**. Unfortunately, no amount of acceptance or approval can fill the black hole in our hearts. No amount of approval will satisfy the need of someone motivated by shame.

We understand that people may function at one extreme today and the other tomorrow. We do tend to be double-minded. Whether we try to exalt others (as the tortoise) or ourselves (as the hare), we are functioning in idolatry!

Defilement

The words used for defilement, in Hebrew and Greek, include concepts that can apply internally or externally. These words refer to ceremonial or moral **contamination**, making a **person** or thing **unclean**. To defile is to **corrupt the purity or perfection** of something or to **desecrate** it. (Merriam-Webster's) This could include gender, identity, or destiny.

In our studies, we have determined that we can defile ourselves, our flesh, the temple (God's house), the land, holy places, food, garments, gold, silver, etc. Although people and things can be defiled, they retain the identity they had before they were contaminated.

I have one identity given to me by my Creator. My identity doesn't change because of what I do. I can act differently, change my appearance, or assume an alias, but my identity remains the same.

If I sit in a garage and make the sounds of a car, have I become a car? If I climb into a tree, swing from the branches, and make the sounds of a monkey, have I become a monkey? If I roll in the mud after a rain and make the sounds of a pig, have I become a pig? In any of these situations, has my **true identity** changed?

If other people see the mud, *they* might be confused; if I look in the mirror, *I* might be confused; but when my heavenly Daddy looks at me, *He* is not confused. He has X-ray vision and can see through the mud. He always sees who I really am. Mud never confuses Him. That is why He always loves me, no matter what I do.

With this in mind, what would happen if I went to a gay bar and did the things a homosexual would do? Have I become a new creation with a new identity? Some people say yes, others say no. Isn't it interesting? When we talk about becoming a car, a monkey, or a pig, people can understand the concept, but when we discuss something about which they have strong feelings, it is not as simple.

Suddenly, our identity can be changed through sinful actions. God, through His **infinite** ability, creates us to be one thing; we, through our **limited** ability, give ourselves a new identity. We accept the lie that what **we have done** defines who, and what, we now are. It may even be possible for our identity to change because of the things someone else **does to us**. Both they and we must be amazingly powerful.

Do you remember the paragraph above? Many things, maybe anything, can be defiled. Did you notice that, even though all these things can be defiled, they remain what they were before? Things can be made imperfect or physically unclean (by being rolled in the mud). From our perspective, any of these effects can represent disaster in our lives. From God's perspective, we need only take a spiritual shower and **wash off the mud**.

In this life, **defilement is normal**. Our Father sent Jesus so we could be free of the mud and its defiling effects. When defiling things are done by or to us, we need Him and the power of a cleansing agent, His blood. This is really not complicated.

Wrong Perceptions

In the heart of a child, the truth of a situation is not what dictates a response. The response will always be based upon the **perception of truth**. (Proverbs 23:6-7) We understand that a person's identity and destiny can be defiled by his perceptions. These perceptions, believed in the heart, can be formed through hatred of the image of father, mother, family, others, or self.

When Glenna was quite small, she was sitting in the front seat of the family car between her parents. Everyone was joking and having fun. For some reason, she reached over to touch the steering wheel. Instantly, her older brothers, dad, and mom all shouted loudly, "No! Don't touch the wheel!"

The motivation of her family was to keep her from doing something that could endanger everyone. They had no desire to hurt or offend her, but that was not her interpretation. Her perception was that she had been treated unjustly and harshly. She thought everyone yelled at her because they were angry. She said, "**You** yelled at me and **hurt my feelings**."

She was offended and produced much negative energy. Is that cause for condemnation? Of course not, it is a normal sinful reaction. In Glenna's situation, the emotional and spiritual effects were the same as they would have been had she been abused. In her heart, she **perceived** that she had been abused.

The reality of a situation is not relevant to the heart; the perception of the person is. Both children and adults may react negatively to something that is for good, when it has been presented badly. When God is quoted as proclaiming, "Thou shalt not," the normal reaction is, "**Who does He think He is**?" Whether an abuse is real or perceived, negative reactions to it are normal. The reactions are based on perception.

Many years later, someone (like John) could say something louder than perceived necessary, and Glenna's reaction could be the same as those of the child. The little voice could say, "You are mad at me; You are yelling at me and you have hurt my feelings."

The triggering situation could be something very insignificant, from an adult perspective. The conditioned response, based in fear, causes "the little girl of Glenna's heart" to react in sin. The reaction isn't logical, nor does it have much to do with what the other person really does, because it has become automatic.

Through the process of renewing our mind we discover the truth. We realize that we are not qualified to judge others or ourselves. We also realize that our old habits and our programmed automatic responses no longer make sense; they are harmful to others and to ourselves. We begin to realize our attitudes and perceptions need to change.

Often, an accusing voice we call *the blackmailer* tells us we dare not expose those shameful, hidden sins because of all the terrible things that will occur if we confess them. He reminds us of the bad things we have done as well as those that have been done to us. The blackmailer tells us how crummy and worthless we are, and how much shame we are supposed to feel.

When we feel the shame, we don't dare tell anyone else. He wants us to maintain the old programming, so he tells our heart it is necessary for our survival. After all, it must be good because we have survived until now.

Instead of listening to him, we need to renew our minds with the truth. As this process continues we are better able to hear the voice of the Spirit of Life. He gives us the understanding that will reprogram our hearts. We can ask Him to bring the blackmailer's lies to our attention so we can reject them.

If we make a list of all the things we don't want to admit to anyone, we should pick the one that represents the greatest dread. That item will usually be the one which has the most fear and shame attached to it. If we *brave it through* and deal with that issue, pulling out the fangs of *the blackmailer*, we will experience the greatest degree of deliverance, healing, and restoration.

As we proceed with the renewing of our minds, and follow the prescription of confessing the hidden things of shame (2 Corinthians 4:2), our lives begin to change. Many of the old attitudes and mindsets are no longer in force. We are able to see ourselves, and the world around us, in a different way.

There are consequences for our sins. Once we have repented of sin, we must deal with the consequences that already exist in our lives resulting from acts of our own free will. God will not be mocked. (Galatians 6:7) After renouncing the hidden things of shame, we proclaim the power of the blood of Christ over those former attitudes and activities. (2 Corinthians 4:2; I John 1:7) We renounce the iniquity that already exists in our lives, souls, and bodies. When we have done our part, the Deliverer does His part.

Christians need to belong to a church that encourages growth and manifests the grace of God, not the condemnation of the enemy. In that environment, we feel free to be transparent concerning our struggles or problems so we can ask for help. If we don't have that kind of relationships we feel isolated and discouraged. If, as the body of Christ, we can't stand together, we fall apart. That is, of course, Satan's goal. It is time we work with one another to be real.

Only Jesus was perfect; so we shouldn't demand perfection in ourselves or in others. We encourage you to take off the church mask and be real.

Idealized or Idolized Self

Another outstanding method for self-defilement is through our efforts to be the infinite Creator. God gave us creative abilities and told us how to use them. He told us what things we are to meditate on and how to take every thought captive to the obedience of Christ.

Many people experience the judgment that nothing they do seems to be good enough. They always feel they have failed, they are worthless and unacceptable, and God could not love them.

The reason they can't become involved in any kind of ministry is because they are not qualified or worthy. We remind them about Moses, David,

Abraham, and the others who did not feel worthy. None of this registers, because *the voice* tells them there is no hope.

A few years ago, we were in a village in southern France conducting a seminar. I asked everybody to close their eyes and see, in their mind, the face of their **greatest critic**. After everyone acknowledged that face, we prayed to be set free from judgments and condemnation.

Glenna had a particularly interesting experience during this exercise. We would like to explore her findings. We'll start with another scenario.

A little girl is feeling depressed. She had been inside trying to get daddy's attention because he was home. He finally responded to her by instructing her to go outside and play. He was busy and didn't have time for her just then.

She wonders why he doesn't want to spend time with her. He is at work most of the time, and when he is home, she wants to be with him. If she were smarter, prettier, taller, or had long hair, would he want to be with her? If she made better grades at school, would he want to be with her? Is there something she could do or be that would change his feelings toward her?

As she wonders, **she sees images in her mind** of all the things she could possibly be that would make her more lovable and acceptable to her daddy. Then, *she begins to imagine* what that girl would be like. *Her fantasies* bring her comfort, because, in them, daddy shows he loves her and isn't too busy to be with her.

Another day, this girl is in school and her *friends* don't want to play with her. They have a new friend and she is now outside of that special circle. As if this weren't enough, the teacher reprimands her for things she's doing to earn acceptance.

During free time *she imagines* who and what she could be to earn acceptance and approval from the teacher and her classmates. She is comforted because the person she creates in her mind is acceptable and lovable to everyone.

She becomes an adolescent with normal adolescent concerns. She notices that the captain of the football team is attracted to taller, cuter girls. The girls accepted for the cheerleading squad are taller, more slender, and have prettier hair than she has. She sees qualities in other people that are attractive, and thinks if she had them, she would be more desirable and acceptable.

As more years go by, *she imagines* being a lover, a friend, the perfect student, or the president of the college class. She meets many people and judges herself by who they seem to be and what they do. Eventually, she meets a special young man who seems to fit her image of someone she could love. Their relationship develops, and they marry.

In her mind they should *live happily ever after*, but it doesn't work that way. She discovers she doesn't know how to be a perfect wife and mother; or how to perfectly take care of a house and family. Once again, she falls into the old pattern. She finds quiet times to imagine and fantasize about what and who *she should be*.

Later, some friends tell her and her husband about Jesus. They agree to attend church the following Sunday and are very impressed by what they hear. As a result, they both go forward and accept Jesus as their Savior, to the applause of everyone around.

Now she has a whole new set of challenges to deal with. She was never trained to be the perfect Christian or the perfect disciple. At church she wonders what other people think of her. She watches others to see how to dress, how to stand, how to worship and praise, and how to respond to other people.

She realizes that she is terribly inadequate for her new position as a Christian. People do and say things to her that she finds embarrassing and she does things that embarrass her. She realizes she is woefully lacking in the faith of a *good* Christian. So now, in her quiet time, *she imagines* what it would be like to be a perfect Christian.

She has been competing with God all her life by trying to *create herself* in the image of what she thought would be acceptable. Each time she sat in thought, fantasized, and imagined, she made additions to the image. This idealized image is like Frankenstein. It has been put together with scraps of this and scraps of that and is the product of death.

She took upon herself the job of being a creator, because she rejected the work of the Creator. She rejected who she was as a girl and continued to reject herself as a woman. She responded to her own self-hatred, self-rejection, and self-condemnation by creating. As life goes on, she continues to add to her *idealized image* and the image she sees in her mind continues to evolve.

This composite image has become a full-sized body mask hiding the identity of a familiar spirit. She invited this familiar spirit into her heart through her own judgments, sinful fantasies, and imaginations. The voice of this spirit always condemns, judges, ridicules, belittles, mocks, and puts her down. It tells her how worthless, unlovable, and imperfect she is.

It is the voice behind *her creation*, that speaks into her mind continually telling her how pitifully inadequate she is. This creation has become her **primary competitor**. It has also become her **primary judge and critic**. Every time she hears the negative words of the condemning voice, she feels defeated.

Her life has become a cycle of unpleasant emotions. *The voice* condemns her, sending her into depression, which progresses to despair, then hopelessness, helplessness, and finally, the pit of doom. As she goes through this process, the voice continues to beat on her without pity, mercy, or grace. It sounds like her voice, but it comes from *the image she created* of who she should be.

Glenna saw an image of her idealized self, her greatest critic. After the meeting, she spoke of the revelation she received, and we decided this would be an appropriate place to focus our attention. Since then, we have heard the clues indicating the presence of this particular enemy. As a result, we've heard hundreds of people describe how condemned, worthless, ugly, and unlovable they feel. They have described the need to compete and the despair of not being able to.

In most cases, we have been able to help them understand the problem by describing a scenario similar to the one above. They could see how this problem had evolved throughout their own lives. They could see how they had been deceived by a familiar spirit wearing a mask.

There are two issues. The first involves our **attempt to be a creator,** like God. Because we hate the way God created us, we try to do something about it. We conclude that our survival or our ability to get our needs met is based upon our ability to re-create ourselves. Does this mean we are bad? No, this means we are normal.

The second issue is the **rejection of self**. The way people respond to us stimulates us to judge ourselves as being unlovable, unworthy, and unacceptable. This produces self-hatred, self-judgment, self-condemnation, and self-destruction. We believe this is why people go through so much effort to change themselves, which is **self-defilement**.

People have described many interesting images to us. One person saw herself as a little girl in royal garb, sitting on a throne. Some have seen themselves as Rambo, Superman, a cowboy, or some other superhero. Others described themselves as slaves, or like Cinderella. Someone dealing with anorexia saw themselves with a *perfect* body with a voice identified as *Anna*. The possibilities are only limited by the imagination.

We have a very diligent enemy. Fantasizing about being someone or something other than we are may create spiritual contracts and agreements that put us in bondage. We may see ourselves as being stronger, smarter, bigger, smaller, more capable, more popular, or more attractive. That idealized image takes on the character of a rival. It becomes the *perfection* we can never achieve no matter how hard we try.

Through our sin, we inevitably open our little door. At some point a servant of Satan puts on the mask, assumes the role, and speaks with a voice that sounds like ours. This voice is terribly powerful because it continually criticizes us and puts us down. The results can be devastating when we believe it.

When we believe we have no value or importance, we tend to feel despair and a sense of futility. We either give up completely or attempt to compensate by striving to establish our worth. We saw a movie once in which the hero was preparing to engage in combat with a creature dedicated to destruction. The hero asked the creature why it was doing all the things it did. The creature's response was to explain that the master it served knew that **people without hope are easy to control**. The movie, in general, was really stupid but this one statement was profound.

We've met many people who seem to think there is no hope. At some point they have decided they might as well give up. It would be hard to estimate how many times we've heard, "Why doesn't God just let me die?" The answer is: BECAUSE HE LOVES YOU!

Our True Identity

Remember our discussion earlier entitled Who Is Man?

When a man and woman join together sexually, there is the possibility of a baby being produced, but in many cases there is no baby. In some instances, the union occurred at the wrong time. It is possible one or both of the parents are *incapable* of producing children. Sometimes, everything seems to be ideal for conception, but nothing happens.

Men and women might join together for many reasons. Sometimes it's because they want children. Often it's just because of animal lust. They could be lonely, afraid, or looking for comfort. They might need to feel needed. Some want to possess another person and have dominion over them. There are many motives having nothing to do with babies.

On the other hand, there are many people who desire to have children, but can't. The medical establishment has fertility clinics and research organizations to help people produce children. There are many people who employ the services of these organizations and still fail. Part of the problem is that they believe this process is purely biological. We don't agree.

When a woman and man join together, they can only provide the egg and sperm necessary to produce a baby. Then again, on some occasions, the finger of God touches the union and says, "I WANT THIS ONE." Now there are three parts: the *spirit part*, and the parts provided by mom and dad. The Lord is never confused or driven by fear-based motivations. He decides He wants THIS ONE, and a baby is conceived.

We are convinced that a human baby cannot happen unless God causes the happening. This being the case, it is **impossible** for a person to be **an accident** or **a mistake**. It is impossible to be from the wrong parents, the wrong family, the wrong city, or the wrong culture. It is impossible to be born with the wrong skin color, hair color, size, or shape.

Because we exist in a world influenced by darkness and death, there are challenges. There are things we don't understand. Many of the things we view as terrible are the products of the sin and death in the world. Some people are born with genetic diseases or problems with their soul. We do not believe the Lord desired that any of His children would have to go through these things.

We do believe He loves all of His spiritual children without reservation or limitation. All of us were created because He wanted us. When we focus only on *here* and *now*, it is easy to lose sight of *forever*. It is not necessary for us to understand His reasoning or His master plan. It is only necessary for Him to understand. He proclaims that His thoughts and ways are much higher than ours. (Isaiah 55:8-9)

We do believe that in the midst of it all, He shows us His love, His mercy, and His acceptance. He understands that we will be taken into a place of captivity, but He also proclaims that He will gather us from all the places of captivity. We view the *here and now* as the only reality, and in that context, it's easy to misunderstand His motivations. It is easy for His critics to condemn Him as being unloving because He allows things of which they do not approve.

On the other hand, He proclaims that His thoughts toward us include **peace** and a **future with hope**. He promises to listen when we call and, when we search for Him with all our heart, He promises we will find Him.

(Jeremiah 29:10-13) He assures us He has a plan for us, and it's all for good because He loves us.

When we know the truth of who we really are according to our heavenly Daddy, we don't have to believe the lies. When we read the parables spoken by Jesus, we get some idea of how valuable we are to our Lord. (Luke 15:4-32)

We have all functioned as prodigal sons and daughters, making covenant with the enemies of our Father. We have wasted the resources God gave us on the defiling things of this world, wallowed in the pigpen, eating with the pigs. We have rebelled against Him, rejected Him, and run from Him **because of shame**. We have allowed fear to rule in our hearts and motivate our judgments against others, against ourselves, and even against Him.

There are people who might look down their noses at us. There are celebrities, governmental officials, people called *royal*, and many others who might disregard us. If we look for the approval and acceptance *of these mortals*, we will probably be disappointed. Many of them wouldn't esteem us worthy of their time or attention.

On the other hand, the King of the universe views us as important. He has time for each of us. He has proclaimed we are worthy of His attention. *"The Lord your God is in the **midst of you**, a Mighty One, a Savior! He will **rejoice over you** with joy; He will rest… in His love; **He will exult over you with singing**"* (Zephaniah 3:17, AB). [Emphasis ours] (Also, Matthew 18:4; 2 Chronicles 7:14; Jeremiah 29:11; Ephesians 1:3-11)

We can stop believing the lies that motivate fear, and learn how to receive God's love and give our love in return. We can reflect His love to others. We can accept the truth of who we are as the highest of His creation. We can give up the shame with its judgments and fears and let Him replace these things with perfect love, acceptance, and approval.

He is not like anyone we've ever known. He is unlike any daddy, brother, friend, any other family member, or authority figure we have ever encountered. He is absolute Love, Power, and Majesty, and He has been waiting thousands of years for *us*.

When He rolls out the scroll spanning *forever past* to *forever future*, He sees things we cannot even imagine. He sees all the good things in eternity only He knows. He sees this reality and views with joy the potential of relationship forever. Can you see the magnitude of this? The King of the universe wants to have fellowship with us forever!

With great anticipation, He has been waiting for the time when we can be His dwelling place and He can be ours. When He can rejoice over us with joy, and exult over us with singing. He has been waiting for the time when we can **enter into eternity** with Him, so we can experience the joys and glories of His creation. Are you getting a sense of the magnitude of this truth? If you are, it is again time to pray.

Sample Proclamation:

In the name of the Lord Jesus Christ, I renounce believing any lies concerning my true identity and destiny. I proclaim that nothing I have ever done, or that has ever been done to me, defines who I am, or assures that my past will always control me.

I renounce all the constructs and images associated with any idealized image representing any other person, place, object, substance, being, or myself. I proclaim that everything spiritual I have received into or onto me, disguising my true identity, is now destroyed by the power of the shed blood of the Lord Jesus Christ.

I renounce every familiar spirit associated with any idealized image. I renounce all real and perceived benefits, received from these spirits. I renounce all judgments, the need to compete and everything else associated with these familiar spirits. I renounce everything I have received from Satan's kingdom that has defiled my true gender, identity, and destiny.

I renounce giving energies, sacrifices, or anything else to Satan's kingdom. I command all these things be given to the Lord Jesus Christ because He has paid for all my sins and He is the only One worthy to receive them.

I renounce everything serving Satan's kingdom associated with shame, defilement, worthlessness, victimization, helplessness, hopelessness, doom, self-hatred, self-rejection, self-condemnation, self-judgment, self-destruction, self-defilement, self-righteousness, pride, selfishness, self-exaltation, and self-pity.

I command all these things to leave every part of my life and being and go where the Lord Jesus Christ sends them.

I renounce seeking my own lusts and desires. I renounce the need to be served and exalted. I proclaim that the Lord Jesus Christ is my Lord. In my own ability and power, I am unable to accomplish any good thing.

I choose to humble myself and give all the glory and honor to my Father in heaven and the Lord Jesus Christ. I am grateful for the privilege of serving Him and being the tool through which He does good works.

I proclaim the victory given to me by the Lord Jesus Christ. I am created in the image of God and am worth the life of His Son, Jesus, who gave His life for me, personally. I am a child of light given the power to overcome and triumph over the trials of this world. I am of God and have overcome because He who is in me is greater than he who is in the world. Amen.

Since God likens us to trees, the base of the tree represents the first year of life. According to Hebrew tradition, the first year of life begins at the moment of conception. It includes the nine months of gestation, the time of being born, and the time of being named and identified as a new member of the community. In Jewish tradition, a person is then one year old. The events that occur during this first year represent the seeds and/or roots of this person's life. We believe the most normal thing is for this new person to perceive him/ her self to be the Center of the Universe.

WHAT ABOUT THE FIRST YEAR?

God tells us **He knew us** and **formed us** in our mother's womb. (Psalm 139: 13-16) He even told the prophet Jeremiah, "Before I formed you in the womb **I knew you**; before you were born I sanctified you; I ordained you a prophet to the nations" (Jeremiah 1:5). [Emphasis ours] As spoken to Jeremiah, the word for "know" is the same as with a familiar friend. The word can also mean to make to be something. Unlike the world around us, He doesn't treat us like a nonentity simply because we haven't yet breathed air.

According to Hebrew tradition, presumably established by God's design, the **first year of life** begins at conception and includes the months in the womb, the birth, a period of prayer and fasting before the baby is named, and a time of purification of the mother. Based on this understanding, the world might state that a person is 12 years old based upon the number of years since being born. The same person would be 13 years old including the first year of life.

When functioning in ministry, we have imposed upon ourselves a simple rule. We can only minister to the issues the recipient of ministry tells us about, or that we **know must exist**. As we are always looking for the deepest roots of any issue, it is logical to explore the one experience everyone has had. This includes everything that concerns *the first year of life*.

The Deepest Roots

A number of years ago, we attended a conference in the Midwest that dealt with issues associated with *ritual abuse* and *satanic ritual abuse*. The only difference between these terms seems to be the religious affiliations of the abusers. In both cases, people who are controlled by evil subject children to incredible abuses.

The principal speakers of this conference didn't seem to believe in spiritual issues such as demons. During one break, I asked one of them to tell us how he dealt with spiritual issues. He explained that when his clients believed in demons and demonic infestation, he would pray with them to exorcise the demons. He found that complying with the wishes of his clients sometimes aided with their therapy. He didn't believe in demons but he did believe in results.

When we began ministering regarding the first year of people's lives, we adopted a similar attitude. Frankly, at that time we hadn't done sufficient biblical study to satisfy ourselves that ministry to this time in a person's life would be valid. At the same time, the purpose of our ministry was to find the beginning of problems, to search for the point at which seeds of emotions and reactions were planted in the heart.

Often, we would do everything we could to resolve adult, teen, and childhood issues. As we were ministering, it became more common for people to relate incidents they believed occurred during the first year of their lives. The problems seemed to be as varied and unique as the people involved. This challenged our *logical approach* to ministry.

Many people have told us of events that occurred during the birthing process or even before. Some knew about them because a family member had told them, but others would say they had *suddenly remembered* something, or they *just knew* something they had not previously known. Because of our ministry model, we would minister to these issues as though they were true.

We had adopted the attitude of the psychiatrist discussed above. If this person believes something is true, we believe their perception should be honored. We didn't know what to believe about these reports but we did believe in results. We have seen many positive results, we've done a great deal more study, and our beliefs have evolved.

Spiritual Death Transmitted

The baby in the womb receives the spiritual components of sin and death automatically through daddy. Receiving these components makes *sinful responses normal*. This being the case, we are convinced that sin begins in the womb.

The definition of sin includes everything that is not produced by faith. (Romans 14:23) Since faith is normally considered to be a positive response, all **fear-based responses** such as worry and dread must be sin. With unfortunate regularity, the seeds of death are planted during the first year. The baby, existing in its own world, must consider itself to be the **center of the universe**.

As the baby develops in the womb, it naturally responds in fear to things experienced by the mother which could affect its survival. In some instances, the mother experiences sickness, pain, or trauma during pregnancy. When this happens, her physical and emotional responses are transmitted to the baby. These responses are processed by the baby, who then reacts **normally**.

If mommy is afraid that daddy is out carousing with other women, the baby will respond according to mommy's fear. The baby can experience feelings of betrayal or insecurity. The baby may assume that, because it is the center of the universe, all of mommy's suffering, unhappiness or trauma is somehow their fault. Because of the emotional charge attached, feelings or responses could represent a threat to the baby's survival. Any such threat would stimulate a normal fearful response.

For example, a thunderstorm terrified a pregnant mother who had been left alone. Her child, now an adult, had always been terrified of thunderstorms and didn't know why. This automatic *sinful response* persisted until the Holy Spirit revealed it in a ministry session.

Other traumas experienced by pregnant moms, such as falling down, having a fight with dad, or being in an auto accident cause strong fear reactions in their babies, and, usually, affect them as adults. In these cases, the *voice* helped the babies judge themselves as being unlovable and unacceptable. These responses, including phobias, are all are *based in sin*.

Former satanists have told us they were tortured while in the womb. They believe their mothers were forced to consume drugs, or poisons, to afflict the babies. Some believe their mothers were tortured with cattle prods, so the babies would also experience the electrical, spiritual, and emotional shock.

They have also described other terrible things that were done to traumatize babies. The perpetrators were doing these things to stimulate *sinful reactions*. We've been told these were deliberate attempts to shatter the soul and subject the babies to the control of those representing Satan's kingdom.

As previously discussed, some people *knew* they were not wanted even while they were in the womb. They were considered an accident or mistake, because mom and/or dad wanted a boy and they were a little girl. They knew they were going to be a disappointment, or a burden, for their family. As a result, they wanted to die. These responses of self-hatred, self-judgment, and the desire to die, are *also sins*.

On the other hand, even in the best situation parents and the medical establishment are imperfect, and babies are born into an imperfect world. Other people have related conversations between their parents that occurred while they were in the womb. In some of these cases, the parents wanted the baby and didn't care whether it was a girl or boy. They were delighted with the fact that the baby would soon be born.

Early in our experience, we would hear this testimony and rejoice. We were glad for this person and would accept this statement without question. We would then move on to some other issue pertaining to ministry. As time went on we discovered we were missing important issues. We needed to find why mom was glad, because it wasn't always a good thing for the baby.

There were so many answers. One child might become a valuable farmhand helping to support the family. Another may have been designated as a *prize pony* the parents could proudly show off. Or maybe they were told mom had always wanted to be a famous ice skater and this child would fulfill her dreams. A child might be expected to compete in the Olympics, play professional football, or become a famous surgeon.

The baby might be told that mommy is giving up an important job or career because of them. The child would be required to compensate mommy by paying this debt. When mommy is old and daddy is gone, this child will be mommy's companion. Only when mommy is gone, no longer needing a caretaker and provider, will this child be allowed to have a life.

Mom or dad may have wanted other significant things in life, and would now enjoy them vicariously through the child. They could have felt cheated because they *had* to get married and this baby would be *their recompense*. On the other hand, maybe the marital relationship is falling apart and this baby is given the job to hold it together. He or she could possibly be given the job to *replace* a child that died.

Maybe mommy is tired of taking care of her spouse and wants someone else to take over the job. Mom could be lonely and this child will be given the job of being her servant. After having three sons, she may desperately want a daughter to function as her *Cinderella*. This will make it possible for her to go back to work or simply have time away from household responsibilities.

There are many *wrong reasons* parents might be pleased to have a baby. In many of these scenarios, this baby is wanted so the parents can have their emotional, or possibly, physical needs met. Isn't this wonderful? The child was wanted, but only to satisfy the selfish agenda of someone else.

After asking the Lord to show them the truth, some people have told us they feared, and even dreaded, coming out of the womb. Their perception was that they clung, as best they could, to the inside of mommy's womb, trying desperately not to be born. They told us they experienced a **terrible fear of life**, because **they knew** they were coming into a world to take on jobs they couldn't possibly do.

These revelations presented us with a dilemma. One possible response to these scenarios is to proclaim, "This is ridiculous. Show me where I can find this in the Bible!" The best we can offer is the reminder that the Lord knew us in the womb.

This doesn't suggest that He will know us someday. We believe this *knowing* suggests a connection of consciousness to consciousness. If we can have a connection of consciousness with Him, why not the mommy within whom we spend the first few months of our lives?

We could be wrong, but if we are, how are we to deal with the testimonies from so many people? How do we dismiss all those who have told us of major life changes once these issues were resolved?

What about the scientific and experiential evidence? When you tickle a pregnant tummy, why does the baby kick if there's no consciousness? When we see sonograms presented in pro-life videos, why do we see babies trying to escape the medical instruments invading their domain and trying to kill them?

We don't believe this is just a fetus, responding instinctively like any other animal. There is ample evidence, for those who want to know, demonstrating that babies in the womb yawn, cry, and respond to physical and emotional stimuli. Every baby exists because **three** free-willed beings made decisions that created it: mom, earthly dad, and heavenly Father. We believe every *baby* has been given consciousness from conception.

We ask the Lord to give you revelation of whatever is important to you concerning your first year of life. He was always there and has perfect understanding concerning all things. He will certainly offer the Father's love, so you can trust Him to deal with you graciously. He won't do anything to hurt you or impose His will on you.

With the help of the Lord, you can know the answers to any questions concerning your first year and infancy. We offer another prayer for you to pray aloud.

> **Sample Prayer:**
>
> **In the name of the Lord Jesus Christ, I renounce all illusions and deceptions concerning my being the center of the universe in place of my heavenly Father.**
>
> **I renounce the voice of the accuser and its function in my mind or in my mouth. I command the destruction of everything associated with demonic goodness or badness applied to, or affecting, any part of my being. I renounce all sinful feelings, emotions, attitudes, beliefs, perceptions, and expectations.**
>
> **I renounce all familiar spirits and everything else serving Satan's kingdom, associated with being the center of the universe. I renounce all their power and control over any part of my life or being, and I renounce all contracts and agreements I have ever made with them.**
>
> **In the name of the Lord Jesus Christ, I command the destruction of everything spiritual which has been put into, or onto, the baby of my heart, causing it to appear ugly, undesirable, unwanted, unlovable, or defiled in any way.**
>
> **I proclaim the destruction of all deceptions that represent the first year of my life, beginning at conception: everything that represents my mother's body; her feelings and emotions; the womb and birth canal; the physical and spiritual umbilical**

cords; and everything that represents the birthing process, including all fear, pain, trauma, rejection, and abandonment.

I proclaim the destruction of all constructs and images that represent real life, dreams, fantasies, or imaginations associated with people, places, objects, events; sights, sounds, smells, tastes, feelings, emotions, body memories, sensations, and stimulations. I command the destruction of everything that would deceive, control, or hold any part of my soul captive to the first year of life, beginning at conception.

I renounce the responsibilities I have taken upon myself for family members, authority figures, or anyone else---for their words, actions, sins, failures, inadequacies, imperfections, and for their unwillingness, or inability, to give me the love, honor, and respect I deserved as a child of God.

I renounce all these things and all the power and control of these things. I renounce the weight of responsibility, the darkness, death, unclean spirits, familiar spirits, voices, tormenters, accusations, guilt, condemnation, all self-destruction, all forms of defilement---everything I received from Satan's kingdom.

I renounce giving anything to Satan's kingdom. I command that all the energies, emotions, or sacrifices received from me by Satan's kingdom must be given to the Lord Jesus Christ. He alone has paid for all my sins and He alone is worthy to receive all these things.

I renounce the fear of life and the desire for death in order to escape life. I command everything serving Satan's kingdom to leave every part of my life and being and go, now, where the Lord Jesus Christ sends them.

Heavenly Father, I now place into your hands all the parts of my soul associated with the first year of my life and my efforts to be the center of the universe. I relinquish this job and the weight of responsibility for this job.

I ask You to replace all the darkness and death with Your life and light, Your perfect love, approval and acceptance, Your peace and joy, satisfaction and security. I ask You to cleanse my spiritual eyes, my mind, and my heart of everything that would deceive me and prevent me from seeing and knowing

> You as You truly are, or from seeing and knowing myself as You created me to be.
>
> I ask You to surround the core of my heart with Your presence and Your power. I ask You to give me the revelation that You are my Father, and I am your child. I ask You to fill me with the Spirit of adoption. I ask You to show the parts of my soul, representing the first year of life, how different You are from any other person or spirit I have ever known.
>
> I ask You to flood my heart with everything I have never received; everything a perfect father, mother, and family would give; whatever is necessary for me to be free from emotional starvation and all associated cravings and yearnings. I ask You to fill my heart with the knowledge of how valuable and important I am to You and Your kingdom.
>
> I ask You to restore everything that I lost, everything I gave away, everything that was killed, stolen, or destroyed, and everything associated with my true identity and destiny. I ask you to restore everything the core of my heart needs to function as the center of my being so I can be everything You created me to be.
>
> **Thank You. Amen.**

Because of the extreme importance of this issue, we ask you to make this proclamation:

> In the name of the Lord Jesus Christ, I proclaim the truth. It is not possible for the baby I was to be at fault for any bad things affecting my mother or father, or for anything happening outside while I was in the womb. I could not have been a mistake or an accident. I could not have been conceived without the approval and participation of the King of the universe. The Daddy of my spirit had to want me or I would not be here.

IMAGE OF THE FATHER

In recent years, representatives of the government, and even the psychological community, have suggested a child doesn't need a *normal family unit* to thrive. Some have said that any combination of people can function as a family unit and that fathers aren't really essential for child development. We've been told the government, nursery schools, public schools, or *a village* can raise our children better than moms and dads.

When we consider these claims, we look at the government's track record of successes in deciding how much to believe.

In past years, our country has engaged in a massive social experiment. References to the Judeo-Christian God have been removed from schools and public places, while other forms of religion are promoted. Women have been programmed to believe it is demeaning to be a mere *housewife*, and significance depends on having a career.

Men have been given the message they are not really important in the lives of their children because they are incompetent and worthless as fathers. This is what children are being programmed to believe in school, on TV, and by the actions and attitudes of some parents. The media preaches this lie tirelessly through cartoons and sitcoms.

The husband, and father, is depicted as a stupid oaf. We have twenty or thirty years of this kind of programming since *Father Knows Best* was popular. We now have stereotyped father figures as depicted in *Archie Bunker, Married With Children*, and *The Simpsons*.

The media has been doing everything in its power to utterly defile the image of the dad. It also seems intent on destroying the image of our heavenly Daddy. It *may* not be doing this consciously, but is certainly being used by the evil one for his purposes. Today, more than ever, there are those who maintain that the government, or the village, is all children need.

Look at the statistics concerning what has happened in the last thirty years in our schools, our inner cities, and in society, in general. Those who consider themselves *the elite* have taken upon themselves the job of deciding what is best for everyone. They do so according to their humanistic ideals and philosophies.

By working through social experimentation, they don't have to receive truth from Him. They seem to prefer figuring it out for themselves. In fact, people seem more inclined to reject simple truths, as stated in the Bible, preferring to do things the hard way. Do we really want this trend to continue?

Having said all this, we are cautiously hopeful that some members of the scientific and psychological communities may be discovering that the teachings of the Bible are true. We have discovered, through reading about controlled studies, that the father in any family unit is extremely important. There are those who are proposing that families without a loving, nurturing, protecting father produce troubled children. This reminds me of my years in junior college.

When I took basic psychology classes back in the early '70s, I was taught that families were important; that a child has to experience tangible nurturing. This included verbal and physical interaction with parents.

I remember seeing a video about chimpanzees that were being used in a study. Some very young chimps were put in an environment with food and water but nothing that represented parental comfort. They grew to be neurotic and extremely antisocial.

Another group was given food, water, and a teddy bear with a built-in speaker that would make chimp noises. These young chimps grew to be slightly more social and well adjusted. Along with this group, there were some who were given interaction with a real female chimpanzee. These chimps had an even higher level of emotional and social development.

The final group was raised in an environment with mommy and daddy chimps. The females spent most of the time with the young and there were adult males present. The young in this study group were well adjusted and social. When they were put into an environment with other chimps, they were able to interact in healthy ways.

Similarly, we have seen statistics in the past concerning the plight of children of the inner city who don't have a healthy family unit. In these studies, it seems there was a much greater percentage of violence and gang-related activity when there was no father present.

These findings were amazingly reminiscent of what I heard in my psychology classes. The conclusions were interpreted as applying to all children, although the focus was on those in the inner city. Isn't it interesting how theories go through cycles? Here we are roughly thirty years later and the psychological community is again considering that dads may be important after all.

When we look at the world around us, as well as the many people to whom we've offered counseling, we see the problem. Boys apparently can't learn how to function as men, husbands, and fathers without a dad as an appropriate role model. Girls apparently don't learn how to function as women, wives, and mothers unless they've had a mom as a good role model, and a healthy father image in their lives.

For both girls and boys, the presence of a father in the family structure is critical for their healthy emotional development, as well as their ability to understand male-female relationships. The people with broken souls we've met have shown us the importance of finding ways to heal the family structure so children can grow to be well adjusted.

The primary motivation of our enemy is to **distort** and **pervert** the image of our fathers. He wants to destroy our relationship with our earthly dad so he can prevent a meaningful relationship with our heavenly Daddy. If he can do this, he believes he will win.

Believing Heavenly Father Is Like Earthly Father

When dad fails to function in an appropriate way, his children interpret what happened with the help of *the voice*. The goal of *the voice* is to project lies and confusion into the hearts and minds of the children. It might say, "See, this is the way all daddies are. They don't care how you feel or what you think. You can't trust them."

The voice belongs to the accuser, or death, and its purpose is to put a barrier of mistrust between children and their earthly fathers, any authority figures, and, especially, their heavenly Father. Unfortunately, many fathers give the voice plenty of material with which to work. When dad is a molester, an abuser, an alcoholic, a drug addict, is violent, or abandons and rejects, *the voice* gladly provides its interpretation of the circumstances.

Curiously, the voice not only accuses fathers, but it also accuses the child of being at fault. Is it any wonder normal people are so dysfunctional? Is it any wonder that the statistics for divorce, child abuse, pornography, and other defilements look the same for both the secular world and the Church?

Is it any wonder that many people feel obligated to go to church when they would much prefer not to go? They may even raise their hands and sing the songs, pretending to enjoy the service so no one will notice the difficulty they are having. Although they may wear their church masks and go through the motions, nothing is happening in their hearts.

When it is safe to speak honestly, they tell us they get nothing out of the service. They perceive that everyone else in the room seems to be experiencing bliss. They say, "I don't feel anything. I don't feel the love of the heavenly Father, and I don't feel any ability to give Him my love. I don't understand why. What's wrong with God that He won't show me His love?" This is spoken with a sense of hopelessness and despair.

Through the interview process, we find there is an adult soul desperately seeking to know the Father's love. Simultaneously, there may be a child soul part hiding in the recesses of the heart saying, "No! You leave me alone. I don't trust you. Daddies have always done bad things to me and You might hurt me too."

The enemy can use any important authority figure in the life of a child as a tool. Sometimes, when the biological father is not a part of the child's life, someone else functions in that role. Grandparents, aunts, uncles, and stepparents also can contribute to this problem with their words, actions, and attitudes. Even when this is the case, we have found that children can blame the father because he did not protect them from the abuse.

The voice might tell the heart of the child it can protect him from bad daddies. So, the child begins to build a shell of protection around himself, with the help of the spirit behind the voice. At this point, he enters into a contract with the spirit. He has been deceived.

Because the earthly father represents God, it is easy for a child to believe that the heavenly Father is responsible for all the bad things that have happened. Since the heavenly Father is also considered to be the enemy, the shell of protection would prevent His access, as well. At some point, we have to *forgive* God of all those bad things for which our hearts have held Him responsible.

We believe this prayer is important because we need to be free from all illusions. Whatever the Holy Spirit has chosen to show us, it is time to be free and receive the Dad Who will never change or be anything but a perfect Father. Let's pray.

Sample Prayer:

Heavenly Father, I now place every part of my soul and humanity that has ever been deceived into Your hands. I ask You to show me who You really are so I can know the truth.

I renounce believing that You are like that man who was, or is, my earthly father, or like any other man I have ever known.

I renounce believing the lies planted in my heart accusing You. I ask You to forgive me for believing those lies and giving them power in my life.

I ask You to forgive me for judging You based upon those lies. I ask You to forgive me for believing that I couldn't trust You to be in control of my life.

I now forgive You for all the bad things that have happened in my life for which I believed You were responsible.

My Lord, I ask you to restore all of my soul and humanity and everything else I gave away. I ask You to make me whole so I can be all You created me to be, and so I can love You, and know Your love. Amen.

Idealized Images: Good and Bad

There are men who truly want to be good, loving dads for their children. They may come home from work with something of special interest. They may sit and talk or play, wrestle, and be silly, showing they really enjoy spending time with their children. As rare as this seems to be, such fathers do exist.

Inevitably, even these dads make mistakes because they are imperfect. When a good daddy is feeling weak, is impatient, angry, or even sick, he is inclined to function imperfectly. These times can have a major impact on the hearts of children.

The accusing voice is always prepared to speak into little hearts. As before, the whole focus of the enemy is to distort dad's image and destroy our relationships with him and our heavenly Daddy. We believe this has affected every person's life.

When dad demonstrates his imperfections, we, as children, can accept them as just a part of dad, or decide not to acknowledge reality. Sometimes, we develop an **idealized image** of dad as someone larger than life and always wonderful.

In our mind, this image is clothed with **demonic goodness** and becomes the **good daddy** of our imaginary world, so we idolize it. After creating this idealized daddy we interpret reality based on the fantasy. Using our imaginations, we can reinterpret real events using images wrapped in demonic goodness. We now function in the idolatry of adoration.

When life becomes unpleasant, we can simply go to the place where we create our own reality. This produces images or constructs in our mind that look like dad, but are only masks concealing the true identity of **familiar spirits** representing the good daddy.

In another case, there is an image of the **invisible daddy**. It might have been created because the real father died or disappeared. Dads are sometimes gone most of the time, due to work and the need to travel. Sometimes they are in the military and are gone for extended periods of time. Many dads are physically present, but are emotionally unavailable to their children. In order to compensate for having an invisible daddy, it might be necessary to create an acceptable replacement.

On other occasions, there is so much shame attached to the real dad that an image of **idealized daddy** is necessary for emotional survival. Dad may have run off with another woman, betraying mom and abandoning the family. Some dads spend most of their time in a bar with their buddies. Some children have dads they would never want their friends to meet. Many people have had shameful dads or family environments; the reasons are as unique as the people involved.

Whenever dad's true image is unacceptable, it is logical to seek an alternative. He could be called the **acceptable daddy**, masking the identity of a familiar spirit.

The created images or constructs always say and do the right thing, and are always there to provide nurturing and comfort, when needed. They are composed of imagination and perception, and are powered by spiritual-emotional energies. They wear masks that could be spiritually superimposed over any face. Once again, we are engaging in **idolatry of adoration**.

At other times, dad is seen as bad, and is clothed with **demonic badness**. Then the idolatry is in the form of hatred, not only of dad, but also of self. We must be bad if we have such a **bad daddy**. The dad image and its associated familiar spirit are powered by sinful emotional energy.

As we experience abuse from dad or any other male authority figure in our lives, the image grows and changes. It may emphasize the face, the eyes, the fists, or other body parts that *represent the badness*. It could also focus on actions such as violence, intimidation, defilement, or any other activity that represents *badness* in our child's heart.

Because this image is clothed in *demonic badness,* it doesn't represent the real person. It is produced from the child's perspective, in the mind of a child, with the help of *the voice* functioning through the image of *bad daddy*. It looks, acts, and sounds like daddy. We live our life being influenced, even controlled, by **this image of daddy**. Sometimes we hear its words, curses, and tormenting accusations in our mind.

This image could continue to evolve even into our adult life. It could take on characteristics or attributes of any male authority figure, such as a college instructor, an employer, a police officer, a pastor, or someone encountered on the street. The spiritual mask representing this image could also be spiritually superimposed over any face. Many people respond to their spouse, or others in their lives, as though they were the one viewed as the abuser.

Our enemy is not our real dad or any other living person; it is the familiar spirit. We are reminded that we do not wrestle against flesh and blood but against spiritual entities serving the powers of darkness. (Ephesians 6:12) If we can keep this in mind, our ability to deal with people and life will be greatly enhanced.

We do not dismiss, condone, or excuse any actions that were harmful to a child. We are concentrating on the way familiar spirits deceive us and gain access into our soul through our sinful responses to those harmful things. Because of **our sin**, the door opens and the spirit representing iniquity enters.

The relationship between the child and the familiar spirits can become very complex. Over the years, the child can confuse fantasy and reality and go to the familiar spirits for friendship or comfort. Sometimes, even abuse could bring comfort to the heart of a child because it is so familiar and *represents security*. It's amazing to see what some people perceive, or would interpret, as benefits. Because of these *perceived benefits*, the child can fall deeper into idolatry.

The idolatrous relationship prevents the child, and later the adult, from having a relationship with their heavenly Father. The idolatry empowers the spirit and gives it a legal place in the heart of the person. The familiar spirit would, from a spiritual perspective, stand between the person and the heavenly Father.

I offer the following testimony as a simple example of how this can work:

My dad has been a big issue for me. Since I started going through my own deliverance and restoration, most of the things I've dealt with pertained to him directly or indirectly.

Some time ago, Glenna and I were in another city doing a seminar and offering ministry to individuals. We were working with a woman we had met on a couple of previous occasions. We dealt with an issue related to her father and I received a flash of revelation for myself. We continued with her and eventually ended the ministry session.

We invited her to lunch. I told her and Glenna about the flash I believed the Lord had given me. This stimulated her to search more deeply into her own heart. After lunch, we returned to the church and did more ministry with her.

When it was completed, I leaned back in my chair to relax. She looked at me and courageously said, "Now, it's your turn. Remember what you said earlier?" I was trying to forget, but I asked the Lord to show me the issue. I don't remember the process, but I can tell you the outcome.

In my mind, I saw an image of myself as Johnny Boy, a scruffy-haired little guy dressed in old, faded jeans. Throughout our ministry with me, the identity of Johnny Boy has been very significant. This identity represented many things in my life because he lived in the shadow of big John, his daddy. In this particular image, he was standing before a huge throne, and sitting on the throne was an image, or construct, that looked like my dad.

The familiar spirit that had wreaked so much havoc in my life looked like my dad. This mental, or spiritual, construct had a particular demonic sneer on its face that my dad would get when he was manipulating me. He was looking directly at the little boy as if he were saying, "I have you in my control; I will always control you."

My emotions went from amazement to fear, and from fear to anger. I knew I finally had to stand up to him. In my mind, I picked up the little boy, turned his face away from that image. Then I started venting the wrath I had *stuffed* for more than forty years. I commanded the destruction of all constructs that would keep any part of my soul captive. I bound that thing, proclaiming my freedom until the image faded away.

Then I asked **the Lord** to provide deliverance and restoration for the part of my soul represented by little Johnny Boy. As I was going through this process, the emotions I had experienced faded away. I find it interesting that I haven't responded to men, or other authority figures, in the same way since that afternoon.

I realized I had been reacting to any male authority figure, and to events in life, in accordance with **my response** to that thing sitting on the throne. Since the ministry, my perceptions and attitudes have changed dramatically and I am very grateful!

As we discussed in a previous section, the familiar spirit can appear to be anything or anyone with whom our soul is familiar. It can look like a mom, brother, sister, teacher, priest, or preacher. It can wear a mask that represents what **we believe** we hate, or need. It can represent what we call *demonic goodness* or *demonic badness*. Both are illusions designed to deceive our soul.

We may all have idealized images associated with dad, mom, or some other authority figure, which aren't realistic. They are idols in our hearts that need to be knocked down and renounced. This is a problem because children usually believe it is better to have a bad daddy than no daddy at all. The idol, or image in our minds, can give us an illusion of security.

It doesn't matter whether we believe dad is good or bad. We desperately want a dad of any kind, because it is in our spiritual genetics. Having a daddy is essential because he represents our Creator; therefore, **we strive** to receive his blessings, love, approval, and acceptance.

When we can't or don't receive these things, we receive a powerful curse defiling our true identity and destiny. When we allow anyone else, through idolatry, to define our identity or destiny, we are mistakenly giving away much of our authority. This is particularly true when we've given that authority to a spiritual entity that hates us absolutely.

Who Am I Supposed to Be?

It is normal for a boy to grow up to be like his earthly father, even when the boy has proclaimed loudly that he would never be like that man, A boy influenced by an *idealized image in his heart*, might believe **he is** supposed to be like this idealized image. That presents a problem because it is impossible.

When a girl grows up being influenced by an idealized image of father, she might believe **she is** supposed to find, and marry, a man like the image. Her quest will prove futile. In both cases, it is **impossible** to replicate an idealized image representing someone who never existed. This image was produced by the creative abilities of a child.

Both problems have the same solution. There is only One who is qualified to define our identity and destiny. He is our Creator and heavenly Father. He is the only One who truly knows us. He is the One whose example boys and men should follow. Women should look for His Spirit in someone they plan to marry.

People frequently think this doesn't apply to them and they struggle with the concept. We remind them the mental image they see can't be the real person, because it is in their mind. We propose it is a mask hiding the identity of a familiar spirit, and they must be **willing** to renounce it. They must be **able** to distinguish reality from fantasy.

If you had a wonderful dad, we are really glad for you. If you had a really bad dad, we understand it must have been very difficult. We don't want to take away anything good. We only want to make sure the dad you see in your mind's eye is the truth, and not some construct. This is our prayer for you.

Heavenly Father, we ask You to show the reader any illusions representing the image of father. We ask You to reveal any mental images the enemy could use to hold the reader in bondage. Whether dad is remembered as being good or bad, we ask You to show the truth. We ask You to give this person the grace and courage needed to see the truth.

*We ask You to comfort the soul of the reader. We ask You to assure them that nothing good will be taken away. If they are willing to pray, anything removed will be replaced with something much better. Please show them the **real God**, who died for them, wants to **adopt** them, and desires to be their **forever Daddy**.*

Once again, we offer you an opportunity to pray for your own freedom.

Sample Proclamation:

In the name of the Lord Jesus Christ, I proclaim the destruction of all images, constructs, or illusions representing that man who was, or is, my earthly father.

I command the destruction of all demonic goodness and demonic badness associated with my earthly father, including any mask, the eyes, the voice, the hands, and all body parts. I command everything associated with this image to be destroyed now, by the power of the shed blood of the Lord Jesus Christ.

I command any familiar spirit representing my earthly father to be stripped of all illusions and deceptions by the light of truth. I command to be allowed to see the truth.

I command the voice of any familiar spirit to be silenced. I command the destruction of all the power and influence of that voice, including all the curses associated with that voice.

I proclaim the destruction of all agreements and contracts I have ever made with any familiar spirit associated with my earthly father or any other authority figure. I renounce everything I received from these spirits.

I renounce receiving darkness, death, all unclean spirit voices, tormenters, accusations, guilt, condemnation, and everything else serving Satan's kingdom, and I renounce giving anything in return.

I command all energies of sacrifice received from me by Satan's kingdom to be given to the Lord Jesus Christ because

He, alone, has paid for all my sins and He, alone, is worthy to receive these sacrifices.

I command everything serving Satan's kingdom, associated with any idealized or counterfeit father, to leave every part of my life and being and go, now, where the Lord Jesus Christ sends them.

In the name of the Lord Jesus Christ, I reclaim all my soul and humanity that I lost, or gave away, to any familiar spirit named, or associated with, my earthly father or any other authority figure. Amen.

Desire to Be the Judge

Now we must deal with the overarching sin of wanting to be the Judge.

Sample Prayer:

In the name of the Lord Jesus Christ, I renounce the voice of the accuser and its function in my mind or mouth. I command the destruction of everything associated with being the judge that has been applied to any part of my being.

I renounce all my efforts to be the judge like my heavenly Father. My Lord, I now place into Your hands all the parts of my soul associated with my efforts to function as the judge. I relinquish this job and the responsibility for this job.

I renounce everything serving Satan's kingdom, as well as all familiar spirits, associated with being the judge. I renounce all their power and control over any part of my life or being, and I renounce all contracts and agreements I have ever made with them.

I command these spirits, and all of Satan's kingdom, to give the Lord Jesus Christ everything received from me as a sacrifice; because He, alone, has paid for all my sins, and He, alone, is worthy to receive these things.

I proclaim the destruction of all constructs and images that represent real life, dreams, fantasies, or imaginations associated with people, places, objects, events, sights, sounds, smells, tastes, feelings, emotions, body memories, sensations, and stimulations.

I command the destruction of all demonic goodness, or demonic badness, and everything that would control, deceive, or hold any part of my soul captive.

I renounce all the sinful feelings, emotions, attitudes, beliefs, perceptions, expectations, lies, and illusions, and all the responsibilities I have taken upon myself for family members, authority figures, or anyone else---for their words, actions, sins, failures, inadequacies and imperfections, and for their inability or unwillingness to give me the love, protection, provision, and respect I deserved as a child of God.

I renounce all these things and the power and control of these things. I renounce the weight of responsibility, all the darkness and death, the unclean spirits, the familiar spirits, the voices, the tormenters, the accusations, guilt, condemnation, and all forms of defilement---everything I have received from Satan's kingdom.

I command everything serving Satan's kingdom to leave every part of my life and being, and go, now, where the Lord Jesus Christ sends them.

Heavenly Father, I ask You to cleanse my spiritual eyes, my mind, and my heart of everything that would deceive me and prevent me from seeing and knowing You as You truly are, or from seeing and knowing myself as You created me to be.

Lord, I ask You to fill my heart with the revelation that You are my Father and I am Your child, and with the Spirit of adoption. I ask You to show the child of my heart how different You are from any other person or spirit they have ever known.

I ask You to surround the child of my heart with Your presence and Your power, and fill my heart with Your perfect love, acceptance, approval, peace, joy, satisfaction, and security, with everything I have never received, everything necessary for me to be free from emotional starvation and all associated cravings and yearnings.

I ask You to restore to me all my soul, humanity, gifts, abilities, talents, skills, dignity, self respect, health, and well-being. Please restore everything associated with my childhood and life, my true identity, destiny, everything I lost, everything I gave away, and everything that has been killed, stolen or destroyed.

I ask You to make me whole so I can be all You created me to be and I can know You as my perfect Father. Thank You. Amen.

Now that you have used your authority to destroy lies and illusions, please allow the Holy Spirit to show you the truth of the following:

The Father's Blessing

My child, I want you to know that I love you. I knew you and wrote your name into My Book of Life at the foundation of the world. I knew who you would be and I loved you. I was there when you were conceived, and I blessed your conception because I loved you. I watched you grow in your mother's womb, and I nurtured you because I loved you. I was there when you were born.

Through the pain, fear, and all the trauma of having to leave that place of comfort and safety, I loved you. When you thought your world was being destroyed, I was there and I comforted you. I blessed your birth, knowing you would have to endure many things.

If you look into the spiritual realm of your mind, and see when you were born, you will see Me there. I have never left you. In all those times when you were small and you cried because you felt alone, I was there. When you cried because you felt unwanted and abandoned, I cried with you. I felt your pain.

When the time came for you to become an adult, and no one else was there to bless you, I was there. I blessed you, My child, to become the adult you were created to be. Throughout your life, I have proclaimed, "You are Mine."

You are My son; you are My daughter; I am proud of you. I am proud to call you My child and a member of My family. When you come to Me, I am filled with joy. I see you through the eyes of silent satisfaction, as already perfected. I exult over you with singing because you are with Me.

I have waited thousands of years for you to be with Me. There is nothing that can affect My love for you. You don't have to perform; you don't have to strive; you don't have to do anything to earn My love; because I have always loved you.

I shall forever love you, no matter what. I have glorious plans for you. I yearn for those plans to come to completion so you will, finally, see the wonderful things I have planned for you. I will do anything I can do to raise you up and exalt you to the highest and best place possible. I LOVE YOU!

A dilemma of identity typically confronts the eight or nine-year old. They are beginning to think about who they are or who they're supposed to be. Frequently, they take on jobs in the family such as the peacemaker, provider, comforter, counselor, protector, rescuer, SAVIOR, the surrogate dad or mom, or surrogate husband or wife, all associated with emotional vampirism; the good person, the bad person, the Christian, the invisible person, the clown, Cinderella and others created to help the person function as Savior for self or someone else. Children can assume these jobs at an earlier age, but we have found that it is more common for them to do so in the middle childhood years.

CAN YOU SAVE LIKE THE SON?

Failure Motivating Actions

Failure is a factor frequently found associated with many other heart issues. We believe it can be traced back to the Garden of Eden. When Adam and Eve were being evicted from the garden, they might have heard the voice of the serpent saying, "You fools have failed. After all God did for you, you betrayed His trust. You are no longer worthy of His love."

The creature behind the voice of *the accuser*, death, is still very active. He relies on deception so he can hide in the shadows. He *accuses us* of being weak, shameful, inadequate failures. He deceives our souls to create misconceptions about God, other people, and ourselves. He *accuses other people, and God*, of doing the things he does, and he *accuses us before God*.

His deceptions are most successful when we are children, because we don't know we can reject his lies. No one has warned us of his wiles or explained that we have options. He plays on our sin nature and fills our hearts with distorted ideas about our circumstances and the people around us. Because of these deceptions, we have fallen into his trap and accepted wrong perspectives, attitudes, beliefs, and perceptions of the world.

In general, we all respond to people and life in the only way we know. Children who grow up with adults accustomed to making nasty comments about people are likely to follow the same pattern. They behave the same way as the adults, because they have no other frame of reference, or life experience, from which to draw. In this case, it is normal for people to *give, even as they have received.*

These children may feel the need to find things they can criticize in others. They seem to feel good about themselves, momentarily, when they tear someone else down. They could use so-called jokes, general sarcasm, or vicious comments. It has little to do with the other people, who just happen to be the focus of attention for the moment. At these times, the ones who function as the voice of condemnation don't feel so worthless, compared to their victims.

Children are masters at figuring out where the buttons are, and, with supreme finesse, pushing those buttons. Any adult who has been around them has seen this work. It is most common with children who are not receiving the necessary emotional sustenance for their souls. It is easy to identify the ones who feel inadequate or **fearful of failure**. They constantly push the emotional buttons of everyone around them, trying to win in the game of emotional jousting.

They do this at home, at school with teachers and classmates, out in public, and in church. They need to win, so they can prove they are not failures. The message could be, "Don't take it personally. I just have to win. Sorry if you have to lose." This deep-seated fear of failure drives them to win, even when there is nothing tangible to win.

If we respond with anger or intimidation, they might conclude they had won, and were receiving some kind of benefit. This would also apply to the need for control, but, in this case, the greater need is to defeat the fear of failure by winning. For someone tormented by the fear of failure, this might offer a temporary reprieve from the oppression of fear.

A child from this environment could become **an exasperator**. With an exasperator you could say, "This is a beautiful day, isn't it?" He would respond, "Maybe, but it is hot and miserable." On the other hand, you might say, "Today sure is hot and miserable," and he would reply, "I think it's beautiful." No matter which side of an issue you take, the exasperator will argue. He or she **has to win**, so you have to lose; nothing personal.

Our life experiences shape our perspectives, attitudes, and beliefs. If we have been put down by authority figures in our childhood, it is reasonable to believe we will manifest the effects in our adult life. When we leave our dysfunctional homes and enter the world, we might subconsciously gravitate to people and social situations we recognize as familiar. We might even gravitate to people who will abuse us in familiar ways. For some, this could represent security.

Surrounded by these familiar situations, we would probably see others being abused in ways to which we could relate. Witnessing these things could trigger something deep inside us, so we take it personally. This could stimulate automatic responses based on the need to survive. We may feel it necessary to *put others down,* in an attempt to feel better about ourselves. We might abuse and mistreat other people, because that is how we were treated.

Glenna and I have both had to minister to an issue pertaining to failure and the fear of failure. This issue is related to the futility of believing that no matter how hard we try, our efforts will be scuttled by the actions of someone else. This is particularly frustrating because there's nothing we can do about it. We are not capable of controlling other people who seem determined to **make us** failures.

In my case, it was associated with my father, and his determination to fail at everything he pursued. This threatened the security of my family and put a great deal of pressure on me. As the eldest son, I had the distorted view that I was somehow responsible for all of his failures. I also believed that I should be able to do something to compensate for him.

In Glenna's case, it was the issue of being the youngest and smallest, who was expected, by others and herself, to be able to do things as well as those around her. When she couldn't perform at the same level as those older and more capable, she felt like a failure. Her older brothers, of course, encouraged this perception. Her response was to feel there was no reason to try; it was futile and her failure was assured.

Fear of Failure

Here is *an example* of programmed perspectives that might control the way we respond. In the mid-80s, I was teaching a small home group in Mesa, Arizona. My pastor asked me to meet with a woman who had been living in Mexico for many years. She had become involved in a variety of metaphysical activities and had many questions.

It was very early in my training for ministry. Because of my involvement with the New Age occult, he thought I would be better able to compare the beliefs of Christianity. We agreed I would meet with this woman and her friend to answer questions. One meeting evolved into several, and then more. Ultimately, these evening sessions lasted several months, during which we became good friends.

One evening she asked me if I would minister in Mexico. I was, of course, filled with trepidation. I stalled as long as I could before agreeing, but we finally established a time when I could schedule a vacation from my engineering job.

I traveled, alone, to the city of Hermosillo, in Sonora, Mexico. I had a wonderful meal with the woman and her family, after which we went to the place of ministry in the outskirts of the city. When we arrived at the location, I was filled with distress and apprehension. We were in an area with a population of roughly 50,000, living in dwellings constructed, primarily, of cardboard and old corrugated metal. I grew up believing I lived in poverty, but I never imagined anything like this.

We were standing outside one of the few masonry buildings in the area, discussing logistics and making arrangements for the next two days. As we talked, some children began gathering, curious to see what was happening. As they ran around laughing and playing, a fruit vendor came down the street, attracting their attention.

One member of our group bought an orange, cut it into pieces, and distributed it among the youngsters. They sat down and began eating with obvious relish. It occurred to me that children in the United States would not spend so much time and effort to scrape the orange rind of every juicy morsel. Even those living in relative poverty would not make such a big deal out of a simple orange.

The depth of poverty in which these children lived touched me profoundly, and my ability to concentrate on the conversation dissolved. Before long, the planning was completed, and we drove back to my friend's home. She must have noticed that something was bothering me, because she was darting glances at me as we drove.

Eventually she asked, "Is there something wrong?" I really didn't want to discuss it, but had little choice. I told her I was feeling overwhelmed and inadequate. I didn't see how I could do any good because the need was so great and my ability was so limited.

I went on and on, trying to explain to her the depth of my feelings. I assumed she was able to understand, and yet, this was the world to which she had grown accustomed. Because of my prejudices, I judged that her perspective would not be the same as mine.

She was attempting to help me deal with these issues when, suddenly, *another voice* invaded my consciousness from way down inside. It spoke calmly but firmly saying, **"Who do you think you are**? You were sent here to do a **specific job** for Me. **Just do your job**. Everything else is My responsibility."

This may have been the first time I was reminded of how small I am compared to Him. My options were to try to do things in my own strength, and fail; or let Him work through me, and succeed. This is a decision we all have to make at some time.

If the fear had continued to fill my heart, it is possible I would not have done the seminar over the next two days. If my friend and the Lord hadn't ministered to my heart, I might have been immobilized with fear and rendered useless. I might have forfeited a great blessing, and the fear of failure would have won.

Failure and the fear of failure are strong influences in our lives. Many of us procrastinate because of the fear of failure. We are so afraid of failing we would rather not even begin a task. We may think it is easier to face the consequences for not doing something rather than risk the possibility of failure.

Are We Institutionalized?

We saw a movie about a man who was convicted of murdering his wife and sent to prison. There he met a wise old con, who decided to function as a mentor and help him survive. At one point in the movie, another old con assaulted a fellow inmate because he had been told he was going to be released on parole.

He was terrified and didn't want to be released. He had lived in a system of rules that were extremely confining, yet represented a form of security. He had a place within that system that gave him a measure of respect, a well-defined schedule, and security. He knew when he would get up, eat, exercise, and sleep. At this point, it seemed safer to stay in prison than to face the potential failure of freedom. Being paroled would strip away the security he knew so well.

He was, eventually, paroled, and struggled terribly with the world outside the prison walls. After a brief time, the pressure became too great and he committed suicide. When the inmates heard of his death, many offered opinions of what had happened. The wise old con finally broke into the conversation. He explained that it was because the other man had been *institutionalized*.

In this case, being paroled would be considered success by any normal con. However, this particular man, because he was institutionalized, had a desperate **fear of success**. With success came great responsibility and the fear of failure. He no longer had the ability to cope in the outside world. It was easier to let others take care of him and be responsible for him.

As I watched the movie, I received a revelation. For many years, all the memories I had of my dad were colored with anger, betrayal, and the judgments of the voice of the accuser. I saw a man who, in spite of being extremely intelligent, seemed determined to sabotage any possibility of his own success.

I knew little of my grandfather and the household my dad grew up in, but I saw some similarities. Based on subtle things he had said, I don't believe my dad was ever able to receive blessings and approval from his own dad. No matter what he did, it was never good enough. As a result, I think he went through life resigned to the *fact* that he simply could not succeed.

As I was growing up, he tried his hand at several careers and always quit just short of success. My judgment, at that time, was that he simply lost interest when the challenge was gone. He would move on to something else, and our family would live with the consequences. I made excuses for him to my friends or others who seemed to be judging our lifestyle. Because of shame, I could judge him, but it wasn't okay for anyone else.

He had, in effect, been institutionalized by his own beliefs, attitudes, and expectations. The prison he created in his mind became, for him, a comfort zone, protecting him from failure. It was easier to quit short of the finish line, so he didn't have to face the threat of losing. It was easier to stay in his self-imposed institution.

In the later years, he spent most of his waking hours studying racing forms for the dogs and horses. He had finally found something at which he couldn't succeed. It was easier to gamble on dogs and horses, so he could blame others when he didn't win. This satisfied the self-fulfilling prophecy in his heart and also drove him day and night. While my mom provided for our family, my dad was controlled by the demons motivating the *fear of failure*, *fear of success,* and the **need to win**.

This isn't unique to the man in the movie or to my own dad. I have, at times, been immobilized by fear. As I faced responsibilities and challenges in life, I was terrified by the prospect of failure. As a husband, father, and engineer, I faced these fears many times. Sometimes I gave in, and had to find excuses to shift the blame.

At other times I faced the fear, climbed over the invisible wall, and moved on to a new level. It was always my decision to become institutionalized or to move on.

Potential for Failure

A number of years ago, we knew a man who was confined to a wheelchair. He requested prayer for healing and the pastor told him he believed the Lord wanted to heal him, and the man agreed, but he was afraid to get out of the chair. He had been disabled a long time and didn't know if he could survive without the government benefits he was receiving. Do you see the irrationality of the situation?

This is another example of someone who was institutionalized, this time by a chair and a benevolent system. He, apparently, could believe God was willing and able to heal him, but he could not believe God would provide for him after he was healed. It didn't matter that God could heal him, because he was **unwilling** to face the responsibilities, and potential failure, of freedom.

Before leaving this issue, it would be good to summarize the magnitude of what it might mean to be institutionalized. Many of us feel trapped in a job or career we hate, because we dare not give up our *perception of security* to try something else. Many of us are trapped in relationships for the same reason.

There are even some of us attending the same church attended by our parents and grandparents, because of tradition. Even if the church is dry, boring, and meaningless, we remain because we have become institutionalized. The familiarity and *illusion of security,* for us becomes a rut, because we are institutionalized in our thinking.

The fear of failure, responsibility, or even success, can immobilize us. Instead of allowing fear to reign in our lives, the Lord tells us to hold onto our confidence. (Hebrews 10:35-39)

Hopelessness and Despair

When we receive the message that we are a failure and are inadequate, we are filled with despair. When these messages are planted as seeds in our heart, they affect every aspect of our lives. We offer an example of how the issue of failure and associated hopelessness can **be programmed** into a person's life.

A young woman was very active in high school. She was enrolled in honors programs and a variety of other activities. Much of this was done in order to receive her father's approval and acceptance. She worked very hard in all her endeavors. Her teachers called her an overachiever.

Her father had an extensive education. As a result, he believed a good education was of supreme importance in everyone's life. He wanted to motivate his daughter to get the best scores possible. His intention was to help her, but due to his upbringing, his parenting skills and ability to motivate in a positive way were very limited.

She brought home her grade card containing one B and the rest A's. She showed her father the card, waiting for his approval. He studied the card awhile and said, "Why is there a B on this card? Can't you work hard enough to get all A's? Is this the best you can do?" Hurt and disappointed, she slumped away, resolving in her heart to do better next time. Dad was satisfied with his method of *encouragement*.

Soon afterward, she reorganized her schedule to have more time for study. She worked even harder and signed up for college preparatory courses. She put aside all free-time activities in her singular motivation to achieve perfect grades. At the semester's end, she again took her grade card home, flushed with success. She had achieved her goal, and dad would surely be pleased.

She presented him the card and stood beaming in anticipation. He looked at the card and was silent for a time. When he spoke, it was to say, "Your classes must be too easy. I don't want you taking fluff courses!"

The message was clear. If you don't receive perfect grades, you have failed; if you do receive perfect grades, you have failed. There is nothing you can do to please that man or receive his approval and acceptance!

The voice of the accuser began speaking into her mind and soul. "It's no use. You might as well give up. There's no point in trying. You can never do well enough to please anyone. You don't want to do that academic stuff anyway. Have some fun and forget studies." At this point, she shrugged her shoulders and gave in to despair.

The following semesters her grades dropped. She started running around with young people who didn't care about grades. She spent much more time in social activities and dating. She began searching for a young man who might offer the love, approval, and acceptance her dad wouldn't give. She found one who was willing to offer, at least, the illusion of what she needed.

Her decisions were an affront to her father. He responded with anger and condemnation, and their relationship took a nosedive, eventually ceasing altogether. She wasn't willing to face his wrath, and he was baffled by her abrupt turnaround.

The young man represented her hope of receiving the satisfaction and acceptance she had never received from dad. As would be expected, this relationship eventually died, as well. The two young people couldn't possibly provide what each one so desperately needed.

Years passed, with failed relationships, unhappiness, and increasing emotional starvation. When men couldn't provide her needs, she tried drugs and alcohol to escape the pain and emptiness. She drifted from potential savior to potential savior, hoping she would, eventually, get her needs met.

Do you see that sex, drugs, and alcohol were never the primary issue? They were the fruit of her despair, and her chosen form of escape. The issue was always a broken heart experiencing starvation. Even though she had an adult body; deep inside, the heart of a girl yearned for daddy's love, approval, and acceptance.

It wasn't unreasonable for her to want these things and expect her dad to provide them. He didn't know how, because he probably hadn't received them from his dad. The result was many years of pain and unhappiness for both of them.

Eventually, she met the real Daddy. She received the gift of salvation with healing and deliverance, and was able to restore her relationship with her earthly dad.

We meet many people in ministry whose story has not yet been resolved. Some have, apparently, received the gift of salvation, but have not yet found the ability to forgive, receive forgiveness, and be healed. They are still institutionalized in that place of pain, hopelessness, and despair. They believe the illusion that it is safer to stay in the **emotional prison** with associated programming, than to face the threat of more pain and failure.

Programmed Failure

Let's look at another example of childhood programming. We begin with the **mythical character** known as Santa Claus, who has a magic toyshop, magical elves, magic flying sled, and magic reindeer. However, this jolly old man seems to have a darker side.

Using either a crystal ball or his elfin spies, he is able to record all the activities of all children. He is able to decide who has been naughty or nice, asleep or awake, and who has been good or bad. *He determines* who receives coal or presents in their stockings.

If we disregard all the magic and witchcraft, there is still a problem. What scale does he use to decide who is *good* and who is *bad*? How much **performance is required** to be considered **good enough**? If we don't get the present we really want, have we FAILED? If we try really hard and still don't receive the desired gift, have we again been subjected to gross injustice?

This is not a tirade against Christmas. The issue for us is the perversion of Christmas and the establishment of programmed failure. How is a child to function in a system of illusions and deceptions, without defined parameters? How are children to deal with all this magical **stuff** and the mysterious being, who has so much power over their lives?

Let's look at this from an adult perspective. Let's say we went to work and found a memo at our workstation telling us that all future wage increases would be determined by satisfactory performance. If this were to happen, wouldn't we like to know the definition of *satisfactory*? Wouldn't it be important to know who was going to make that determination, and on what basis?

Wouldn't it be frustrating to find the definition to be arbitrary, based on unknown factors outside of our control? What if this *judge* were going to be like Santa Claus, hidden away somewhere in his cubicle? What if the judgments were going to be based upon hidden cameras, bugged telephones, or computers that would be randomly monitored?

What if we would never be allowed to confront our judge to determine the accuracy of his judgments? What if there were no consistent guidelines to follow, because the one making the rules was inconsistent? What if we knew the decisions made were based on politics?

Guaranteed Failure

What if that inconsistent judge is mom or dad, and the definition of **good enough** is dependent upon someone having had a sound night's sleep? Maybe a headache or a hangover determines their reactions. Maybe their desire to punish one another dictates the way they respond to the children. They might project their own inadequacies and perceived failures on their children. These are disturbingly common behaviors from fouled-up parents.

A parent might play head games, use manipulation and control, or guilt and intimidation as methods of deciding the success or failure of a child's performance. He or she might respond to their children's activities with, "You kids are making so much noise, you're driving me crazy!" They use this threat for control. Then, when the parent acts irrationally, the children assume they have failed somehow.

Most children are willing to take the blame and responsibility for adults who are not willing to be responsible for them. These children experience the terrible fear and insecurity that mom or dad is going crazy and they are to blame. Some parents actually want to be unstable so *those crummy kids* will suffer. For them it may have been a way of getting attention or sympathy.

If people decide that noisy children, problems at work, or frustrations in marriage are good excuses for going crazy, it is their decision. Perhaps their desire is to escape responsibility and the things in life they desperately don't want to face. Whatever their motivation, the effects are the same. The souls of the children are filled with seeds that grow to produce the fruit of failure, despair, hopelessness, and the desire to die.

Need to Be Perfect

Many people feel they are expected to be perfect. Their parents always demanded perfect performance in any endeavor. Most of us are familiar with these parents. You enter *her* house and find everything exactly in order, while she's apologizing for how messy it is. You go into *his* garage and he explains to you that there's a place for everything, and everything is in its place.

This man wouldn't consider allowing his son to work with him in the garage, because the boy might misplace something or make a mess. Since the son is not allowed to have any real interaction with dad, he attempts to receive some approval and acceptance from mom. He asks if he can do anything for her and she tells him to set the table for dinner.

He gathers up the dishes, flatware, glasses, and napkins, and puts them all in place. When he's finished, he asks if he can do anything else. Instead of responding to his question, she inspects what he has done. Rather than giving him the approval he desperately seeks, she gives him that special *look* that tells him he failed again. She doesn't say anything but rearranges everything to her satisfaction.

She could have accomplished her goal without sending him that terrible message. She could have said, "You did very well. I normally arrange these things a little differently. Would you like to see how, so it will help you remember? I really appreciate your help."

Do you see the difference between giving him *the look* and affirming what he did with positive instruction? These are two clearly different messages which can be sent to his heart. Later, mom will ask him to do something and he might *forget*. It has now become easier to face her anger for not doing something than to face the potential failure when he doesn't perform perfectly. Once again, we have a person programmed with the expectation of failure and its consequences.

In our view, **procrastination** is a symptom of perfectionism and a result of the fear of failure. Many people go through life unable to function in even the most fundamental ways. They don't balance their checking account or pay their bills on time. It is very hard for them to keep a job because they believe that anything short of perfection is failure.

The fear of failure is so immobilizing, it can cause some people to sit at their workstation daydreaming. Others will do a simple task over and over again, trying to achieve perfection. In their mind they may see that familiar face with *the look*, rejecting their work no matter how well it has been done.

Need to Perform

We met a man who grew up as an only child surrounded by adults. His parents were very intolerant when he *acted like a child*. He was expected to think, converse, and behave like a grown up. He was told he had to be brilliant in everything in order to be accepted.

His response was to strive, throughout his life, to achieve the level of perfection that was required. When we met him as a middle-aged man, he was still striving. He told us all about his achievements, his intelligence, his abilities, and all the reasons we should like and approve of him.

People usually want to have conversations that include a variety of subjects. They don't always want to hear about how wonderful we are. They get tired of having to affirm us and assure us that we are acceptable and lovable. They eventually get exasperated with our constant need for affirmation, and drift away. Then we wonder why we are always rejected. The result can often be a form of self-imposed isolation.

This man felt isolated as a child, so he was familiar with that feeling. His response to the apparent rejection of other adults was to return to his place of isolation and blame them. Although he yearned for social interaction, he didn't know how to successfully engage in it. His emotions fluctuated between intense frustration, anger, injustice, fear, and an overwhelming sense of failure.

People like this man can flop back and forth between perceptions of grandeur and intense feelings of inferiority. They grew up with conflicting messages, feeling powerful and powerless, brilliant and incapable, needed and unwanted. Their identity was always defined by the will and the needs of others.

As adults, they don't know how to find an identity of their own. They have tried identities that served the needs of others and those produced by their own creative imagination. Their only hope for satisfactory resolution is to go to the Creator and let Him restore their true identity and destiny.

Sibling Rivalry and Competition

Very early in life we are taught to compete in a variety of ways. Most of us have experienced **sibling rivalry**. In most cases, parents function as referees in the heat of battle. On the other hand, we have encountered situations in which the parents' role was entirely different. They would pit one child against another and encourage the rivalry.

In some families, each child is presented with the challenge of accomplishing as much as, or more than, the other children. Perhaps satisfactory performance is based upon a comparison with a sibling or some other person. This situation may be established with family members older, more experienced, or more gifted in certain areas than we. For the older, this is a great time to receive positive reinforcement. For the younger, this is a great time to set up a no-win scenario filling their heart with the expectations of failure.

My dad was an example of this type of parent. I don't remember my older sister being involved except when it came to comparing grades in school. I was reminded many times that she always got good grades. His question was, "Why can't you be more like your sister?" I remember deciding I didn't care about my school grades. It was *impossible* to compete with my sister, and the injustice of being expected to do so was intolerable.

Typically, my dad would set up competitions between my brothers and me. He was constantly telling each of us how proud he was of the other two. No matter how well I did, I always felt I had fallen short.

He managed to convey these messages verbally, with mannerisms, and sometimes by shaking his head. The latter action was done in such a way as to convey the message, "You are hopeless." The nearest thing to positive reinforcement I remember receiving from him was, "Johnny, get your head out of your ass!"

There were also times when two or three of us weren't getting along or weren't performing well enough. In these times dad would relate stories of families he had known in the past with kids like us. He would tell us how they had found a solution to these problems.

Out of frustration, these other parents sent their kids to orphanages and foster homes. The parents went happily on with their lives, and the kids never saw each other again. These threats were extremely traumatic for me. Even the thought that my dad would throw us out like old garbage would fill my heart with a storm of emotions.

I can't speak for my brothers, but I remember the effects on me. One time he told the story with yelling and gestures. I was flooded with feelings of failure, despair, anger, and shame. At that moment, I felt the only escape from all the pain and failure was death.

This put us in a double bind. My dad would force us boys to compete for his approval and acceptance. Then, when the competition bugged him, he used threats and intimidation to maintain control. In our experience, my dad was more typical than most of us would like to think. We've met many people whose parents demanded competition for approval and acceptance.

In other cases, children may also be compared to other role models at school, in their neighborhoods, or at church. In such a system, everyone is expected to excel in such things as academics, sports, social skills, and behavior.

In school, contests and competitions are regularly used to motivate students, retain their attention, and evaluate their progress. All sports involve some form of competition. If you ask a coach the value of sports they would tell you all the physical and emotional benefits. We would probably agree with most of the statements but we also believe this coin has two sides.

We are not opposed to sports, school activities, or anything else that helps children grow. The problem isn't with the activity; it is with the attitudes and perceptions being planted in the hearts of the children. These attitudes permeate every aspect of life. There is so much fear of losing, or being a failure that people automatically compete. We are driven by the need to win at something, or anything!

In Las Vegas, we see an interesting phenomenon associated with this issue. If we're traveling on the highway through town, we've noticed it can be dangerous to turn on our turn signal. We discovered that there are those so competitive they will do everything in their power to cut us off. In many cases, it is safer to change lanes suddenly without giving notice. In my opinion, this is a classic example of someone wanting to win, even when there's nothing tangible to gain.

Competition for Parents' Attention

Competition within the family can present some interesting situations. We've met people who were required to compete in very creative ways for dad's attention, love, acceptance, or approval. Some children were required to compete with mom for dad's attention. In these situations, each member of the family, including mom, competed as though their survival depended on it.

In other cases, children were required to compete with dad's job, his need to succeed, or his lust for money. Generally, dad can spend most of his time at work giving children the impression they are not very significant. Then, he might come home from work and immediately go to the garage to work on something important to him. The message sent to the hearts of his children is that they are not as important as his work or hobby.

In other cases, a child might have to compete with dad's bottle of liquor, gambling, or a variety of other things. I grew up with the absolute certainty that I could never compete with my father's need to gamble. No matter what the obsession or addiction is, the effect it has on the hearts of children is the same. When we realize we can't compete successfully, hopelessness and despair can overwhelm us.

This doesn't only apply to dad. People have told us of their despair in knowing that mom loved alcohol more than she loved them. They were required to find creative ways to postpone mom's *happy hour*. Once she started drinking there would be no more social interaction.

Anytime a child is sent the message that they are required to compete with a career, a lifestyle, any other person, a thing, or an activity, they face failure. This expectation of failure, based on worthlessness, can manifest with a variety of emotions, including the desire to die. This really isn't the same as sibling rivalry because the competition can be with anyone or anything.

School Activities and Sports

We compete on the playground, in sports activities, for the approval of teachers, parents, and authority figures. We are told it doesn't matter whether we win or lose, but how we play the game. We hear that, but no one believes it. When we see the obvious conflict between the words and the actions, we know winning really is all-important.

Even if the coach manages to stay balanced, the children still have to deal with the parents. There are moms and dads who act like lunatics at Little League games, screaming, yelling, and cursing the coach, umpires, and children, even their own.

If *their* team fails to win, they rage and act like it's a major disaster. They might say, "We were going to go out for a pizza, but not for a bunch of losers." We believe it would almost be impossible for a child to grow up in our culture without being programmed for failure through competition.

In the Media

Recently we have seen the explosion of what is called *Reality TV*. Contestants compete for survival, prizes, a spouse, or titles, and the distinction of being the last one standing. During the course of this so-called game, the contestants typically lie, cheat, steal, and do whatever else is required to win.

We've heard contestants proclaim that they will do anything to win. People are being programmed to believe that it's OK to *do anything to win*. This includes all the young people who see the adults around them approving of the contestants' tactics. Is this really the message we want to be planted in their hearts?

In Marriage

What about the *need to win* in the marriage relationship? Often, husbands and wives compete for dominance, wanting decisions to *go their way*. They may, like siblings, strive to please their own parents or those they inherited with their spouse. They may compete over careers, housing, priorities, finances, and other life considerations.

People we've ministered with have told us of manipulation and control, intimidation and violence, including amazing tactics to maintain dominance. In the struggles of competition, is God being glorified or is Satan running people in circles? Because competitive motivations are self-serving and fear-based, they cannot glorify God.

In Business

When this need to win enters the business environment, we see a variety of injustices. Supervisors oppress and dominate. Subordinates look for any opportunity to do less work for more money. There is a management mentality that treats employees like the enemy and vice versa. There might even be the desire to sabotage others with whom we work to gain an advantage and possibly a promotion.

Road rage can, at least to some extent, be explained by this programmed need to compete. We treat driving a car as though it were a business endeavor. We want to win because we have been programmed to win. Losing is not an acceptable option. Competing with other drivers for some perceived advantage, in order to win some intangible prize, is irrational, particularly when we resort to recklessness.

Many people expend great amounts of energy to win. Once again, the message seems to be, "This is just business. It's nothing personal. I have to win; so you have to lose."

In the Church

How does this affect the church? In Ezekiel 34, God instructs His prophet to proclaim that the shepherds have fed and ministered to themselves, but not to the needs of their flocks. God directs a number of accusations at the shepherds. He proclaims they shall be removed from their positions. He seems to have very strong feelings about their behavior. What is He referring to? Was it just those priests of old He was talking about?

There are pastors and leaders today who desperately want to win. As a result, they function the same way they would in any other corporate environment. These *corporate executives* look upon the other members of the church as a resource to be utilized. In some cases they treat the members of the church as servants whose purpose is to serve the executive. A number of people have told us they have left a church for this reason.

Pastors can also compete with one another. This severely limits their ability to work together. The lack of unity within the body, or in a community, can cripple any projects requiring cooperation. This presents a great challenge in the body of Christ.

We are convinced that resistance to unity is primarily rooted in the fear of failure and the need to compete. Pastors ask each other, "How many attended your service on Sunday? What were your offerings?" They remind us of kids engaged in sibling rivalry, trying to impress everyone else and convince themselves they are successful.

Did Jesus exhort us to build big congregations, or did He tell us to go and make disciples? Did He say to compete for and steal sheep, or to feed them? Whose sheep are they, anyway? What about sabotaging others so we, or our ministry, can have greater perceived success? Whose kingdom does this kind of activity really benefit?

Competition is **not necessary** and definitely **not beneficial**. In competition, we function as agents of Satan, because he is the winner. When we do our job *for the Lord*, failure is impossible! Looking at this from a purely selfish standpoint, which is better for us?

When we were born again, we were adopted into a **new family**. In this new family, when one of us suffers, we all suffer; when one of us is honored, we all rejoice. As the expression says, *a high tide raises all the boats*. (1 Corinthians 12:26) Our Father has set up a system in which **we can all win**. According to his system, when we help others to succeed our success is increased.

Are We in Savior Mode?

Our enemy never gets tired and never sleeps. He has been deceiving people for a long time. If he can plant the seeds of failure and competition in our hearts, he will remain in control until we discover the truth.

When we know the truth, we can crawl out of the rut and choose new life patterns, attitudes, and perceptions. From the memory banks of our soul we can delete all the beliefs based on lies, illusions, and deceptions.

For many of us, whatever our age, our emotional needs are not being met. We're not experiencing satisfaction and are looking desperately for something else. That is why so many of us, including many in the church, are making bad decisions concerning important life issues such as marriage.

Many of us are not satisfied with our marriages, relationships, jobs, careers, churches, or our situation in life. We meet people of every age who appear to be going through midlife crises. This is another case in which people are trying to do what only God can do. We are told God is Love. He is the Source of love; therefore, He is the only One who can fill our hearts with all the love-based things we need.

People often struggle in their marriage because of this. We suspect they have tried desperately to do the job they were given. The relationship has probably gone through a downward spiral, as both parties believe they are failures. It isn't because they are bad, don't care, or don't want to satisfy the other person's needs. What they are striving to do is impossible. They often come to us, barely holding on to a small ray of hope.

They ask if we do marriage counseling. We do, in a manner of speaking. We allow very little spousal accusation in our sessions. Otherwise we could spend an infinite amount of time hearing everything wrong with the spouse. This doesn't accomplish anything useful. We want to go into the catacombs of the soul where the real issues are.

As previously discussed if they each establish a great vertical relationship with their real Daddy, the horizontal relationship between the two of them will be much easier. When we go to the infinite Resource for our provision, emotional starvation and failure issues begin to fade.

Emotional Vampirism

Children are not given as the property of parents, but are always to be considered children of God. The role of the parent is to represent God as accurately as possible so children will be able to discover Him. They should present the image of an abundant provider for their children.

As children's hearts are filled with good things, they can experience satisfaction and security. These children would have no trouble discovering and accepting the nurturing love of their heavenly Daddy.

Unfortunately, we've never met anyone whose parents had the ability to provide and accurately reflect an image of God. Many people to whom we have ministered live in a world of depression, anxiety, and low self-esteem. As a result, they become easy prey for those who would feed upon them physically or emotionally.

Many were never given permission to establish healthy boundaries to protect themselves. Since they were never allowed to establish boundaries for themselves, they are unable to honor the boundaries of others. As a result, they have problems with all forms of relationships.

When we, **as children**, are asked to provide for others in inappropriate ways, we are being subjected to emotional vampirism. In such cases, we may take on jobs associated with the Savior for which we are hopelessly inadequate.

Have Any Jobs for Me?

We have ministered with a surprising number of people who have told us about the jobs they accepted as children, and why they accepted them. They became caretakers, comforters, providers, peacemakers, confidants, counselors, or **saviors** for other family members.

Being daddy's comforter, mommy's caretaker, or the protector for their siblings gives a child a sense of importance and power. When someone has jobs like these, their role and importance in the family is secure. Don't we all want a sense of security? These jobs, and the weight of responsibility associated with them, become both a powerful **source of significance** and a **terrible burden.**

As one would expect, taking on the job of savior is a guaranteed, no-win proposition. We cannot succeed, because we are dealing with the free will of other people. There is no way any of us is qualified to do the job of savior, and yet *the voice* says, "You can be like God." This deception is very seductive because we all want to be powerful.

Since children usually view themselves to be the center of the universe, they tend to assume they are responsible for all family problems. Therefore, it is easy to manipulate them into taking on inappropriate jobs. If mom or dad needs a best friend, a surrogate spouse, intimacy, companionship, or a scapegoat, the child is available. If brothers and sisters need a surrogate mom or dad, the child is available. If mom or dad is emotionally or physically sick or dependent on drugs or alcohol, the child is available. When there is a need to establish the illusion of security, the child is available.

We have ministered to people who, as children, were raped, molested, or were sent out to function as prostitutes by their parents. Sometimes they stoically describe the events; and sometimes they cry and rage. Regardless of the offense, children who are used by their parents experience tremendous pain.

They have been betrayed and victimized by those who should have been protecting and providing for them. They have been unjustly treated by being asked to do jobs that guaranteed failure. They have been fed upon by those who should be feeding and nurturing them. God's system has been turned upside down and **everyone** within the system of vampirism is **defiled.**

Even when trying to do the jobs described above, a normal child might perceive they are not having their needs met or their survival is threatened. When this occurs, the logical thing to do is to take on other jobs, with associated masks, that might secure survival. These jobs can be assumed earlier in life, but we have found that children of roughly eight or nine years old take on these **mask identities**. There are a variety of other jobs children take upon themselves, but these seem to be some of the more frequent choices.

The good person, the Christian, Cinderella and a variety of other jobs are designed to help the child receive enough attention or acceptance to survive. When a person wearing any of these masks is performing their role, they hope to receive an appropriate pat on the head. This can help them feel accepted and approved.

The bad person acts bad in order to receive attention, because bad attention is better than no attention.

The invisible person wears a mask of invisibility to escape the attention of those engaged in violent conflict. This person might hide under the kitchen table and hope that no one notices them. They might also hide under their bed or in their closet in an effort to escape being a part of this family.

The clown responds to the violent actions of parents in a different way. This person waits for daddy to come home and immediately begins performing. The hope is that telling jokes, singing songs, and keeping everyone laughing will prevent the violence. Later in life, the clown might perform in every aspect of life in the hope of preventing unpleasant situations.

The jobs described above and their associated **masks** indicate a person is using their assumed identity. When someone grows up wearing these masks, it can influence relationship with their family, and the world around them. These masks can also affect a person's ability to have a relationship with our Heavenly Father.

Someone wearing the mask of the **invisible person** will also wear that mask in their relationship with Him. They will hide from Him in an effort to prevent Him from hurting them the way others have. The person wearing the mask of the **clown** will perform compulsively to keep everybody, including Him, laughing and happy so there won't be violence and unhappiness.

The person wearing the mask of **Cinderella** will work hard to please everyone, including Him, in the desperate hope they will receive acceptance and approval. We can apply this principle to all the masks people wear.

When we see mommies, daddies, family, and others experiencing pain, abuse, or unhappiness, we would all like to put on our Superman suit and save the day. In this case, the S stands for savior. In addition, we begin to feel responsible for their inadequacies and failures. Our **failure is guaranteed,** because none of us is qualified to be the Savior.

Desperate Needs

Some people have needs so profound they might create a fantasy or an idealized world. They create as *memories* only what they want to believe concerning their childhood, their families, and their lives. For them, it is easier to believe in the illusions of having had their needs met, than to deal with the realities of life.

Those who tell us they grew up with an idyllic life, might tell us how good things were with tears streaming down her faces. They might also tell us about the fouled-up relationships and life patterns they live in now with great emphasis. When we ask where all the emotion is coming from, their response is usually that they don't know. We are then faced with the challenge of finding the truth behind the fantasy, if they are willing.

Let's use some normal, broken people as our example. They have trouble functioning as man and wife in a healthy way. In spite of this, they produce a child who represents responsibility and the distinct possibility of failure to adequately handle it.

If the child is a girl, in many cases an alliance will be established with dad. If he is a boy, most often the alliance will be with mom. This assumes that both mom and dad are still present in the family structure. When such an alliance is formed, the child will usually have a more distant relationship with the estranged parent.

Remember, the two adults have trouble relating to, supplying the emotional needs for, and nurturing one another. The estranged parent is likely to retreat, even more, from the relationship. The act of retreating might be due to anger, resentment, and jealousy. It could also be a method of defense or relief from responsibility.

If mom is experiencing fear of failure concerning her relationship with dad, she might reduce that fear by pushing the little girl into dad's arms. In mom's mind it is the girl's responsibility to satisfy dad's needs. So, now, dad comes home from work and his little princess climbs into his lap in front of the TV. Mom doesn't have to be bothered to interact with him in any significant way. She can do her own thing because she's no longer responsible.

Now let's look at the other side of the coin. Let's say the child is a boy. Dad goes off to work and mom fixes breakfast for the little boy. She tells him he needs to be her little man because daddy doesn't provide for her. He works most of the time and she is lonely and afraid. She says, "If you'll be my little man, everything will be okay."

The message to the little boy proclaims he is someone very powerful and important in mom's life. That seems really cool for him, because it's normal to enjoy being powerful and important to someone.

Many people have stated their dad was a really good provider. They had a nice house, a good car, and all the benefits of a middle-class family. Later in the interview, we found that the important heart needs were never addressed because dad had no idea they even existed. He didn't know how to support or provide for them in any way but materially.

Our need for acceptance, approval, and love never goes away. Without these things we grow up with empty hearts, yearning for what we can't name and have never experienced. We call this condition **empty heart syndrome**. This condition stimulates fear that prompts us to search desperately for ways to fill the emptiness. We believe this is one of the primary motivations for sin.

This didn't begin with our generation, or even in the recent past. We believe it would have begun with the eviction of Adam and Eve from the Garden of Eden. Because of their feelings of abandonment, they must have experienced the sensations of an empty heart. Therefore, many generations of people with empty hearts have come and gone.

An adult trying to be a savior might be called codependent. In our view, a codependent would be a person saying through their words and actions, "I need you to need me." Often this is what we mean when we proclaim, "I love you." Many people believe the codependent person wants very badly to give to someone else. The exact opposite may be true in some cases.

What if the adult codependent is actually functioning as an **emotional vampire**? What if this empty-hearted person needs us to need them so they can feed on us? Any relationship built on this foundation has nothing to do with love but with emotional hunger. It is possible that many marriages are based upon this defiled contract offering.

For parents who have never had their needs met, who have children so willing to give, taking seems natural. Another adult, similarly suffering from **empty heart syndrome**, isn't likely to give as freely. They are more likely to make demands of their own.

They may actually want to have their own needs met. They may want meaningful communication or expect someone to comfort them and offer encouragement. They may want things an empty-hearted person is unable to give. It is much easier to go to a child.

The child is dependent upon the adults in their life and motivated by **a need** for security, love, and acceptance. In response to these desperate needs, most children would be willing to do anything to protect even an illusion of security. Although we believe it's erroneous, this is sometimes described as love. While love could be the motivation for the child's actions, it is more likely the child is responding in *survival mode*.

Parents, or other adults, threaten children with the lie that they are responsible for bad things that take place. If the child were to tell what really happened in the home, someone might be killed or mom or dad might go to jail, or get divorced, and the family unit would be destroyed. We don't believe it is surprising that children, subjected to various abuses, would lie to authorities at school, at church, and to the police.

Young children are particularly inclined to view themselves as the center of the universe. If daddy brings home a carton of chocolate ice cream, it's because they are wonderful. If mommy and daddy fight, it's because there's something wrong with the child.

If someone dies, children often believe it's because they did something wrong. If mommy and daddy are vampires, the children feel responsible and must do something to take care of the problem. The illusion of security can be based on **the need to be needed**.

Emotional Starvation

When we read in Genesis about Cain and Abel offering their gifts to God, we see it as a two-way transaction. They were offering something they thought was good, and were hoping for His approval and acceptance. God accepted Abel's sacrifice and rejected the one offered by Cain.

God confronted Cain, who was feeling very angry and rejected. It is possible that Cain believed he had been deprived of something **he needed** and God wasn't providing his needs. His security and survival were being threatened. Cain's anger could have been stimulated by this fear.

Many generations later, we live in a world inhabited by billions of people. Most of us are struggling with the effects of empty heart syndrome, and the fear we will never have our needs met. With this fear controlling and motivating, is it hard to understand why many of us want so badly to be like God?

Many of us react in the same way Cain did. We decide to give up on God and function as savior for ourselves or for those around us. When we dismiss God as the provider, it becomes necessary for us to find another way to have our needs met.

One of the normal consequences of being fed upon is **emotional starvation**. Since we are asked to provide for the emotional needs of others, we are not allowed to have feelings, emotions, wants, or needs. As a result, we search for ways to get our own needs met. Often we also become emotional vampires.

Picture a man with an empty heart searching for love in *all the wrong places*. He meets a woman whose heart is just as empty as his. A one-night stand becomes a relationship. They conclude they have much in common and begin considering marriage.

They proclaim their *love* for one another which may actually be lust, need, codependency, or emotional hunger. It is very unlikely this is love, because neither one has ever experienced love. They can't give something they don't have.

While they plan the wedding, each unconsciously harbors unspoken expectations. As they recite the vows, they are covertly placing upon one another the responsibility for filling the black hole in their hearts. The messages are transmitted in a variety of ways. "I'm now expecting you to provide all the love, approval, and acceptance I never received. It is now your responsibility, as my spouse, to fill my heart with everything I need to be free from emotional starvation."

This is so efficient; it guarantees failure for both parties. If we were to approach an adult and ask them to pick up the corner of a building, they might laugh and call us crazy. If we go to that same person and ask them to fill our heart with everything we need, they might go into *savior mode* and try to do the job.

No human father, no mother, spouse, or friend can ever hope to fill that black hole. Anyone who tries experiences failure. We can see it in the other person's eyes and mannerisms, and they can see it in ours. Both parties feel betrayed and hear the voice proclaiming their failure. When we go to the Infinite Resource for our provision, emotional starvation and failure issues will fade. When these issues no longer matter, fear is no longer motivating the production of defensiveness and anger.

The system that God ordained would have all needs being met from top to bottom. God is at the top. He is the *Bread of Life*, the *Water of Life*, and the *Source* of love, acceptance, and approval. He is the Source of everything good because He is the only perfect Father. He has the ability and the desire to provide perfectly for all His children. He **never** asks His children to **provide for Him**.

Self-Destructive Behavior

In this discussion we're talking about **lust** and **perversions**. We may resort to alcohol, drugs, sexual perversions, or lust in order to have the illusion that our needs are being met. These categories include such things as adultery, fornication, homosexuality, sexual fantasies, erotic dreams, pornography, prostitution, licentiousness, and over-indulgence stimulated by cravings and yearnings.

Typical Christians will pull out their swords when they see these things manifesting in *someone else's life* and start swinging. Because smoking, drinking, and sexual sins are so detectable, people focus on them. We believe these behaviors are simply fruit indicating deep, unmet needs and are never the primary issues.

Jesus didn't condemn people for such things. When he met the woman who had been caught in adultery, He didn't condemn her. He confronted her accusers; then said to her, *"I don't accuse you either. Go and sin no more" (John 8:11)*.

He confronted the Pharisees and others who were full of self-righteousness, hypocrisy, pride, and arrogance. Her accusers would have stoned her to death but were convicted by His simple instruction. He told them that the one without sin should throw the first stone. (John 8:7)

We must take our eyes off the fruit in order to find healing. We don't accept or condone sin, but we look behind the action to its cause. The things of the heart are much more important than outward manifestations. We look down the tree, to find the bigger branches, the trunk, and the roots in order to discover why a particular sin fruit exists. In our view, **lust is based in fear** and **emotional starvation**.

Throughout the years, a few people have told us that these testimonies were unpleasant to them and should never be discussed in the open. At the same time, there have been many people who have told us these testimonies gave them the courage to face their hidden things of shame. While we honor the few, we have chosen to serve the many. In order to protect others to whom we have ministered, we can give you examples from our own lives.

At the end of one summer, when I was twelve or thirteen, I went to a James Bond movie with my brothers and a neighbor boy. As I watched, I compared Bond and his exploits to my dad, who was not the ideal father figure or satisfactory male role model. He was so fouled up he didn't know how to be a good father or husband. In my mind he wasn't *anything* he was *supposed* to be.

My dad spent all the money he could beg, borrow, or steal on the dogs and horses. Earlier, I described our relationship. As a result, I felt abused, unwanted, and inadequate. I was desperately afraid that I would grow up to be like him. I was his namesake and believed the enemy's lies about me.

As a result, I was desperately looking for a *real* man I could emulate. This guy in the movie could do anything. Every woman who laid eyes on him wanted him. He could kill the bad guys and bed down the women in the same scene. He met every challenge with ease. This was a male identity I longed to attain.

I had been trying to figure out what a man was supposed to be, and the movie was telling me Bond was a real man. I felt overwhelming waves of inadequacy and fear wash over me. I knew I could never be like him.

After the movie, I was standing in the lobby waiting for my brothers and watching the people coming out of the theater. Most of them were couples around my age. I had been working all summer and didn't have time for a girlfriend. Even if I had the time, I didn't have the confidence to attempt such a relationship. I felt cheated and empty.

As I stood there, another series of devastating thoughts hit me: *You're never going to have that. You're never going to find someone who really wants to be with you, love you, and receive your love. You'll never find someone who wants to provide for your needs, or be everything you need her to be. You're never going to find that person.* A desperate new level of fear was planted in my heart that day.

Soon after that event, I started masturbating. I began with, what I would now call, soft-core pornography, doing everything I could to disprove that fear. Later, I began seeking more hard-core pornography. The fantasies became more explicit and weird, as I tried desperately to **be my own savior** and satisfy my own needs.

No matter what I did or how hard I tried, the needs were never satisfied. I could do something really perverted and, fifteen minutes later, the same hollow, desperate feeling would return. This behavior continued until amazingly, a few years later, I found someone who was willing to marry me.

I thought my needs would finally be satisfied, but they weren't. No matter how willing she was to satisfy me, it was never enough. My body could be drained of energy, but my emotional needs were never met. That voice of doom would come back over and over again reinforcing the fears planted years before. I suspect she must've known and received a message that she was a failure. I look back with great sadness now.

I believe we each entered into marriage thinking we would finally have our needs satisfied. Since neither of us could, both of us were unhappy. I continued to masturbate and use pornography, opening the door for the powers of iniquity. Real life couldn't compete with the fantasies and stimulations provided by my *helpers*. I believe that is why many people end up cheating on their marriages. Eventually, our marriage died and we both went looking elsewhere for satisfaction.

Many years went by. I accepted Jesus as my Savior and more years went by. At last, I was willing to think about *them* again. If God would take control and give me the right one, I might consider a woman friend. About that time, I was transferred to Winslow, Arizona, and met Glenna. After nearly a year we were married. We then moved to Las Vegas. At last I was married in a Christian covenant. Everything should have been fine.

Then again, why should it? I had spent thirty-plus years defiling myself, living in my fantasies and imaginations, and providing for my own needs by doing all kinds of weird stuff. I had turned parts of my mind, my nervous system, and my body over to those who promised to help me find satisfaction. Those creatures knew how to put images into my mind and tickle my nervous system in ways a *mere* woman couldn't.

I could be watching TV, see a woman in a bikini, and get all excited; but as soon as Glenna and I began to get intimate, everything went wrong. Strange stuff began happening in my head, and I would see weird pictures. Strange things would be going on in my body; nothing worked right.

Every time I did the things Satan wanted me to do to satisfy my needs, the little door opened and *something* came in. I was giving those *things* control over my mind because I wanted to have wonderful fantasies. Then I gave them control over my nervous system because I wanted to have wonderful sensations. I wanted all the sexual perversions I was involved in to be intensely enjoyable.

I'd believed I was able to function as my own savior by providing my own needs. I didn't have to depend on anyone else. I had thought this pertained only to men, but, amazingly, I discovered that Glenna had done similar things. She had never been married and had defiled herself with fantasies and imaginations using romance novels. They can be used in the same way I used pornography to accomplish the same thing.

Due to my need to perform like *Bond* and my fear of failure, I was willing to blame her, even though I knew I was responsible. It was the same with Glenna. Because of her feelings of shame and self-judgment, she was willing to accept responsibility for the failure of those early times of intimacy. Both of us believed the lies of the enemy and were miserable. Both of us had turned control of our minds and our bodies over to darkness, allowing it to rule. We finally grew desperate enough to go to our only Hope.

We stopped assigning blame and began asking the Lord for help. **He reminded us** of all the years of masturbation, sexual fantasies, and the pornography we had used to meet our own needs. There were many sins and hurts we wanted to go away. We assumed they were all under the blood and gone. However, that isn't what Scripture tells us.

Glenna's story:

"As a little girl I was molested. Not long after that, I began masturbating and continued throughout most of my adult life. As a young woman, I had a painful affair and vowed never to go through *that* again. I would not give anyone else the opportunity to hurt me. I stuck by that vow for many years, until I met John.

"In the interim, I tried to be my own savior and to meet my own needs. I used a slightly different method than John, but experienced essentially the same results. Even in my first few years as a Christian, I was attempting to provide for my needs, knowing it was wrong but being unable and/or unwilling to stop.

"The same kind of thing that John did in his own unique way, I also did. I was single until we got married in 1990 and *celibate* for most of that time. During that period I read many romance novels. I also fantasized and masturbated. I allowed those spirits of darkness to have control of my mind and my nervous system.

"We joined into what was supposed to be a godly relationship, but you can't enjoy a godly relationship when you have all those *bugs,* formerly our *helpers,* interfering. Frequently, we had to stop and pray in the middle of our attempts at intimacy. This had never been mentioned in any of the novels!

Satan, the Blackmailer

"There is a tendency to continue in a downward spiral of perversion, constantly seeking to meet the needs of our bodies and souls. We experience feelings of self-hatred, self-condemnation, self-judgment, failure, guilt, despair, and the drive to do more to feel better. We see no way out of this vicious cycle. (Romans 1:24-32; 1 Corinthians 10:6)

"We had to admit those hidden things of shame to one another. That was the hardest thing I ever had to do. The voice of the blackmailer is determined to maintain secrecy. As long as our shameful secrets are kept in the shadows and hidden, we are under the power of the enemy and subject to his control.

"It is much easier to say, 'Father, this clown You gave me is not doing his job right,' while John was saying, 'Lord, this woman is a mess.' Then, we were honest with each other and began working together to drive out the darkness coming between us. In answer to our requests, the Lord made it possible for us to more honestly communicate with one another.

"A big issue in our relationship was the *performance thing*. In order to be acceptable we had to perform well sexually. All our programming said we had to be *good in bed* to be acceptable as partners. Whether it comes from the gospel of Hollywood, pornography, sweet stories where you live happily ever after, steamy novels, or just your imagination; it is a lie. Sexual prowess has surprisingly little to do with a real relationship.

"When John and I were first married we both believed the performance lies. After many painful *performance* sessions, we realized we were focusing on the wrong thing. As our communication skills improved, our relationship and our intimacy began to improve.

"Instead of blaming or bottling up our frustration, and feeling cheated and angry, we began to share our hearts with one another. We began admitting something was wrong in our own hearts and minds. The Lord began to speak to us in this process. We began to look at the root of this thing and seek solutions. The answers didn't come all at once.

"We now understood that for some period of time we turned both our minds and bodies over to something malevolent for the purpose of heightening *the experience*. We empowered the things *helping* to give us better and better experiences. We gave them permission to stimulate our senses, not realizing how damaging this would be.

"When we decide to have a godly marriage relationship, that *something* has the attitude that it's still in control. When we want to do one thing; it wants to do the opposite. It will do anything to defile a good relationship with our spouse, because that will serve its lord. When we decide to stop fantasizing, so we can have intimate time with our spouse, instead of the fantasy lover, we will begin to heal.

"With this new understanding, before we even started our times of intimacy, we would pray, 'Lord, You created these bodies with their needs. We don't want anything from our enemy; we only want what comes from You. We dedicate ourselves to You, and we ask You to work in every aspect of our relationship. Take control of our bodies and minds.'

"I know that sounds a bit extreme, but it did help. At times, we would catch ourselves slipping into old habits and behavior patterns. We would stop and shift our focus, reminding ourselves we had dedicated our relationship, in all its aspects, to the Lord. If it didn't glorify Him, it was not acceptable. Before long, we began to see positive results.

"We cannot allow *the creatures of defilement* to be in control any longer. We must deal with all of the manipulations of these enemies, and all the ways in which they influence us. We must command these things to let go and get out every time they manifest their presence. We don't have to be subject to the blackmailer's tyranny. We can be free. Our Lord promises to provide **all our needs** according to his riches in glory. (Philippians 4:19)

"We can stop trying to do a job we have never been equipped to do. He is the only One who can satisfy the cravings of our hearts. He wants to pull us into His embrace and give us all the love for which our hearts desperately yearn.

"If we are willing to give up all the jobs at which we cannot succeed and take the jobs for which the Lord has equipped us, we will be able to say, with confidence, *'I can do all things through Christ who strengthens me'"* (Philippians 4:13).

What Is Wrong With God?

Why does God allow each baby to be born through the womb of a person as imperfect as mommy, with an imperfect family, under the spiritual headship of an imperfect father? Why are babies born to be so dependent?

What is wrong with God that He allows these things to take place? Wouldn't it have been better to guarantee that all children would be born into families with perfect parents and perfect family dynamics? Wasn't this possible for God?

When Adam and Eve were first put in the Garden, they were given dominion in this realm. When Jesus came to earth, He achieved what was necessary to pay for all the sins of the world. In doing so, He nullified Satan's claim of control over parts of our soul. After Jesus paid for all the sins, He proclaimed He was giving authority to His followers. Remember, the gifts and the callings of God are irrevocable.

The result of these events is that people wearing clay bodies have both dominion and authority. When God was talking to Cain, He proclaimed that Cain should have dominion over that creature crouching at his door. How much more do Christians have dominion and authority over all the creatures serving the powers of sin and death?

Our goal is to help people realize that the prison holding parts of their soul and humanity is an illusion. This is based upon the miraculous process of healing our Creator provides. Jesus gave us the ability to release all the negative feelings and emotions resulting from trauma. He told us to give Him all those things because He paid for them on the cross. All parents have to do is give their children the opportunity to release them in a natural way.

Many of the people with whom we minister had normal, dysfunctional parents who discouraged their children from using the natural mechanisms for dealing with trauma. Instead, they stifled their children's natural reactions using anger, intimidation, overprotection, and smothering. They may have done this because of their own needs, fear of failure, or feelings of guilt.

They projected the message, "You are not allowed to experience or express feelings, emotions, wants, or needs. In this family system, **our** wants and needs are all that matter." This is not always the case; however, it has been a factor in a surprisingly large number of families of those with whom we minister.

Maybe God isn't so confused after all. In this ministry, we have seen the results of God's creative power. People have experienced terrible things and yet survived. He has obviously built within us a miraculous ability for healing and restoration. Once again, our God is not the one creating the problem. Once again, He gets the credit for what normal, dysfunctional people, inspired by death, do.

How About This for That?

Satan comes to steal, kill, and destroy, and he can accomplish these things through imperfect parents and family. He usually uses people who are unwittingly serving as his agents to offer children subtle emotional contracts.

The contract may offer the **promise** of love, acceptance, and approval, if we give something in return. He might promise we'll never miss it. He only wants some *insignificant* part of our soul or humanity. Although the transaction is done on an unconscious level, it is as binding as if it were done consciously. Children are usually willing to give up parts of their identity, soul, and humanity in the hope they can receive their perceived needs.

Every child desperately wants to receive love, acceptance, and approval. Having these needs met seems to be essential for the survival of a healthy soul. Parents have the power to determine which of these needs will be met. The result can be a form of negotiation.

In order to receive acceptance and approval, we might have to give up our independent thought and expression. We may be allowed to develop our talents to please our parents, if we don't bother anyone with our need for comfort and nurturing. We might grow up to be a compulsive achiever in the hope of receiving acceptance and approval.

Just as we are capable of giving away talents and skills, we can also give away our mental capabilities. We've met people who were told they were too smart, too pretty or too talented. If mom was feeling threatened because of their intelligence, their looks or talent, the safest thing to do was *give it away*.

People don't do these things because they are evil, but because they, too, are victims. All of us have been born into a world in which the need to enter contract negotiations like these is normal. The reason that parents subject their children to these kinds of negotiations is most likely because they grew up with dysfunctional parents.

Many years ago, I saw a movie entitled *The Snake Pit*. In this movie, a woman had **decided** she had become mentally ill. She displayed all the symptoms of dissociation and of being delusional. She was eventually placed into an institution and was diagnosed by members of the staff.

During the movie, she was put into a ward called the snake pit, where she was surrounded by people who were profoundly insane. As the movie progressed, she experienced a revelation about her own mental stability.

She then called for her doctor and told him she didn't belong in the snake pit. He told her he had always known she didn't belong there. He was just waiting for her to discover the truth. We believe it's the same for most people. They simply need to discover the old beliefs and contracts are no longer required for survival. When they do, anything can be restored.

Some people come for ministry expecting us to say a prayer or two so they will be instantly healed. It doesn't work that way. Our job is to help them understand that God has given them the authority. We don't have dominion and authority over their soul. We only facilitate their recovery.

We interview them about significant issues in their lives and mirror back to them what they have said, from a different perspective. Usually they experience revelation and remember events they haven't thought about for many years. We help them discover that behaviors and attitudes they thought were normal are not acceptable, from a biblical perspective. They can decide whether or not to adopt a new perspective and receive healing.

In this process, we may tap into a well of emotions. We assure people they are in a safe environment. They are allowed to **have and express** feelings, emotions, wants, and needs. Some have never before been given this permission. When they are able to express what has been bottled up, they find it both cleansing and freeing. This can help destroy the programming they received growing up.

Earlier we asked the question, *what is wrong with God?* We have concluded there is nothing wrong with God. He has made provision for all our needs. He has given us the way by which we can be free of all the emotional, physical, and spiritual baggage we have accumulated through the years. He has given us the dominion and authority to appropriate these things.

All we have to do is **decide** to accept the gift so we can **experience** the freedom for which He paid such a high price, and **leave the snake pit**.

Refuse Satan's Offer!

The common denominator in all the examples we have described is a desire to be like God. When mom is sad or dad is lonely, depressed, and despairing, the comforter pats their shoulder and tells them everything will be OK. The enemy of our soul lies to us, telling us we need to be like God so we can handle this big job. Even though we do our best, none of us can do these things.

We feel emotionally starved as a result of being fed upon by emotional vampires. We have a fear of failure and sense of inadequacy that require us to perform in every aspect of life, while being terrified of having to perform. These fears are mingled with words of defeat spoken constantly in our hearts.

We are frequently reminded that no matter what we do, it will never be enough. Then *the voice* tells us we might as well die. We were a mistake, anyway. They never really wanted us. Everyone would be better off if we were dead. Somewhere deep in our hearts, even though we don't fulfill the act, there is a fear of life with all its failures and unhappiness and a desire for death. When we entertain this desire, the little door opens and we receive the consequences of our sin.

If you were ever given any of the jobs of savior, you can resign today. If you had to perform to earn approval and attention, you can resign from the job now. The badge of Savior is too heavy. We can't be peacemakers, comforters, or providers. These jobs are just too big for us, and not because we're bad or are failures. We are not qualified. No child can provide for the needs of mom or dad.

Therefore, since Christ suffered for us...we have spent **enough of our past**...when we walked in lewdness, **lusts**, drunkenness, revelries, drinking parties, and abominable **idolatries**. (1 Peter 4:1-3) We've spent enough of our life **under the control** of these things.

Our Conclusions

Your heavenly Daddy doesn't require any of these things. He just wants you to jump into His lap and accept His perfect love, approval, acceptance, grace, and abundance. He truly can provide everything you never received. Daddy, because of what Jesus did, can fill all the empty hearts. Even *you* can have your heart filled. God is the only one big and powerful enough to do this job. This is His heart's desire.

None of us is perfect, especially Glenna and me. We've made a lot of headway over the last few years, and we're much better off now than we were then.

We **can** help people discover they were deceived into taking responsibility for jobs that were never theirs, so they haven't failed. They can give Jesus all the despair, failure, and hopelessness. They can renounce all the jobs, responsibilities, titles, the badges associated with being a savior, and all their efforts to be like God. They can give Him all the responsibility and weight. He doesn't know how to fail.

During ministry we lead people through prayers for cleansing, deliverance, and restoration. They reclaim parts of their soul, humanity, gifts, abilities, dignity, self-respect, and everything pertaining to their true identity and destiny.

They discover they have the right and the ability to rescue parts of their soul and humanity from the snake pit. They can explore the labyrinth of their soul, with all its emotions and traumas, from the perspective of an adult Christian. They don't become the person being traumatized again, but they function as rescuer. The authority given to them by the Lord makes it all possible.

We ask the Holy Spirit to show you if you're being ruled by the fear that your needs won't be met, or that your heavenly Daddy is incapable or unwilling to satisfy all of your needs. We ask that He would shine His light so you can see the truth. We ask Him to show you where the seeds were planted, and what lies have taken root in your heart.

It is time to give Him the job of being the Savior, so you can experience guaranteed success and have your needs met. *"As **His divine power** has given to us all things that pertain to life and godliness... that... you... having **escaped the corruption** that is in the world **through lust**" (2 Peter 1:3-4).* (Also, Galatians 5:16-18; 1 Thessalonians 4:3-5; James 4:17; Philippians 2:15; 2 Timothy 2:21-22)

Once again, it is time to do the most selfish thing so you can be free.

<u>**Sample Prayer**</u>:

In the name of the Lord Jesus Christ, I renounce trying to provide for my own needs through any form of lust, perversions, or over-indulgence of the flesh. I renounce everything serving Satan's kingdom associated with any form of lust.

I renounce the fear, and associated torment, that my spiritual, emotional, or physical needs will not be satisfied, and everything serving Satan's kingdom associated with this fear.

I renounce all bondages, responsibilities, and sin-based jobs associated with being the savior. I renounce the need to be the provider, peacemaker, comforter, companion, confessor, or confidant associated with emotional vampirism.

I renounce the need to compete with anything or anyone for my heavenly Father's love, acceptance, and approval. I renounce all the sinful thoughts, attitudes, beliefs, perceptions, expectations, feelings, emotions, and body memories designed to control me and keep me in bondage. I renounce all failure, despair, hopelessness, helplessness, and the desire to die.

I command all these lies, powers, effects, controls, spirits, and everything I've received from Satan's kingdom to leave every part of my life and being and go where the Lord Jesus Christ sends them. I proclaim my freedom from all sins and their

control in my life through the power of the shed blood of the Lord Jesus Christ.

I choose to maintain my own vessel in sanctification and honor for the glory of the Lord Jesus Christ, who bought me with His shed blood.

I ask my heavenly Father to fill my body and soul with His presence and power. I now dedicate my body and my soul to His glory. Amen.

Desire to Be a Savior

Now we must deal with the "umbrella" sin of wanting to be like the Savior.

Sample Prayer:

In the name of the Lord Jesus Christ, I renounce the voice of the accuser and its function in my mind or mouth; I command the destruction of everything associated with being a savior that has been applied to any part of my being.

I renounce all my efforts to be the savior like the Lord Jesus Christ. I renounce all my efforts to be a savior like the Lord Jesus, everything serving Satan's kingdom as well as all familiar spirits, associated with being a savior. I renounce all their power and control over any part of my life or being, and I renounce all contracts and agreements I have ever made with them.

I renounce everything I have received from Satan's kingdom including all perceived benefits. I command everything serving Satan's kingdom, to give the Lord Jesus Christ everything received from me as a sacrifice because He, alone, has paid for all my sins and He, alone, is worthy to receive all these things.

I proclaim the destruction of all constructs and images that represent real life, dreams, fantasies, or imaginations associated with people, places, objects, events, sights, sounds, smells, tastes, feelings, emotions, body memories, sensations, and stimulations.

I command the destruction of all demonic goodness or demonic badness and everything that would control, deceive, or hold any part of my soul captive.

I renounce all sinful feelings, emotions, attitudes, beliefs, perceptions, expectations, lies, and illusions. I renounce all the responsibilities, including those associated with being a savior, I have taken upon myself for family members, authority figures, or anyone else; for their words, actions, sins, failures, inadequacies, and imperfections; for their inability or unwillingness to protect me, provide for me or to give me the love and respect I deserved as a child of God.

I renounce all these things and the power and control of these things. I renounce the weight of responsibility, all the darkness, death, unclean spirits, familiar spirits, the voices, tormenters, accusations, guilt, condemnation, and all forms of defilement; everything I have received from Satan's kingdom.

I command everything serving Satan's kingdom to leave every part of my life and being, now, to go where the Lord Jesus Christ sends them.

Heavenly Father, I place into Your hands all the parts of my soul associated with my efforts to function as a savior. I relinquish this job and the weight of responsibility for this job.

I ask You to cleanse my spiritual eyes, my mind, and my heart of everything that would deceive me and prevent me from seeing and knowing You as You truly are, or from seeing and knowing myself as You created me to be.

I ask You to give me the revelation that You are my Father, my Brother, and Friend, and I am Your child and friend. I ask You to show the child of my heart how different You are from any one else they have ever known.

I ask You to surround the child of my heart with Your presence and Your power, and flood my heart with Your perfect love, acceptance, approval, Your peace, joy, satisfaction, and security, with everything I have never received so I can be free from emotional starvation and all associated cravings and yearnings.

I ask You to restore everything associated with my childhood, life, my true identity, destiny, everything I lost, everything I gave away, and everything that has been killed, stolen or destroyed, because I was trying to be a savior.

I ask You to make me whole so I can be all You created me to be and know You as my perfect Father. Thank You. Amen.

We liken a person's life to a tree. It has a primary trunk, and many branches. The branches signify the different functions of a person's adult life. All these branches function together, just as do all the different parts of a person's body (brain, lungs, heart, etc.), or soul (the Christian, the worker, the driver, the mom, the dad, etc.). Connecting the trunk to the branches and functioning as the union of the childhood and the adult are the adolescent years. This point of connection occurs when a person is twelve or thirteen.

This is the time, in Hebrew tradition, when a person goes through a ceremony in the temple. In this ceremony, the priest and/or father bless the person's transition from a child to an adult. This is a very important time in a person's life. Both God and Satan orchestrate events to influence who the person will become, as an adult. Adolescents tend to be supersensitive to injustices and betrayals and can be obsessed with the need for control. This need for control can dominate the entire adult life, unless healing takes place.

CAN YOU CONTROL LIKE THE TRUE HOLY SPIRIT?

To control is to regulate, rule, or exercise authority over someone or something. A control is a restraint or something used to guide or manage. In striving for control, we seek the power of the **Judge**, the **Savior** and different aspects of the **Holy Spirit**. Control plays some part in all the issues previously discussed and is worthy of much more attention.

We believe all the issues we have been discussing are rooted in fear. This issue concerning control has been saved for last because it is the most comprehensive way we strive to *be like God*. Most of us grew up in dysfunctional households. It is normal to grow up with inappropriate and oppressive controls placed upon our lives.

On the other hand, when it comes to family, we want to love them and have a good relationship. Everyone knows it's better to have a bad family than none at all. In spite of this desire, we may not dare to trust them because of past experiences. As a result, we have no reason to believe *they* will **provide** for us, **secure** our survival, or **protect** us in any way.

We have all experienced times in our lives when family, friends, parents, classmates, or people in church have **abused** us or **betrayed** our trust. When we experience the *normal abuses* of control and manipulation, we develop automatic defenses. They are designed to protect us from unreasonable control and can apply in every aspect of our lives. Because of being subjected to unjust control, we might reject all forms of control by others. We begin to judge the motives of others.

When we believe someone in our family, pastors in church, or others in leadership positions are trying to control us, we resist automatically. As a process, we decide to limit other people's control in our lives. In truth, we want to be in control ourselves! As we grow and mature, we decide to **take control** of our own lives, the lives of others, and forces that would affect us or threaten our survival.

Next, we must find ways to **maintain control**. Sometimes, the best way to do it is overtly. If someone yells at us, we yell back. If we are hit, we hit back. If someone threatens our survival, we threaten back. While these methods can be employed by anyone, they are usually considered masculine behaviors and might be more risky for females.

Females are usually not as physically powerful; therefore they are more likely to adopt more subtle means of control. They can establish a variety of passive-aggressive activities. They might pretend to agree with someone bigger and stronger, and then, when the other person isn't watching, do what they had planned all along. Or they might find ways to control verbally.

Physical force isn't necessary when the tongue can be used more effectively. Take, for example, a woman who might tell us her husband is so abusive she doesn't know what to do. They might be having a normal conversation and suddenly he would explode like a rocket, screaming, yelling, threatening, and sometimes using violence.

Then, she gives details of their conversation. It followed a time of sexual intimacy and began affectionately. Her husband then said something she interpreted to be a criticism of her ability as a lover. She was hurt and angry and began to tear into him with words. She said, "You think you are such a great lover? Who do you think you could please, you pathetic little man?" At first he looked confused; then, he exploded.

The complete story involves different forms of attack. He was the first to manifest physically; she was first to throw a poison-tipped word dagger. When did the fight really start and who started it? Do we consider physical attacks as the only form of abuse, or are verbal attacks just as abusive?

Which will heal first, the physical bruise or the emotional injury? Most of us consider both physical and verbal violence as attacks on our identity or security. We respond in whatever way we consider appropriate to secure our protection or survival.

Injustice Produces Rebellion

This is our paraphrase of Scripture. If a father **exasperates** his child with commands, demands, or **unjust treatment**, it will precipitate the **need for vengeance** in the heart of his child. (Ephesians 6:4) If, by his actions, the father stimulates sin in the heart of his child, the father shares responsibility for that sin. Instead of properly representing the image of God, he represents a defiled image. Because dad who represents God is unjust, the child perceives God as unjust.

The normal response is to rebel against God and His law. We are convinced the normal response to **perceived injustice** is rebellion. Therefore, this need for vengeance manifests as the **sin of rebellion**.

We can imagine what took place between the serpent, Eve, and Adam in the Garden of Eden. The snake suggested, "I think this is injustice. Why won't God give you this secret knowledge that will make you like Him?

Why does He diminish you and restrict your development? What does He have to fear? Will you be able to threaten His position? You won't have to submit to His unreasonable restrictions if you learn the truth. You were created to be like God, and He is preventing the fulfillment of your destiny!"

We can imagine Adam sitting on a log in a pose like *The Thinker* with his chin propped on his fist pondering these words. We can almost see the computer in his head comparing the pros and cons of the serpent's suggestion.

We also imagine Eve standing with her hands on her hips, giving him *that look* that said, "Come on Adam, I really think this is a good idea. Maybe the snake is right and God is just being unjust. Maybe we'll be much better off, if we know *all the secrets* and can *be like God*." If rebellion is the normal response to the perception of injustice, Satan had only to convince them that *God was being unjust*.

He is doing the same thing today. Does this make people bad? We don't think so because we do believe rebellion is the natural response to **perceived injustice**. If anything serving the serpent can deceive us into believing we are being treated unjustly, we will react in the most normal way. The problem is that rebellion is sin. When we sin, we reap the consequences of that sin.

How do we first rebel? Let's look at an example. Picture a baby in a crib. The baby's diaper is wet and he is uncomfortable. He lets out a squawk to let the adult caretakers know he needs help, but no one responds. He cries vigorously and thrashes around in the crib.

Finally, someone comes to change the diaper, but does it very impatiently, treating the baby roughly and mumbling under their breath. The baby wonders what the problem is. Caretakers should understand these are normal needs. The baby may respond with a sense of outrage, thinking, "This person should not be treating **me** this way."

The baby may assume he was treated roughly because there was something wrong with him. Maybe he is defective in some way, and that's why he has to potty so often. Maybe this defect is the reason that mommy, daddy, or babysitter are always so grumpy and impatient.

Since he feels he is the center of the universe, he must have created the problem. Remember, perception is everything. Maybe it's the baby's fault, and he needs to make amends. Maybe…maybe…maybe…the lies are planted in his heart. As a result of the lies, he might feel fear, shame, or even self-hatred. These perceptions demand a defensive response that may appear to be offensive.

Let's say the baby responds with outrage and a sense of injustice: "How dare this person treat me in this way? Don't they know I'm the center of the universe, and they should respond to all my needs? Don't they know **it's all about me** and what I need to be comfortable? My survival is being threatened, and it's their fault! This is intolerable, and I should not be subjected to this kind of abuse!"

It is a short step from **injustice to rebellion**. Babies are not able to manifest rebellion in too many ways, but can certainly make their dissatisfaction known. They can become fussy and uncooperative with all attempts to establish a routine. They might keep parents up all night. Feelings of injustice and seeds of rebellion lodge deep in the soul.

Does this seem too farfetched for you? Do you think babies don't sense the feelings, attitudes, and even words of those around them and draw conclusions? We think they do. We have ministered to many people who, as babies, understood they were loved, were rejected, or were expected to perform in some way to satisfy their parents or others.

Rebellion Equals Witchcraft and Lawlessness

Following this chain of thought, when others try to **control** us in ways **we decide** are unreasonable, we naturally rebel. Although they could be trying to help or teach us, we may misinterpret their actions and judge them to be unjust or oppressive. Our perception of truth is what motivates our responses.

Our resistance of the control of others and **our perceived need** for control stimulates us to respond in rebellion, which God says is **witchcraft**. (1 Samuel 15:23; Isaiah 30:1 and Deuteronomy 9:7) Do you see what this chain of thought has produced? This is an algebraic equivalence: *control = rebellion = witchcraft = control = rebellion = witchcraft!*

Rebellion is also the **same as lawlessness**. Adam functioned in lawlessness. The Bible says in the last days God will deal with the *man of lawlessness*. This is the one who will rebel against all God's laws and blaspheme the Name of God. In those days, God says that people will be doing what is good in their own eyes and deciding for themselves what is right and what is wrong.

This sounds like many of the teachings that exist in American society today. They proclaim there is no absolute right or wrong. Everything is relative and dependent upon situation ethics.

Here is another algebraic equivalence: **control = rebellion = witchcraft = lawlessness = control = rebellion = witchcraft = lawlessness!** Can you see that all these are woven together as a cord? There are four words with four definitions and they all represent the same sin.

The Importance of Vows

People who have been subjected to injustice tend to focus on the injustice they see around them. It is true there are many injustices and evils in our world. It is also true that people are more concerned about the injustices in their own lives. The abuses and injustices of a typical dysfunctional environment are sources of frustration and exasperation.

Why would anyone choose to respect the laws of God when they believe those laws are unjust? Why would anyone honor God, and His authority, when they believe He is unjust? When people believe these things, it doesn't matter what their mouth says. Rebellion will be apparent in their actions and the fruit of their lives.

This is a similar situation to the one we imagined previously concerning Adam and Eve. The snake speaks into the hearts of people challenging God's goodness. He accuses God, planting the seeds of injustice in their hearts that become the seeds of rebellion.

If we have been abused in some way **we may vow** never to let anyone hurt us again. We might have spoken the vows with our mouths, or only in our hearts. We may have expressed them loudly or very softly. The issue of control, and the sin of wanting to be in control, is based in the hope of avoiding further pain.

We mistakenly believe that such vows put us in control. Quite the opposite is true. These vows give the enemy an open door to torment and control us in various ways. Because such vows are usually made with emotional intensity and fervency, they typically represent sin. As such, they have considerable power in our lives, even long after such vows are forgotten. The Bible warns us about making vows due to their spiritual significance. (See Matthew 5:37 and James 5:12)

Just as God honors our proclamations and vows, we are sure Satan works to help us make vows **based in sin**. This gives him control of parts of our soul or humanity. When a sin creature knocks and we choose to open our door, it is allowed to establish residence in our *condo*. If this sin creature gained access as a result of a sinful vow, we come under the influence of the creature and the consequences of the vow.

A typical scenario might include a small child being abused and victimized by older brothers and sisters. At some time, the child decides never again to allow these things to happen to them. They resolve with a **vow** to become strong and powerful so in the future they will not be subject to abuse.

In effect, they renounce the parts of their soul and humanity they perceive to be weak and worthless. In order to survive, this person would gladly relinquish the God-given attributes they perceive threaten their survival. These attributes could pertain to our natural gender.

We believe something like this takes place, although not on a conscious level. When the contract is offered and accepted, Satan has a legal claim in our hearts. He cannot claim the sins of other people against us. He can only claim our own sins, including vows and proclamations.

Gender Defilement

The book of Proverbs tells us an evil man functions in rebellion and, as a result, a **cruel messenger** will afflict him. (Proverbs 17:11) We remind you that *messenger* means an angel, ambassador, or deputy. This word identifies a subordinate working for its master. In this case, the messenger is described as cruel; therefore, we assume its master is Satan.

"That isn't fair," we protest, "I was the victim. Do I have to suffer twice for something someone else did to me?" As we have said before, the enemy cannot torment us because of someone else's sin, only because of our sin. Our sinful reactions to injustice (such as anger, outrage, offense, or rebellion) invite torment.

We have found another sinful reaction the enemy can use. We believe there are specific spirits of defilement associated with male and female homosexuality, but we don't believe this is the only way gender defilement manifests. There is a phenomenon we call **gender defilement** that affects many people.

This is primarily an issue of self-hatred and doesn't necessarily affect sexuality. The spirit of defilement does not always manifest as homosexuality or lesbianism. It does work tirelessly to pervert godly, man-woman relationships. We often meet men and women who strongly manifest the attributes of the opposite gender and are heterosexual.

In order to protect ourselves, provide for ourselves, or survive, we might receive gifts and abilities from the spirit of defilement. In doing so, we give away the things of our natural birthright and gender, and make it more difficult to receive what Jesus has for us.

A common scenario could involve a little girl arguing with her older brother. He throws her to the floor, sits on her, and slaps her around while laughing and mocking her weakness. She is humiliated and outraged by this abusive treatment **and vows** she'll never let it happen again.

Satan seizes the opportunity to offer the girl a contract. He may offer to help with the problem by providing the demonic armor, demonic protection, demonic powers, strengths, abilities, weapons, and anything else she *needs* for survival.

All he wants in return is her natural femininity, strength, gentleness, and the nurturing tendencies that would make her a good mother. He whispers into her mind, "You'll never miss them."

She agrees to the contract and receives those things she believes are necessary to accomplish her goal. She might receive spiritual entities, attitudes, perceptions, strengths, and the inclination to compete *like a boy*. After this transaction, it's possible she'll assume the attributes of what could be called *a tomboy*.

Does this make her bad? No. She is simply trying to survive. Does this make her a lesbian? She can certainly behave like a lesbian, but we don't believe it is the required outcome of her decision. She may wear her hair like a man, walk like a man, and look for opportunities to compete with men.

The spirit of defilement dwelling in her never sleeps. It is always doing its job to defile its human host. The true identity and destiny of the person has not changed, but the person has taken **upon themselves** a counterfeit identity and destiny.

Let's look at another situation. Imagine that dad has come home in a drunken state. He is angry and belligerent, and demands to know what mom has fixed for dinner. She tells him she's fixed spaghetti.

He yells, "Don't you know how to make anything but spaghetti? How many times a week do we have to eat this slop?" He picks up the pan of spaghetti and throws it against the wall. At this point, Mom explodes and starts yelling back. Dad's response is to grab Mom by the throat, throw her across the dinner table, and choke her into unconsciousness.

(You might be surprised by how many times we've heard scenarios like this related during ministry sessions.)

While mom and dad are fighting, a little boy and a little girl are hiding in the corner, hoping they won't be observed. Both of the children feel terrible because they really want to help mommy but they can't.

They think they should be able to do something but they don't know what. They think they might be able to help mommy in some way, but they don't know how. If they were stronger and braver, they could help but they are too frightened. As a result, they feel guilty and responsible for what is happening.

The little girl thinks, "I don't ever want to be weak and vulnerable like mommy. I want to be strong and powerful so I won't be abused by any man. If someone is going to be abused; it won't be me." At this point, Satan comes with his contract offering, "Do I have a deal for you!"

The little boy thinks, "I don't want to be mean and abusive like that man. I don't want to hurt people like my mommy. I hate that man because of what he does to my mommy, and I hate me because there's nothing I can do about it. When I grow up, I want to be more like my mommy: warm, nurturing, loving, gentle, and good." Again, Satan comes with his contract offering.

What efficiency! One event takes place and massively affects the hearts of two children. Both decided they hated the gender God gave them. Both decided they would become what they *wanted to be*. They would *correct* the injustice and forsake the identity they despised.

Everywhere we have ministered, people have told us they desperately want to serve God and function in significant ways as Christians. They felt they were being *blocked* in some way. They didn't know what the problem was but they could see its effects.

They may have been experiencing difficulties in their marriage, because they didn't have an appropriate relationship with their spouse. They knew there were issues with other relationships, because they couldn't respond to other people the way they should. They knew there were challenges in church, because they couldn't get along with anyone functioning in authority. All these things caused confusion and frustration.

When Jesus was in the garden preparing to be crucified, He responded to His heavenly Father with the heart of submission. In spite of not wanting to do what He had to do, He proclaimed, "Thy will be done."

The issue here is similar, but opposite, because people have decided, "Not Your will, but my will be done." We want God to fix our problems; we also want our will to be done.

While we can understand these motivations, we also understand it creates a whole new set of problems. When **we reject** our true identity and destiny and **take a counterfeit**, our role in the kingdom of God is greatly affected. God can't honor or bless our sin. He won't bless rebellion, because that would make Him an accomplice in the sin. He has to honor our right to defile ourselves.

When we want to live according to our will, even if we want to go to hell, God's response has to be, "Thy will be done." He is grieved by our decision, but His hands are tied by our will.

What is Honor?

In spite of the fact that Glenna grew up in a *good family*, there were events in her life affecting her responses to many things. Prior to our meeting, she went through a tough time that caused her to seek the Lord's help. As a result, she was drawn to a church in the city in which she lived and accepted the offer of salvation.

Later, in a new believers' class, she was confronted with the teaching that she was a bondservant of the Lord. The teaching also covered the way God ordered families, making the husband the spiritual authority over his wife and children. She proclaimed in class, "I'll never submit to any man or to God."

Some years later, she was confronted with the death of her mother and other personal crises. It was only at this time she was sufficiently broken to fall to her knees. Her prayer was, "Lord, I've made a complete mess of my life so I'm turning it over to you." This was the first time she was willing to let him be her Lord, also.

Christian women are told they are supposed to honor their husbands because that represents God's order. Wives are told to submit and yet their man is nothing like Christ. So, why should they submit to him? The husbands may not have any idea what it means to treat their wives the way Jesus would.

At the same time, women today are encouraged by society and the media to resist all forms of male authority, including God's authority. This presents Christian women with an even greater dilemma. They must decide whether to follow God's prescription for wives, or rebel against it and follow the world's view, which we believe is a doctrine of lawlessness.

The problem isn't primarily with the women, but with the men. We've talked to men about the proper way to deal with their wives and have been told, "The Bible says I'm supposed to love my wife like Christ loves the church. I do, I would be willing to kill or die for her. I just want her respect and obedience." (Ephesians 5:22-24)

This guy is just reading one verse and ignoring the rest. If he really would love his wife the way Christ loves the church, he would never oppress her or put her down. He would always raise her up, exalt her, disciple her, and help her become everything Christ created her to be. He would never function as an unjust ruler and stimulate the sin of rebellion.

Ephesians, chapter five, is advice to all Christians. Some of it specifically addresses husbands and wives. If we are to get a clear picture of what the Lord is calling us to do, we must read the whole thing. (Ephesians 5:25-33)

In the book of Acts, the rulers of the temple confronted Peter and John while they were teaching in the temple. The rulers arrested them for healing the cripple and instructed them to stop preaching about Jesus. They also ordered them to stop praying and doing works in the name of Jesus. (Acts 4:18-20) The Apostles were faced with a dilemma. Jesus had told them to comply with the rulers of the land, because God had established the rulers.

Peter's response was to proclaim that if he had to choose between God's command and their command, he would do what God had instructed him to do. This is an example of Peter and John refusing to comply with sinful instructions, despite the fact that the instructions came from an established authority.

The message is clear. When we receive *appropriate instructions and commands*, we comply. When we receive *sinful, oppressive, or inappropriate instructions*, we refuse. God's Word is the ultimate authority. It is our guide for determining what we should do in any situation.

In our opinion, this would apply to a woman married to a man who is not functioning in a godly way. When he gives commands that are ungodly, she should refuse. When he tells her not to do things that God has told her to do, she should reject his command. When he tells her to do things that are defiling, degrading, or sinful, she should refuse.

When he is violent, abusive, or destructive, she should call the police and have him arrested. We simply can't believe that God wants His daughters, or any of His little sheep, **abused by** dysfunctional men or **any** other **unjust ruler**.

We have also ministered with people who have dominating, controlling, and manipulating mothers or fathers. These parents have typically functioned as emotional vampires, and may still be functioning in that way.

The people tell us, "I have to do what they say don't I? The Bible tells me I'm supposed to honor my father and my mother. When I resist, they hit me with, 'I thought you were a Christian. Christians are supposed to honor their father and their mother.'" This causes them to feel trapped and helpless.

What does the Bible really say about this? We must look at all the information, not just part. Usually, people point to the Fifth Commandment to honor father and mother.

This was part of the Law given to Moses by God. It is clear what we are to do, but not clear **how to do it**. The same God, in the Person of Jesus, showed us how He interpreted the Law in practical life situations.

At age twelve, He was left behind in the temple as His family's caravan headed for home. He was asking questions and listening to the teachers. When His mother asked Him why He had stayed behind, causing them worry, He told her He had to be about His Father's business. He obviously believed His heavenly Father's business took precedence over **any** earthly considerations. (See Luke 2:40-49)

Another interesting event is recorded early in the book of Mark. The scribes and the Pharisees accused Jesus of being possessed by Beelzebub (the Devil). They were offended because Jesus had been performing miracles. Apparently, some of Jesus' family heard this and came to take Him away by force, saying He was out of His mind. They attempted to interfere with the work His Father had called Him to do.

They may have been maintaining a safe distance from Him. The rulers of the synagogue were watching the activities of Jesus and His companions very closely. There was a real threat that those connected with Jesus could be thrown out of the synagogue and lose their standing as members of the community.

While He was teaching in the temple, someone told Jesus His mother and brothers were outside and wanted to talk to Him. He refused to go out to them by inferring that the ones He was teaching, those doing the will of His Father, were His mother and brothers. (Mark 3:31-35) In this case, Jesus, Who was without sin, apparently disrespected His mother.

If Jesus is the same God who authored the Ten Commandments, why didn't He honor His mother? Not only did He refuse to go out to her, He did so rather sternly.

His statement suggested she was not doing the will of His father and He would only respond to those who were. If she was not doing the will of His Father, she must have been **functioning in sin**. Did Jesus see their fear of the people and the rulers as sin? Is it possible that, for the sake of **His righteousness**, He could not be a party to their sin? We believe this was the problem.

When we participate in sinful activities with anyone, we become a party to the sin. Even if we are not actively participating, civil law says we are accomplices and are also guilty. Following Jesus' example, for the sake of **our righteousness, we** should **never** be a party to someone else's sin, even if that someone is our father, mother, or family.

We should **separate ourselves** from sinful activity and proclaim, "Who are my parents, my family, or my friends, but those who do the will of my Father."

If our father called us and commanded we purchase drugs, or perhaps some poison for him, what would we do? If we knowingly do something to or for someone and they die as a result, are we responsible? Is their blood on our hands because we helped them commit suicide? We think so. If this is true for the sin of suicide, then it is true for any other sin.

If our parents or family want to engage in witchcraft, rebellion, manipulation, control, emotional vampirism, spreading rumors, or slandering people and we participate, we **are also guilty** of these sins. Engaging in sin does **not honor** anyone. Engaging in sinful activities not only harms us, but also **enables others** to continue in their sinful lifestyle.

This is a very important point to understand. It doesn't mean our lifestyle will instantly change or we will suddenly learn how to **establish healthy boundaries**. It does mean we have some new information with which to make better decisions. Whether this applies to relationships with parents, family, spouses, or any authority figure, we can make more beneficial decisions.

God tells us to **give honor to all people**, because all people are made in the likeness of God. **We honor** the right of another person, no matter who they are, to function in their own sinful lifestyle. **We honor** their right to make really bad decisions and live with the consequences of those decisions. That is how **we give honor**.

Religious Environments and Programming

Previously, we discussed being institutionalized. We believe this happens regularly within family environments that have rigid, or religious, rules for behavior.

If we ask people about their past involvement with religion, they might tell us they don't have any. They grew up with parents who didn't have anything to do with the church or religion. Then, they tell us about all the rules and regulations associated with their family life; that everyone's behavior was controlled by those rules and regulations.

In our view, this is a religious environment. In this case, it might be described as humanism, because no one was acknowledging the real God. In spite of this fact, there definitely were gods demanding worship and obedience. They wore masks that looked like mom, dad, or other family members.

These **counterfeit gods** are always imperfect and usually unjust. They do not present an accurate image of the real God. In their need for control, they establish rules and regulations. If these are not followed, the consequences can include violence, intimidation, various abuses, guilt, condemnation, accusations, and manipulation.

We expect to find all these things in normal religious systems. Used as weapons, these consequences function to program children, causing them to become institutionalized. They also create *double binds*, or lose-lose situations.

When faced with aggression, children must decide how to respond. Their security and survival could depend on the decision they make. If they try to be too strong in meeting the aggression, they could be hurt. If they show weakness, they become easy prey and could be hurt. Whichever way they choose, they could lose and be hurt. This is another example of injustice that fills hearts with frustration and rebellion.

The response to programming could go in another direction, and a child could just give up. They could become passive, compliant, and easily molded. We describe this phenomenon as **rape of the soul**.

Rape has many variations, such as attack, maltreatment, assault, abuse, molestation, or force. It can be defined as theft or **outrageous violation**.

Studies of rape and rapists have been conducted in prisons, and seem to conclude that physical rape had less to do with sexual appetite than with the need to dominate. The rapists functioned as predators and the victims were perceived as pray.

The rapists' goal, and desperate need, is to impose their will on another person to establish their dominance and control. We conclude that people who have been deprived of the *reasonable* controls they should have had, can manifest their need to control using various forms of rape.

For our discussion, rape doesn't require the use of a penis. We are not talking about sexual activity, but about the act of outrageously violating someone's soul or will. This could occur when an attacker rages in someone's face until the victim wilts, totally subjecting his or her will to the attacker. The victim's soul has been subjected to rape, in the form of **domination**.

These behavior patterns usually begin during childhood. Children can be conditioned not to make decisions or exercise healthy controls in their own lives. They experience unpleasant consequences when those in control do not approve of their decisions. Some combination of spiritual, emotional, and physical abuse is often employed against children to **punish and dominate them**.

Punishment can be used to vent the anger and wrath of parents who feel they must have absolute control. Can you see that abusive punishment is something we would associate with Satan's kingdom? Punishment instills fear. Satanism uses fear as a control mechanism, even normal dysfunctional homes, run with strict arbitrary laws and requirements.

The system of relationships, rules, requirements, and programming that surrounded us from childhood is all we know. We don't recognize unconditional love, because we have never seen it. As loving and caring as our parents may have been, they were not perfect. As a result, we tend to raise our children the way we were raised. In doing so, we often use injustice to establish control and program those under our control.

The same pattern can be true in working as supervisors, teachers, or any other position of authority. If we have only seen control established in one way, we will naturally establish control in the same way, because we are programmed to do so.

Are we evil if we are unable to function like our heavenly Daddy? We don't think so; we believe this makes us normal. We all want to survive, have our needs met, and protect ourselves, particularly when we can't depend on anyone else. It would be strange if we didn't respond this way. When a contract is presented that will enable us to survive, we naturally accept.

Alternative to Rape

Because Jesus became sin on our behalf, God's requirement for a perfect sacrifice was met. Jesus took away the need for us to carry the burden of all our sins. God gives us choices. When He tells us to choose, He is never angry or wrathful.

He explains that there will be consequences for all our choices, good and bad. There is no attempt to control, simply a statement of fact. This has nothing to do with whether or not we are saved, but how victoriously we will live in this world, and what our eternal position will be in heaven.

God has managed to blend perfect righteousness, just consequences, and perfect love to establish relationship with His highest and greatest creation. The book of Hebrews states very clearly that the covenant we now have with God is based on His righteousness and love. He interacts with us with grace and mercy.

He is not like people who function imperfectly as they interact with children. His goal is never to control, manipulate, intimidate, or program His children. He is not intimidated when His children function imperfectly. He doesn't want children who are institutionalized. He wants children who love Him and are willing to receive His love.

How Can We Be in Control?

Most people are controlled by their own fears, insecurities, and brokenness. If mom and dad were controlled and tormented by familiar spirits, they would not always attend to our welfare. We might think we are dealing with our parents, but may, instead, be dealing with something functioning through them.

It might look at us through their eyes and speak to us through their mouths, but it is something that can't be pleased or satisfied. This something will never give approval or acceptance, because it is incapable of these feelings and responses. It doesn't feel pity, remorse, or mercy, because these spirits are supernatural beings, functioning through people, to serve the lord of darkness and death.

If we encounter these things, we might eventually decide there is no hope or reason to believe we will receive just treatment from our parents or families. Our hearts might be filled with pain, anger, and rage.

At some point, we might decide *our survival* depends on our being in control. If we can't trust mom, dad, or any other authority figure, we need an alternative plan. There is an expression, *if you want something done right, you have to do it yourself.*

We don't have a chance, but our illusions keep driving us. We have been created with a powerful survival instinct, and most of us will do anything we believe necessary in order to survive. This includes trying to do the impossible.

Many of us follow this line of thinking. However, **we can't be in control**. As children, we are dealing with larger, more powerful people and a system of supernatural beings. We aren't big enough, strong enough, or powerful enough to control adults or anyone else.

When we strive to be in control, we attempt to function in the role of God. We try to replace the Holy Spirit, even though we don't have His infinite power or wisdom. We put on a **big, heavy badge** that says *controller*, and walk through life carrying the weight of that badge.

No mere mortal is capable of carrying that weight or employing the wisdom needed to use that great power. When we try to do these things, we **set ourselves up for failure**. No one likes the feeling of failure. We want to be successful in all our endeavors, and yet, we often guarantee our own failure by trying to do this job.

I have read the Bible many times since accepting Jesus as Savior, and I always had trouble understanding what it meant. I read about God's people in the wilderness, and His command that they take a day off each week to rest. I read His commands concerning weeklong celebrations followed by a holy convocation. He commanded His people to feast, drink, and rejoice in all the good things He had provided.

Paul told us to live in *the rest of the Lord*, and I always struggled with the idea. (Hebrews 4:10, 11) He doesn't tell us to rest one day a week or to take a vacation occasionally. If I understand correctly, Paul tells us we should be living in the rest of the Lord all the time. This flies in the face of all my programming.

I grew up being told *God helps those who help themselves*. I looked for that *Scripture*, because it conflicted with the idea that I'm supposed to be living in God's rest all the time. I studied, checked the concordance, and pored over the Bible, but I couldn't find that verse.

Finally, I found the opposite is actually the truth. **God helps those who allow Him to**! The other quotation, which is not from scripture, has encouraged many people to function in sin. The statement proclaiming I have to help myself emphasizes the contrast between popular beliefs and what Scripture really says.

We also find the Bible warning us not to become entangled in a yoke of bondage once Jesus has set us free. (Galatians 5:1) Jesus encourages us to **take His yoke**, because it is easy and His burden is light, and **He will give us rest**. (Matthew 11:28-30. Also, 1 Corinthians 6:17, 19-20 and Galatians 5:16-26)

Philosophically, I could understand what Jesus said and knew it must be good for me. Beyond this mental assent, however, there was no real understanding. I couldn't imagine turning over *my* problems to someone else. I had no frame of reference, because my father was not a provider.

I couldn't imagine a father who really would provide for me. My programming demanded I do things for myself, because I dare not trust anyone else. Instead of telling Him, "Thy will be done," I would usually say say, "Stand back, God, I can handle this." We've met many people who would follow this line of reasoning. Apparently, we are not willing or able to trust Him.

One night, when I was feeling particularly frustrated, I was complaining to the Lord. If He really is God, nothing is going to happen without His approval or instigation. I was listing all the problems with my business, my marriage, and the challenges of the ministry **He had put on my back**. Logically, I concluded that He was producing these problems in my life for some inscrutable purpose. I was angry and I wanted Him to know it.

As I struggled with these feelings and ideas, I saw a mental image that really surprised me. I could see Him from the rear, as He stood in front of me. In this image, He must have been fifty or sixty feet tall, and had a massive wooden yoke on His shoulders. On the right side, just past His shoulder, the structure of the yoke reduced significantly and extended a little farther out. Built into this very small part, was an indentation that looked like a very small yoke. Hanging from the small part were cords, and attached to these cords appeared to be a piece of wood.

As I was studying this image, He bent down very low and invited me to sit on that little piece of wood. It turned out to be a swing, sized just for me. I took the cords in my hands and steadied myself as He stood up again.

At first I felt somewhat uncomfortable, and He seemed to look over at me, out of the corner of His eye, and smile. As He started walking forward, I swung back and forth gently. Soon I began to enjoy my place in the swing.

As He walked, I would make note of what was happening way down on the ground. I could see what appeared to be a battlefield in an old movie, with bomb craters and burned-out trees. I could see skirmishes and warfare going on all around us.

All the events taking place were very distressing, because they were things with which I had always thought I should help. People were being subjected to various forms of demonic attacks and heavy oppression. In some cases, it appeared they were losing the battle.

It was really strange that He seemed not to notice any of these things. When I couldn't stand it any longer, I asked, "Lord, can You see what's going on down there?" At my prompting, He looked down, smiled, and said, "No problem." He stretched out His hand and pointed at the event, and suddenly everything was okay.

I thought, "Wow!" All I had to do was draw His attention to a particular problem and it became no problem. As we walked along, with me swinging in the swing, I saw more issues that needed to be fixed. As I pointed out these issues, the Lord would smile, stretch out His hand, and everything would be okay. Finally, it seemed very natural. I was enjoying the process.

Even so, I wanted to get out of the swing and get involved in the events around us. Before I even verbalized my desire, He bent down. I slipped out of the swing and began walking forward.

I struggled to get through the charred vegetation and thorny bushes. I carefully worked myself around the bomb craters and through the rubble. The going was very hard, but occasionally, from the low vantage point, I could still see a problem. I would point at the problem and yell up at Him to get His attention.

He would smile and gesture at the problem just as before. The process seemed to be the same, except that now I was on the battlefield experiencing the rigors of moving forward. Eventually, I was getting very tired so I decided I wanted to get back into the swing.

As soon as I made this decision, the Lord bent down very low so I could climb up again. As He stood up, I realized how good it felt. Not only was I out of the dirt and the thorn bushes, but from this new vantage point, I could also feel the cool breeze.

I could see much farther, and I had a much better perspective of what was really happening below. In every way, my ability to function was greatly enhanced while I was in the swing.

I decided to get out of the swing at other times. When I got tired of the struggle, the Lord allowed me to get back in again. Eventually, the time spent in the swing became much greater than the time spent on the ground.

I suppose this is the process of discovering wisdom. We try things in different ways and have an opportunity to discover which is best. In this case, being in the swing was much better than being on the ground.

Later, as I was thinking about this whole thing, it occurred to me that this is what it means to be in His rest. I can try to do the work by fighting my way through the battlefield and becoming tired and burned-out. My other option is to stay in His swing, let Him do all the work so I don't have to get tired and burned-out. I had to ask myself a question. **Which is better for me?**

Now I have a much better understanding. If I want rest for my soul, I need to put all the weight on Him. As long as He is carrying the weight, I can be at rest. I can choose to trust Him, and quit trusting in my own strength and ability. I can give up the illusion that I am, or ever can be, in control.

We're Never in Control

We live in a world influenced by supernatural forces. We live between two spiritual kingdoms: one ruled by darkness and death, the other ruled by Light and Life. We have a very simple choice. God tells us to choose to function either in righteousness or in sin.

We can proclaim, "My will be done," function in sin, and give control to the kingdom of darkness and supernatural beings that want to destroy us. Our attempt to control everything ourselves opens the door for the enemy of our soul. (Proverbs 17:11)

These cruel beings serve Satan's kingdom and can do us harm using powers and abilities beyond our understanding. When we give control of our lives to them through sin, we experience the consequences of our sin.

Or we can proclaim, "Father, Your will be done in my life, even as it is in heaven." When we respond humbly, there are other supernatural beings that want to minister to our needs and help us experience victory in our lives. They serve our heavenly Daddy and have abilities and powers beyond our comprehension to do good for us.

All around us are supernatural beings, and **we have the illusion** that we're going to be in control? It's obvious **we only decide who will** be in control. We can give control to our **greatest enemy** or to our **greatest Friend**. The question is, and this is a hard one, **which is better for us**?

As always, the choice is ours alone. Relinquishing control to our heavenly Father allows **Him** to work in our lives and gives us true freedom. **This is rest for our souls**. Now, if you are ready, it's time to pray.

Sample Prayer:

In the name of the Lord Jesus Christ, I renounce believing that my God and Father cannot be trusted to control my life. I renounce the fear of relinquishing control to God, and all vows, oaths, and contracts I have made, turning any part of my soul or humanity over to anything serving Satan's kingdom.

I renounce all rebellion and the sin of witchcraft whereby I have tried to maintain control of my life or the lives of others.

I renounce all forms of spiritual armor, protection, powers and strengths, abilities and weapons, everything I have received from Satan's kingdom in order to survive, protect myself, or provide for my own needs.

I bind and renounce everything serving Satan's kingdom associated with control, rebellion, witchcraft, and all associated fears. **I command all these to go where the Lord Jesus Christ sends them.**

I ask the Lord to replace these things with His armor of light, His power and protection, His strengths, abilities and weapons; with glory, righteousness and royalty so I can know myself as He knows me.

I proclaim that I trust God to control my life, and I ask the Lord to free me from the bondage to fear. I choose to give my Heavenly Father control. Amen.

CONTROLLING THROUGH SICKNESS OR INJURY

We have chosen to separate this issue from the previous chapter because we perceive it to be significant to many people. There's a special aspect to control that has to do with our physical bodies and our souls. We believe this is so important it needs to be addressed separately. We certainly would not propose that all sickness is self-imposed. However, some people **use sickness** for various purposes. There is usually a **perceived benefit** of some kind.

Some people seem to be complying with the will of others. We have ministered with people who have been programmed for sickness by family or the medical establishment. Imagine, for example, a little girl who had been taught by her mother she was supposed to have pneumonia at the same time every year. We don't know how or why this pattern began but we've seen the outcome.

As an adult woman, it didn't matter what the weather was or what else was going on in her life. At the specified time each year, she and her mom expected pneumonia to manifest and it did. She was programmed. For a week or two, this woman had a very powerful position. She might go to the hospital or she might stay at home maintaining control of the family. We've discovered variations of the same phenomenon many times, in many places.

I have no reason to believe my father was ever programming us. On the other hand, he manipulated and controlled people using techniques that, I believe, had a spiritual component. Frequently, when he and my mom would fight, he would get sick. When she was ready to give in and let him win, he would get well.

I remember one particular night when he goaded her into walking to the liquor store in the rain to buy him some whiskey. This served as her peace offering. I walked with her that night because I was the oldest son and felt it was my duty. As I recall, a similar scenario re-occurred a number of times. I felt that sense of anger and outrage on my mother's behalf each time.

I felt angry because of the way he was treating and controlling her. I also felt another dimension of anger because I wanted to protect my mother from his abuse but there was nothing I could do. This produced a sense of shame and the fear of being worthless, which manifested as anger.

Something else intrigued me. My dad apparently had the ability to be sick whenever it suited his purpose. There was power in that ability. I don't remember the process of considering the potentials of this power, but I must have at some level of mind.

One morning when I was nine or ten, I woke up and realized I hadn't studied for a test at school. Immediately I thought, "I'll be sick." By the time my mom came to get me up, I had a fever and nausea. My mom even smelled my breath and said, "Yes, you're sick," and called the school to tell them I wasn't coming in that day.

She went to work, and ten minutes later I was miraculously healed. It was cool. I couldn't use this ploy very often, because I knew she would catch on, and I'd be busted. However, I used it every now and then.

As an adult, when the pressures and responsibilities seemed too big and oppressive, I would get sick. I could decide I *needed* to be sick, and within a few days I would have pneumonia. The doctor would give me a note, and I'd send it to work so I could be off, with pay, for a week.

There was another interesting phenomenon that occurred in the Miller household. My dad apparently wasn't allowed to punish us with spanking or physical violence. I believe my mom had read a book on child psychology.

It seems this was one rare issue where my mother prevailed, because I only remember physical punishment being administered on rare occasions. We did hear many times, "I'll give you something to cry about," but he rarely used physical punishment. Looking back, I am sure this was frustrating for my dad. As a result, he had to find creative ways to punish us and vent his anger and frustration.

One of his methods of punishment was to put us in the closet. In the summertime that closet was very hot, dark, and unpleasant. Occasionally I would feel something crawl across my foot and hoped it wouldn't bite or sting.

Sometimes I would sit in that closet and fantasize about all the bad things that were going to happen. I would see myself break out in big bleeding sores, or I would imagine having terrible problems in my lungs. Sometimes, I would even imagine dying and, "Boy, will **they** be sorry."

I thought I was the only one who did that. I had never verbalized these things to anybody until Glenna and I watched a movie called, *The Christmas Story*.

The little boy in the movie desperately wanted a BB gun. At one point in the movie he said a bad word and his mother made him *wash his mouth out* by sucking on a bar of soap. When he went to bed, he fantasized about going blind.

In his fantasy, after he was blind, he visited his parents, handed them a note, and sat down on the sofa. The note said the blindness was due to soap poisoning.

As his parents wailed and moaned, the boy sat there with a huge grin of glee on his face. He, of course, was thinking, "If something terrible happens to me, or if I die, they'll really suffer." He thought it would be worth the pain, suffering, or even death, if he could have his vengeance and WIN. That's the payoff!

I looked at Glenna and said, "I used to do that." She gave me a funny look and said, "I did too."

As it turns out, that little boy isn't unique, and neither are we. Since then, many others have confessed to us of doing the same kind of thing. Our question is, what are the spiritual effects of iniquity that we experience as a result of **wanting to be sick** or **wanting to die**?

Another example of wanting sickness or infirmity occurred when I was a young man. I was in an auto accident during the seventies when whiplash was so popular. My car was rear-ended. Almost instantly, after recovering my senses, I thought, "Whiplash!" I really wanted to have whiplash and be hurt bad enough that I would get millions, but not bad enough to prevent me from enjoying them.

I experienced a couple of weeks of real misery, with pain in my neck, shoulders, and head. It was hard to sleep, and if I moved my head too quickly, everything would go black for a moment. There were times when I was just plain miserable. However, when I thought about the millions, I was glad for the pain.

With the doctor's report and other considerations, my attorney decided I didn't have a significant case. We negotiated with the other driver's insurance company to reach a settlement. My attorney, who seemed to have done very little, received much of the settlement while I suffered the pain.

It was just another case of **wanting to experience infirmity**. I had been fairly successful at it, as a youngster. In this case, I did manage to get out of work for a week, so there was a small payoff.

Glenna offers the following from her own experience.

"In ministry, anytime we ask the Lord to reveal the root of some issue in a person's life, we accept what the person receives, and minister to it. We have discovered it makes no difference whether the revelation concerns a real event, a dream, or an imaginary event. Perception is the key. Our object is to find how an event affected the person adversely and minister based on the information.

"Part of the reason we do this is because of the ministry we have done with one another. One evening, at John's urging, I asked the Lord to show me the root of some physical problems I was experiencing. We were both greatly surprised at what I vaguely perceived. While the actual events were hazy, my feelings were extremely vivid and sharp.

"I had known for quite some time that I was molested as a child. Because of the molestation, I believed I was dirty, bad, and nasty. Self-hatred, self-rejection, self-judgment, and self-condemnation were very strong. They worked together with other things I've experienced to create strongholds. I believed I was at fault for being molested. Because of the shame and fear of rejection, I didn't speak of it for many years.

"After becoming involved in ministry and with the Lord's help, I discovered there were earlier incidents in my life that greatly affected me. Both of the following incidents occurred as a result of what would seem to be unimportant events. Even so, my reactions opened the door for the enemy to afflict me.

"When I was about eighteen months old, someone changing my diaper was a little rough. I felt offended at being so roughly handled. I experienced a variety of emotions including outrage, anger, betrayal, shame, and feelings of being violated. I also experienced the perception of being treated as though I was not important.

"I had an intense sense of dissatisfaction because my needs were not being *properly* met. I was bombarded with self-pity. I definitely saw myself as a victim, and yet also suspected I must be at fault, somehow, or it wouldn't have happened. I felt yucky.

"When I was a little older, I again felt misused or roughly treated by an adult, not in punishment, but in an ordinary social situation. The Holy Spirit showed me a picture of the little girl pitching a fit over this perceived offence, causing my parents much embarrassment. They were quick to show their disapproval and disgust at my behavior.

"In my mind, this was even more reason for me to be upset and offended. I felt unjustly accused, betrayed, and victimized. Because of my parents' reaction, I looked for ways to justify my actions and shift blame.

"I also looked for ways to establish a measure of control. In those very early years, I began to use **sickness to escape** the consequences of my own behavior, or **avoid responsibility** for assigned tasks. I was able to receive the attention I always craved as well as punish *the abusers*, and exert some control in my family. As I was the youngest and the only girl of three children, I was always looking for ways **to be in control**.

"I had dissociated these events until I asked the Lord to reveal the source of my feelings and physical manifestations. My fear of losing control of myself, of not being in control of situations, or of being controlled by others was causing problems in my relationship with John. I learned that my attitudes, beliefs, and responses were being shaped by my childhood experiences and perceptions."

There are many forms of sickness and many forms of death. The issues we have discussed all pertain to physical illnesses. In our experience as ministers, we have discovered that sickness and disease can also **affect the mind**. In our need for control we can resort to extremes. Some of the people we have interviewed have used **mental illness** as a **form of control**. We have also been told about children who were subjected to parents using this form of control.

People have recounted memories of a parent threatening to go insane, saying, "You kids are driving me crazy! You'll really be sorry when I go into an institution and you won't have me around anymore. It will all be your fault." This is a classic form of punishment for those who will not honor someone's right to exercise absolute control.

In some cases, these parents actually did have a breakdown and were hospitalized. The children felt terribly guilty, even though the adults were responsible for their own words and choices.

Some parents threaten to commit suicide. Children have been lined up against a wall and forced to witness their parent cut them self with a butcher knife. The blood begins to flow, the children cry and scream, and the adult rants and raves about how they are going to suffer when he or she is gone. We believe that many of the people exhibiting these aberrations do so to receive attention, establish importance, or maintain control over those around them.

Let's review the different options. Sometimes we want to be sick to **escape pain or responsibility**. We could choose infirmity because we **want to receive money** from a whiplash case. We might want to be sick because in that way, **they will suffer**. We may want to **receive attention, sympathy, importance, or exercise control** through the sickness.

Although we believe we are crummy and worthless, we may use any or all of these devices to prove to ourselves that someone does care. Otherwise, we might be overcome by the fear that others would agree with our self-assessment.

Maybe we just **like jerking people's chains**. If we like **being in charge**, we exert control through manipulation. We enjoy knowing that when we are sick, or decide to be sick, **everybody's going to jump**. Children, particularly, would be willing to do almost anything to protect their illusion of security. Imagine the feeling of power!

Is Sickness an Illusion?

Please understand, we don't believe this is the same as hypochondria. We are not talking about pretend or imaginary sickness. We believe the symptoms are real, the sicknesses are real, and the effects are real, because we have experienced it.

In the early 90's, we were heavily involved in deliverance with some very *special* people. We were spending virtually all our spare time doing so-called ministry. At the same time, we were experiencing a variety of unpleasant emotional and physical manifestations. We often prayed for hedges of protection around our home and around us. In spite of our prayers, we continued to experience these things. We couldn't understand why.

One day I was, once again, complaining to God. I told Him how hard we were working to serve Him, holding down full-time jobs and doing ministry in our spare time. Sometimes the pain was so great, if I moved my head from side to side, I felt I was going to black out. He was allowing all this *stuff* to happen, and I was sniveling and whining.

I continued by reminding Him that we were doing all this to take care of His people, and He wasn't even helping us. I was telling Him how much of a failure I thought He was. It didn't take long before He began giving me little flashes of insight. They included wanting to have whiplash.

When I arrived home, I started telling Glenna. The flashes of insight really began to flow. I remembered sitting in the closet and wanting to have terrible things happen to me. I remembered the times I'd wanted to be sick to escape school, work, and responsibility, or to manipulate and control. I remembered so many things I had done, willingly, to be sick. Glenna was remembering similar things in her life.

The Lord told us the reason we were experiencing pain **wasn't** because the problem was **out there**; it was because the problem was **in us**. Tilt! **Here we were trying to fix everyone else, and we needed fixing the most!** This process of discovery was pretty rough. We were receiving understanding about our own sinful motives and their effects on our lives.

We prayed, renounced, and repented throughout the evening. When we went to bed that night, it seemed as though nothing had happened. When I woke up the next morning, the pain in my neck had reduced significantly. Over the next few days, the pain actually diminished to almost nothing. Over the next couple of weeks, other physical manifestations faded.

During this process, it occurred to me that I experienced the pain because I wanted *those things* in my life. Of my own free will, I had given them control over my body. Once they came into me, they would gladly make me sick when *I* wanted, but they would also make me sick when *they* wanted.

Before, **there had been a payoff**. We could escape from life and responsibilities. We could get sympathy, attention, and things we wanted, maybe even five million dollars. We were face to face with the consequences of our sins, and they weren't at all pleasant or attractive. All we were getting was pain.

That was a turning point for us. There are many aspects to this thing. As we prayed and renounced giving control over our bodies and souls to Satan, the manifestations decreased. We received so much relief from suffering we began sharing with some of the people with whom we were ministering. We would tell them what we had experienced and why, and ask them if they could relate.

Somewhat reluctantly, they might agree and we would take them through prayers similar to the ones we prayed for ourselves. Later, we would receive a praise report about some benefit they experienced. After receiving these testimonies, we added this discussion to our seminar material along with associated prayers. We frequently see examples of this phenomenon working in people's lives.

A day or so after a scheduled seminar, someone may tell us they were really planning to come, but the morning of the seminar they felt ill and went back to bed. Then they assure us they won't miss the next one. You have no idea how many times we've heard something like this, sometimes from the same people.

From this we conclude there may be others who are just as deceived, in this way, as we were. Is it any wonder that on Sundays, when the Lord moves in an awesome and magnificent way, some people don't come to church because *they are sick*? It is no surprise at all. When we invite the powers of sickness and death into us, they receive control. We become the slave of sin.

The contract might read something like this, "We will be glad to make you sick any time you want. We will employ the power of death in your body and soul, whenever it pleases you, and, since you invited us in, we will impose death and/or sickness on you when it pleases us. When you schedule something to serve the Lord, or to receive His blessing, we will be pleased to do our work."

Now, if this makes sense to you, it is time to pray.

Sample Prayer:

In the name of the Lord Jesus Christ, I renounce ever desiring any form of sickness, infirmity or death for any reason. I renounce giving death, sickness, disease, injury, or infirmity a place in my body or soul. I renounce all the perceived benefits I received.

I renounce giving control of any part of my soul or body to Satan's kingdom as an act of my will, through programming or by any vows spoken aloud or in my heart. I renounce everything spiritual or physical associated with sin, iniquity, and defilement I have received onto or into me.

I command everything serving Satan's kingdom to which I have given access to my soul or body, including all sickness, disease, manifestations, symptoms, illusions, and body memories to go now where the Lord Jesus Christ sends them.

Heavenly Father, I ask You to flood my body and soul with Your light, life, healing, and restoration. Thank you Lord. Amen.

Desiring to Be the Controller

Now we must deal with the "umbrella" sin of wanting to be like the Controller.

<u>Sample Prayer:</u>

In the name of the Lord Jesus Christ, I renounce the voice of the accuser and its function in my mind or mouth. I command the destruction of everything associated with being a controller that has been applied to any part of my being. I command the destruction of all demonic goodness or demonic badness I have received. I renounce all my efforts to be a controller like the Holy Spirit.

I renounce everything serving Satan's kingdom, as well as all familiar spirits, associated with being a controller. I renounce all their power and control over any part of my life or being, and I renounce all contracts and agreements I have ever made with them. I renounce everything I have received from them.

I command everything serving Satan's kingdom, to give the Lord Jesus Christ everything received from me, as a sacrifice, because He has paid for all my sins and He, alone, is worthy to receive all these things.

I proclaim the destruction of all constructs and images that represent real life, dreams, fantasies, or imaginations associated with people, places, objects, events, sights, sounds, smells, tastes, feelings, emotions, body memories, sensations, and stimulations. I command the destruction of everything that would control, deceive, or hold any part of my soul captive.

I renounce all sinful feelings, emotions, attitudes, beliefs, perceptions, expectations, lies and illusions. I renounce all the responsibilities I have taken upon myself for family members, authority figures, or anyone else; for their words, actions, sins, failures, inadequacies, imperfections, and their inability to give me the love, honor, and respect I deserved as a child of God.

I renounce all these things and the power and control of these things. I renounce the weight of responsibility, all darkness and death, unclean spirits, familiar spirits, the voices, tormenters, accusations, guilt, condemnation, all forms of defilement, and everything I have received from Satan's kingdom.

I command everything serving Satan's kingdom to leave every part of my life and being and go, now, where the Lord Jesus Christ sends them.

Heavenly Father, I ask You to cleanse my spiritual eyes, my mind, and my heart of everything that would deceive me and prevent me from seeing and knowing You as You truly are, or from seeing and knowing myself as You created me to be.

Lord, I ask You to give me the revelation that You are my Father, my Brother, and Friend, and I am Your child, Your family, and Your friend. I ask You to show the adolescent of my heart how different You are from anyone else they have ever known.

I now place into Your hands all the parts of my soul associated with my efforts to function as a controller. I relinquish this job and the weight of responsibility for this job.

I ask You to surround the adolescent of my heart with Your presence and Your power, and flood my heart with Your perfect love, acceptance, approval, peace, joy, satisfaction, and security, with everything I have never received, everything necessary for me to be free from emotional starvation and all associated cravings and yearnings.

I ask You to restore everything associated with my adolescent years and my life: my true identity, destiny, everything I lost, everything I gave away, as well as everything that has been killed, stolen, or destroyed in my attempts to be a controller.

I ask You to make me whole, so I can be all You created me to be and know You as my perfect Father. Thank You. Amen.

YOU CAN BE EVERYTHING HE CREATED YOU TO BE!

Throughout this book, we have been discussing the desire of normal people to be like God. In the Garden of Eden, this was Adam's sin. The serpent came to Adam and Eve and sold them a lie, convincing them that God was being unjust. He convinced them that they could, *in their own ability*, become like God; all they had to do was *learn the secret knowledge*.

Since then, the prophets of hell and the religious systems of the world have propagated this lie. The worship of philosophies, all based in humanism, has been the predominant religious system throughout the centuries. Today, governmental systems, religious systems, educational systems, and cultural systems continue to teach this lie.

People are being taught that they can earn the right to be like God by learning the mysteries of the universe, by doing good works, or by paying for their own sins. There is no difference between these religious systems and the religious system introduced in the Garden of Eden by Satan. We have endeavored to illustrate this truth: through our own abilities, it is **absolutely impossible** to be like God.

It is essential that we understand what God says. Throughout the centuries, He has been reestablishing relationship with mankind. He has been unfolding His master plan to bring us **back to Him**, to a **place of life**, from the death that has bound us. Now, we see, in the light of truth, the gospel of Christ and what **it offers us**.

Righteous

Faith in Jesus Christ causes the **righteousness of God** to be given to all that believe. (3:21-26) What does this mean?

We don't receive the righteousness of God because we have a philosophical understanding. Believing in Him means believing in Him as the Savior for us, personally. It has nothing to do with **our** works; it has entirely to do with **His** works. In Romans, chapter 4, **God imputed righteousness,** without works. We are **justified by faith** and we receive **peace with God.** We accomplish this by **allowing Him** to be the Savior.

The good news is that when we allow Him to be our Savior and accept His works, we receive His righteousness. We receive justification, and peace with God. These are not just possibilities; they are guaranteed by His righteousness.

The Bible says that God is Love. This is a proclamation of His identity and His nature that is constant and forever. He is absolute Love. God **commanded His love** toward us before we even had relationship with Him. While we still hated Him, He loved us with a love we cannot comprehend. (Romans, chapter 5)

We were **reconciled to God** by the **free gift** that provides **justification,** despite our many sins. **His gift of righteousness** is given as an act of **abundant grace.** Jesus paid for all the sins of the world, so this righteousness must apply to past, present, and future.

Free From the Law of Sin and Death

If we have been given righteousness as a gift, can the law of sin and death still hold us in bondage? Paul proclaims there is **no condemnation** to those who are in Christ Jesus. The **law of the Spirit of life** in Christ Jesus has made us free from **the law of sin and death.** (Romans, Chapter 8) Can you see that the law of the Spirit of life is **preeminent** over, and has **nullified** the law of sin and death? (Romans 8:33-35)

If God, alone, gave justification, He, alone, can take it away. He won't, because the gifts and the calling of God are irrevocable. It is Christ who died and now makes intercession for us. His prayers are perfect and will always be honored by His Father.

The Lord guarantees to **complete the work** He has begun in us. This gives us the ability to cry out, "Daddy, Father!" That we still function imperfectly is normal. Nothing we can do is powerful enough to nullify what He has done, or the identity He has given us. It is impossible for us to scuttle His master plan.

Heirs with Christ

He continues by telling us that the Holy Spirit tells our spirit the truth: we are **children of God.** If we are His children, we are heirs of God and **joint heirs with Christ.** We are told that we will suffer with Him, but we will also be **glorified together with Him.**

We can imagine Him sitting at the right hand of God the Father. We can imagine the glory radiating from Him, brighter than lightning. Does this suggest that **if** we are glorified together with Him, the glory applies to us also?

If Jesus is really the Christ, and the Christ has been made Lord over creation, what does this mean to us? Trying to figure out what it means to be a joint heir with Christ is mind-boggling. It may be impossible for us to comprehend the magnitude of this concept with our finite minds. We believe that one day we will understand and will be moved to joy beyond anything we could experience now.

The Spirit searches our hearts and minds and makes intercession for us according to the will of God. Even when we are not praying for ourselves, **He is praying for us**. This is how He will be able to complete that work He has begun.

When we invited Him through our door, we received His perfect intercession. He always prays in accordance with what is best for us, even when we don't understand it. It is His job to function as our Teacher and our Trainer, so we can become everything an heir of God should be, as a part of His royal household.

Guaranteed God's Love

Because of all this, we know that all things work together for good for those who love Him and are called according to His purpose. Before the foundation of the world, He knew what His master plan was going to include. He knew who we were going to be, what we were going to be, and how we, individually, would fit into His plan.

In spite of all those things that have mystified us, nothing has been a surprise to Him. **He foreknew us** and **predestined** us to **be conformed** to the **image of His Son**. We have been called, **justified,** and **glorified**. We are given the guarantee that **nothing can separate us from the infinite love of God!** (See Romans 8:28-30; 35-39)

When Joshua led God's people into the Promised Land, God told them He wasn't going to give them all the land at one time. They would take part of it and then learn to occupy it. He would then help them take another part of the land and help them learn to occupy it. Thus the process would continue. Our goal is to possess all the spiritual land the Lord has ordained as our inheritance.

He is teaching us how to give up the roles, jobs, and responsibilities associated with being the Creator, the Judge, the Savior, and the Holy Spirit. He is teaching us how to let Him do those jobs, so we can become more victorious and successful in our lives. We believe that, as we go through the ministry of deliverance and restoration, our inclination to sin will be greatly reduced.

His Divine Nature

He is taking us from glory to glory. (2 Corinthians 3:18) Did you notice it is all about what **He is doing**? It is not about what **we are doing**. Earlier, we said that our efforts to become like God guaranteed our failure. Being like God, **in our own ability**, is absolutely impossible. Remember those words; **absolutely impossible**.

On the other hand, look at all the Scriptures we have already presented concerning our inheritance as His children. Look at all He has already done to guarantee our position in eternity.

This is a glorious guarantee. He uses **His own divine power** to give us everything pertaining to **life** and **godliness**. Through the knowledge of Him Who has called us to **glory** and **virtue**, we may become **partakers of the divine nature.** (2 Peter 1:3)

Did you see that? Through His own divine power, He has done what is absolutely impossible for us to do. He has given us everything pertaining to life and godliness, and everything necessary to become like Him. Furthermore, He has called us to glory and virtue as His children.

Finally, He makes the most awesome statement of all. As we get to know Him better, we become partakers of the divine nature. This is part of His master plan, and a guaranteed end result. We don't know how long it will take, or even if it will occur in this life. We don't know to what extent we can take on His divine nature while in our clay bodies. We do know it is **inevitable**. We do know it is **absolutely impossible to fail**!

Do you see the contrast? When we try to do it in our own ability, it is **absolutely impossible to succeed**! When we allow Him to do it, in accordance with His infinite ability, it is **absolutely impossible to fail**! Now, this is a really tough question. Which is better for you, guaranteed failure or guaranteed success?

When we know Him as our **Father**, **Brother**, and **Friend**, we are able to establish a greater level of fellowship with Him. The goal is to allow Him to make us to be like Him. The goal is to **reflect Him**, **represent Him**, **channel Him**, and **allow Him** to exalt us to the highest and best place He has for us. One more time, let's pray.

Sample Prayer:

My God, Father, and Savior, I acknowledge You as the only Lord over all creation.

I praise You for the gift of righteousness. I praise You for justifying me and for the gift of peace. I praise You for the amazing gift of love. I praise You for the promise that nothing can separate me from Your infinite love!

I thank You for adopting me and making me a joint heir with the Lord Jesus Christ. I thank You for completing the work You have begun in me, and I ask You to do whatever it takes to complete that work.

I know that all things work together for my good because I love You and I am called according to Your purpose. Please teach me how to take Your yoke so my soul can, finally, be at rest in You.

I ask You, Lord of heaven and earth, to restore to me everything I need for Your perfect will to manifest in my life.

I am going to rely on You to raise me up to the highest and best place You have created for me. I want to reflect, represent, and glorify You.

Thank You for everything You are and everything You do! Amen!

In Closing

The Lord has commanded us to be whole, so we can love, serve, and worship Him with all our heart, mind, will, and strength. If this were not possible, He would be unrighteous to command it. We believe it is possible to find the best path He has for each of us and receive all of our inheritance. This will also include the highest and best place in His kingdom.

Some people are not going to accomplish this for various reasons. It doesn't, in any way, affect His love or acceptance of them. We believe it fills His heart with sadness that they won't receive the best.

The focus of our ministry is to facilitate a process of restoration to accomplish everything described above. We suspect the coming days will include many hardships and challenges, and the Lord has given this ministry for a time such as this. Our greatest blessing is to help equip His army. We believe restoration will include our physical bodies, because no army can survive without dependable vehicles.

We believe we can and should be healed, because it is a part of our salvation. He bought it for us, so we believe we should receive our healing in this life. We also believe He has given us a great responsibility as stewards of our bodies. He expects us to do what we can do to keep our vehicle functioning efficiently. He will do what we are not capable of accomplishing.

We trust the promise in Romans 8:11, *"He who raised Christ from the dead will also **give life to your mortal bodies** through His Spirit who dwells in you."*

We have faith that He will complete the work He has begun in all of us. It will be done, for sure, when we stand before the Judgment Seat. Then, all the hay, straw, and stubble will be burned up in the light of truth. What we hope is that He will be able to do it in most of us before we leave this earthly realm.

Everything will be brought into the light, dealt with, recompensed, and finished. We believe His judgment will be the toughest time we will go through. We may be in a big room with millions of others watching. It seems to us that it is much easier and more beneficial to get as much as possible done, here and now.

He has promised that, if we will judge ourselves, we will be saved another judgment. Then, because we've been healed, He can raise us up to be everything He created us to be.

You, and everyone you know, can receive healing NOW. This isn't complicated! Whenever that still small voice makes you aware of something that needs healing, you must be willing to deal with it. You don't have to obsessively look for things. Just give Him permission and He will show you the truth. This is not the John and Glenna show; this is the **JESUS** show.

THE END, OR MAYBE THE BEGINNING.

BIBLIOGRAPHY

Achtemeier, Paul J., General Editor. *Harper's Bible Dictionary*. San Francisco, California: Harper & Row, 1985.
The Amplified Bible, Expanded Edition. Grand Rapids, Michigan: Zondervan Publishing House. 1987.

Anderson, Neil T. *Living Free in Christ*. Ventura, California: Regal, 1993.
_____. *Victory Over the Darkness*. Ventura, California: Regal, 1990.
_____. *The Bondage Breaker*. Eugene, Ore: Harvest House, 1990.

Billheimer, Paul E. *Destined for the Throne*. Minneapolis, Minnesota: Bethany House Publishers, 1975.
_____. *Destined to Overcome*. Minneapolis, Minnesota: Bethany House, 1982.

Bubeck, Mark. *The Adversary*. Chicago, Ill: Moody Press, 1975.
_____. *Overcoming the Adversary*. Chicago, Ill: Moody Press, 1984.

Cloud, Henry and John Townsend. *12 "Christian" Beliefs That Can Drive You Crazy*. Grand Rapids, Michigan: Zondervan Publishing House, 1994.
_____. *Boundaries, When to say YES, When to Say NO to Take Control of Your Life*. Grand Rapids, Michigan: Zondervan Publishing House, 1992.
_____. *How People Grow, What the Bible Reveals About Personal Growth*. Grand Rapids, Michigan: Zondervan Publishing House, 2001.

Curtis, Brent and John Eldredge. *The Sacred Romance, Drawing Closer to the Heart of God*. Nashville, Tennessee: Thomas Nelson Publishers, 1997.

Flexner, Stuart Berg, Editor in Chief. *The Random House Dictionary of the English Language, Second Edition, Unabridged*. New York, N.Y: Random House, 1987.

Frangipane, Francis. *The Three Battlegrounds*. Cedar Rapids, Iowa: Advancing Church Publications, 1989.

Gill, A.L. *Destined for Dominion*. Fawnskin, California. Powerhouse Publishing,1987. (For other publications by A.L. and Joyce Gill, visit gillministries.com)

Hill, Craig S. *The Ancient Paths*. Northglenn, Colorado: Harvest Books, 1992.
_____. *Deceived? Who Me?* Northglenn, Colorado: Harvest Books, 1986.
The Holy Bible, The New King James Version. Nashville, Tennessee: Thomas Nelson Publishers, 1992.

Hudson, Robert, General Editor. *The Christian Writer's Manual of Style, Updated and Expanded Edition*. Grand Rapids, Michigan: Zondervan Corporation, 2004.

Joyner, Rick.*The Final Quest*. Charlotte, N. C: Morning Star Publications, 1996.
_____. *The Call*. Charlotte, N. C: Morning Star Publications, 1999.
Love, Patricia with Jo Robinson. *The Emotional Incest Syndrome, What to Do When a Parent's Love Rules Your Life*. New York, N.Y: Bantam Books, 1990.

Merriam-Webster's Collegiate Dictionary, Eleventh Edition. Springfield, Massachusetts: Merriam-Webster, Incorporated, 2003.

Sabin, William A. *The Gregg Reference Manual, Ninth Edition.* New York: Glencoe McGraw-Hill, 2001.

Smalley, Gary and Trent, John, Ph.D. *The Blessing.* Nashville, Tennessee: Thomas Nelson, 1986.

Strong, James. *Strong's Exhaustive Concordance of the Bible.* Nashville, Tennessee: Thomas Nelson Publishers, 1990.

Virkler, Mark and Patti., *Counseled by God.* Shippensburg, Penn: Destiny Image Publishers, 1989.

Wagner, C. Peter. *Warfare Prayer.* Ventura, California: Regal, 1992.

Zondervan NIV Study Bible, Fully Revised. Grand Rapids, Michigan: Zondervan Publishing House, 2002.

www.ingramcontent.com/pod-product-compliance
Lightning Source LLC
Chambersburg PA
CBHW030136170426
43199CB00008B/84